"By focusing students' attention on one extended reading from 1–2 Kings and emphasizing a communicative approach to pedagogy, *Intermediate Biblical Hebrew* offers an experience unmatched by other intermediate-level textbooks. It preserves the best aspects of the authors' *Beginning Biblical Hebrew*, while shifting to a model in which grammatical and syntactical instruction responds to features of the text being studied. It thus prepares students to continue their study of Biblical Hebrew beyond the intermediate course. Instructors who disagree with the authors' minority view on word order can easily supplement that discussion and still benefit from the book's many strengths."

—**Christopher Heard**, Seaver College, Pepperdine University

"Picking up where they left off in *Beginning Biblical Hebrew*, Cook and Holmstedt deliver an exciting intermediate grammar that engages the senses and proves that learning a dead language does not have to be a lifeless prerequisite to further studies. What students already know is helpfully reinforced, and what they need to know is presented in memorable ways. By focusing their attention on the Elijah story, Cook and Holmstedt allow students to see how the language serves the narrative. Vocabulary, grammatical concepts, and other insights such as geography are all correlated to this entertaining unit of biblical text. The linguistic approach to the instruction in *Intermediate Biblical Hebrew* results in more than additional vocabulary words and paradigms; students will come away with a genuine love of the language and an ability to use it effectively."

—**Julie C. Möller**, Grove City College

"Cook and Holmstedt are two of the most linguistically sophisticated scholars working in Biblical Hebrew today. In this book, a sequel to their earlier beginner's textbook, they show that they are also among the most pedagogically sophisticated. Their descriptions of the language are linguistically rich, and their presentation of the material applies the findings of research into second-language acquisition to make the task of learning as painless and fruitful as possible."

—**Aaron J. Koller**, Yeshiva University

"Cook and Holmstedt move the student toward natural use and assimilation of the language, replacing Latinate grammatical and syntactical terms and concepts with ones natural to Hebrew itself. A joy to read and use, *Intermediate Biblical Hebrew* will be a favorite of instructors and students alike!"

—**John Bergsma**, Franciscan University of Steubenville; coauthor of *A Catholic Introduction to the Bible: Old Testament*

I0809053

Intermediate BIBLICAL HEBREW

An Illustrated Grammar

JOHN A. COOK AND
ROBERT D. HOLMSTEDT
ILLUSTRATED by PHILIP WILLIAMS

Baker Academic
a division of Baker Publishing Group
Grand Rapids, Michigan

Online resources for this textbook are available at www.bakeracademic.com/intermediatebiblical hebrew. Students can view flashcards for reviewing vocabulary and hear audio files of Hebrew exercise sentences, lesson vocabulary, and readings. Professors can request sample quizzes and exams, lesson plans, and an instructor's manual with answer key.

Published by Baker Academic
a division of Baker Publishing Group
Grand Rapids, Michigan
BakerAcademic.com

Printed in the United States of America

Library of Congress Cataloging-in-Publication Data
Names: Cook, John A., 1968– author. | Holmstedt, Robert D. author. | Williams, Philip John, 1983– illustrator.
Title: Intermediate biblical Hebrew : an illustrated grammar / John A. Cook and Robert D. Holmstedt ; illustrated by Philip Williams.
Description: Grand Rapids, MI : Baker Academic, a division of Baker Publishing Group, [2020] | Series: Learning biblical Hebrew | Summary: "This full-color, intermediate textbook by two leading experts in biblical Hebrew features pedagogical advancements that enhance student outcomes"—Provided by publisher.
Identifiers: LCCN 2019041774 | ISBN 9780801097621 (paperback)
Subjects: LCSH: Hebrew language—Grammar—Textbooks.
Classification: LCC PJ4567.3 .C67 2019 | DDC 492.4/82421—dc23
LC record available at https://lccn.loc.gov/2019041774

Unless otherwise indicated, all Scripture quotations are the authors' translations.

Baker Publishing Group publications use paper produced from sustainable forestry practices and postconsumer waste whenever possible.

Contents

Introduction

This textbook is intended to fill a surprising lacuna in the Biblical Hebrew textbook market. Although the number and variety of introductory textbooks is great (and sometimes bewildering), there are startlingly few textbooks for the next stage of learning the language. And yet this is the stage when what is learned becomes embedded and the skills that students work so hard to acquire in the introductory course become useful for longer-term Hebrew study.

We are aware of only four other textbooks aimed at the intermediate language audience:

Ehud Ben Zvi and Maxine Hancock, *Readings in Biblical Hebrew: An Intermediate Textbook* (New Haven: Yale University Press, 1993)

Andrew E. Steinmann, *Intermediate Biblical Hebrew: A Reference Grammar with Charts and Exercises* (St. Louis: Concordia, 2009)

Robert B. Chisholm, *A Workbook for Intermediate Hebrew: Grammar, Exegesis, and Commentary on Jonah and Ruth* (Grand Rapids: Kregel Academic, 2016)

Eric D. Reymond, *Intermediate Biblical Hebrew Grammar: A Student's Guide to Phonology and Morphology* (Atlanta: SBL Press, 2018)

The Ben Zvi and Hancock textbook is keyed to various reference grammars and introduces students to a wide variety of short textual passages, asking basic parsing and syntax questions along the way. Steinmann's book is transparently a summary of traditional reference grammars with some exercises. Chisholm's workbook includes a very brief overview of narrative and poetry, walks through the texts of Jonah and Ruth, and ends with a guide to parsing verbs. And Reymond's volume clearly lacks any description of syntax or pragmatics.

All four existing volumes reflect a view of the typical intermediate Biblical Hebrew course as a continuation of passive language learning and assume that, for example, paradigm learning, verb parsing, and applying Latinate-based case language labels (e.g., genitive, accusative) leads to a mastery of the grammar and in turn to reading ability. Unfortunately, all the language acquisition research shows that this pattern, even for ancient languages, does not lead to true proficiency. Authentic reading ability proceeds from an aural-oral proficiency: the learner must be able to both *hear* and *speak* the language, even an ancient one! Our introductory textbook, *Beginning Biblical Hebrew* (Baker Academic, 2013), was our attempt to move strongly in this direction for the university and seminary classroom. In *Beginning Biblical Hebrew* (*BBH*) we used visual cues (illustrations of biblical texts, vocabulary icons) and Hebrew grammatical terms and exercise instructions to encourage instructors and students to be as immersive as possible in the classroom.

The Distinctives of This Textbook

This textbook continues our focus in providing a learning tool that allows for a more immersive, communicative learning experience at the next stage of Biblical Hebrew acquisition. Certainly an instructor can use this textbook in a more traditional way, encouraging translation in the student's first language (e.g., English), reviewing paradigms, parsing verbs, and memorizing the grammatical terminology that we introduce (which is not traditional but based on modern linguistic study), thus substituting an older approach for a newer one.

However, we encourage a different method, one that eschews mechanical translation exercises in favor of a more dynamic and communicative approach. For example, we do not ask for full translations of the passages in the illustrations but focus instead on more active language activities, such as reading the passages out loud in class with students taking part. Even memorizing small sections and having the students perform the passages as plays is immensely useful, not to mention fun. We often take turns (instructor and students) reading the passages aloud in class, followed by spontaneous questions relating to comprehension (sometimes asking the questions in Hebrew). Or for exercises that require more engagement with grammatical issues, we set students to rewriting verses or larger passages to change, for example, the gender of the characters or the time setting.

As for actual long-term reading comprehension, we encourage students to make the following process a deep habit. For each Hebrew text, the student should search for the "what" (verb), the "who" (subject), the "who or what else" (complements or adjuncts [modifiers]), the "where" (spatial adjunct), the "when" (temporal adjunct), and the "why" (causal or purpose adjunct). Whether or not the student can specify the lexical content of the "what" (verb), the very process of identifying it as a "what" (verb) is itself a critical step forward in acquiring authentic reading skills.

Finally, to encourage an immersive mindset in studying Hebrew and to crack open the door to Jewish resources, we cite biblical references using the Hebrew book names and the Hebrew numbering system: א = 1, ב = 2, י = 10, יא = 11, and so on. (Note that 15 is expressed as טו rather than יה, and 16 as טז rather than יו, to avoid forms resembling the divine name.) Students may need to keep the chart below near at hand until this reference system is learned.

Further Information

Though we have tried to create an intermediate textbook that can be used following any introductory textbook, the most seamless transition will occur when moving from our *BBH* to the present volume. And since we base our student materials on our linguistic research and so teach concepts and terms proceeding from that research,

Biblical Reference Systems for English and Hebrew

English book name	Hebrew book name
Genesis	בראשית
Exodus	שמות
Leviticus	ויקרא
Numbers	במדבר
Deuteronomy	דברים
Joshua	יהושע
Judges	שפטים
1–2 Samuel	שמואל א–ב
1–2 Kings	מלכים א–ב
Isaiah	ישעיהו
Jeremiah	ירמיהו
Ezekiel	יחזקאל
Hosea	הושע
Joel	יואל
Amos	עמוס
Obadiah	עבדיה
Jonah	יונה
Micah	מיכה
Nahum	נחום
Habakkuk	חבקוק
Zephaniah	צפניה
Haggai	חגי
Zechariah	זכריה
Malachi	מלאכי
Psalms	תהלים
Job	איוב
Proverbs	משלי
Ruth	רות
Song of Songs	שיר השירים
Ecclesiastes	קהלת
Lamentations	איכה
Esther	אסתר
Daniel	דניאל
Ezra	עזרא
Nehemiah	נחמיה
1–2 Chronicles	דברי הימים א–ב

Arabic numeral	Hebrew numeral
1	א
2	ב
3	ג
4	ד
5	ה
6	ו
7	ז
8	ח
9	ט
10	י
11	יא
12	יב
13	יג
14	יד
15	טו
16	טז
17	יז
18	יח
19	יט
20	כ
30	ל
40	מ
50	נ
60	ס
70	ע
80	פ
90	צ
100	ק

we provide a short list of the most common terms below and provide cross-references to our *BBH* throughout this volume.[1] Also, because many of the standard reference works on Hebrew (primarily lexica and grammars) employ the traditional Latin-based grammatical terms to describe Hebrew, the following list provides equivalencies between the terminology of this grammar and the traditional Latin-based terminology.

Grammatical Terminology

Term used in this grammar	Traditional term
adverbial infinitive	infinitive absolute
enclitic pronouns	suffixed pronouns
first-person jussive	cohortative
infinitive	infinitive construct
irreal Perfect	waw-consecutive Perfect
Past Narrative	waw-consecutive Imperfect
proclitic preposition	inseparable preposition
subject pronoun	independent pronoun
vowel letter	mater lectionis ("mother of reading")
בִּנְיָן/בִּנְיָנִים	verb stem(s)
דָּגֵשׁ חָזָק	dagesh forte
דָּגֵשׁ קַל	dagesh lene
נִסְמָךְ	construct form
סוֹמֵךְ	absolute form
סְמִיכוּת	construct relationship
פַּ֫תַח גְּנוּבָה	furtive patach
שֹׁ֫רֶשׁ	(triconsonantal) root

Structure of This Textbook

The textbook readings are divided into twenty-four chapters. The reason is twofold: (1) covering two readings per week approximates a typical university or seminary semester, allowing time for review and examination, and (2) the number accords with the illustrated pages the artist, Philip Williams, created to cover the biblical story of Elijah's interactions with Ahab (beginning at 1 Kings 16:29) until he passes the prophetic mantle to Elisha (ending at 2 Kings 2:14).

The presentation of grammatical concepts follows two simple principles. First, we tried to balance syntactic and semantic topics in each chapter, though this was not an unbreakable rule. Second, the topics had to correspond to the grammatical issue arising from the biblical text. This more inductive approach has resulted in grammatical concepts being scattered throughout the textbook rather than appearing in a sequence more typical of standard reference grammars. This was deliberate

1. Forthcoming Baker Academic volumes that the instructor or student might also find helpful include books on Biblical Hebrew syntax (Holmstedt) and the verbal system (Cook).

because we do not think a reference grammar is what an intermediate language course requires. Rather, at this stage the student still needs to acquire proficiency in using the language, and variation, repetition, and the engagement of as many senses as possible is vital to the acquisition process.

Finally, the instructor and student should be aware that the first time a grammatical concept is introduced is likely not the first time it occurs in the larger story; this is intentional. In fact, it is only reasonable, since if we tried to address every grammatical issue on its first occurrence, all the topics would be covered in the first three readings! Additionally, we are convinced that a good part of developing both comfort and proficiency in reading an ancient language is being able to see something unknown and set it aside for later investigation while maintaining the reading flow.

Each chapter has six components:

1. The biblical passage within the illustrations. The illustrations incorporate the text either as narrative (square text boxes), human speech (rounded speech bubbles), or divine speech (cloud-like speech bubbles). Moreover, on each page an open Bible icon gives the biblical reference (in Hebrew) for the text included on that page.
2. A list of vocabulary words from the passage, titled "Words to Learn." The list includes all words occurring less than 200 times in the Hebrew Bible, with the assumption that in their introductory Hebrew course students learned vocabulary occurring more than 200 times.[2] Grammatical labels are provided, along with blanks for filling in the English meaning of the word. For verbs not appearing in the Qal stem, three blanks appear in parentheses next to the verb for recording the triconsonantal Hebrew root.
3. Two or three new grammatical topics under the heading "Going Deeper with Grammar." The topics presented move students beyond information typical of introductory textbooks. If the student's introductory textbook represented the "mini-reference grammar" model, then our presentation can be understood to pick up from the typical limit of a beginning student's ability to absorb and retain. Questions in the grammatical discussion are always based on the passage.
4. A section titled "Challenge." This section isolates one or two features of the text that will likely be difficult for the intermediate student to sort out.
5. Aids for reading the passage under the heading "Reading Insights." One or two features of the passage are explained here that will aid in its reading. Often this section demonstrates how knowledge of grammar directly relates to an accurate understanding of the text.
6. Review questions. In early chapters these questions can be answered with only the basic knowledge gained at the introductory level. Questions in later chapters draw on knowledge gained from previous chapters in the textbook. Here students are also asked to review the weak verb morphology, so we have included cross-references to the relevant weak verb discussions and paradigms

2. In *BBH*, students learn almost all vocabulary appearing 200 times or more except for 40 items that are listed in an appendix in the instructor's manual for *BBH*.

appearing in appendix B. Questions ask the student to identify examples in the passage of the weak verb form under discussion.

Nine chapters (chaps. 2, 5, 8, 11, 14, 17, 19, 22, and 24) also require use of the Aleppo Codex, selected pages of which appear in appendix A. The Aleppo Codex is an important medieval Masoretic work (ca. 925 CE) and represents this textbook's focus on text, visual beauty, and deeper language learning. We hope that students and instructors—particularly those interested in the textual history of the Hebrew Bible—will enjoy integrating readings from this codex with the illustrated text readings. In our classroom experience, we have found that students generally appreciate the opportunity to discover and explore the features of an actual handwritten manuscript.

We think that the Elijah story is dynamic and engaging and is therefore an excellent piece of the Bible for students to enjoy as they seek to embed their knowledge of Hebrew more deeply and move toward authentic reading proficiency. We are sincerely grateful for the artistic abilities of Philip Williams, whose colorful and entertaining Elijah illustrations were critical in helping us achieve our vision for this textbook.

John A. Cook
Wilmore, Kentucky

Robert D. Holmstedt
Toronto, Ontario

A Word from the Artist

My goal in illustrating the life of Elijah was to create a comic book that was dutifully faithful to the biblical narrative yet so lively and engaging that it caused readers to consider things that they'd never before noticed in the text. I designed the characters in an overly exaggerated way to avoid modern offensive stereotypes.

To my knowledge, Jezebel is the only character in the Bible who is said to have worn makeup (2 Kings 9:30), so I illustrated her with a pale, overly painted face. I designed Ahab to be reminiscent of a self-centered king from classic children's fairytale illustrations. Elijah's messy hair and stick-thin figure is intended to emphasize his life as an outcast, living in the wild.

Some of the characters and their clothing were inspired by archeological artifacts. The Black Obelisk of Shalmaneser III contains a portrait of Jehu. I tried to mimic that depiction with Jehu's big nose and long, flowing hair. The costumes worn by the prophets of Baal came from what some historians believe the prophets of that time period may have worn. To add to the pagan appearance, I gave them bulging eyes and yellowed teeth, like fairytale sorcerers.

Overall, I wanted the overly exaggerated character designs to pull readers into the emotion of the story.

Philip Williams

Abbreviations

General and Bibliographic

BBH	*Beginning Biblical Hebrew*, by John A. Cook and Robert D. Holmstedt (Grand Rapids: Baker Academic, 2013)
DCH	*Dictionary of Classical Hebrew*, ed. David J. A. Clines, 9 vols. (Sheffield, UK: Sheffield Phoenix, 1993–2016)
HALOT	*Hebrew and Aramaic Lexicon of the Old Testament*, by Ludwig Koehler, Walter Baumgartner, and Johann J. Stamm, trans. and ed. Mervyn E. J. Richardson (Leiden: Brill, 2001)
NIV	New International Version
NRSV	New Revised Standard Version

Grammatical and Syntactical

*	designates a hypothetical Hebrew form
ADJ	adjective
ADJP	adjective phrase
ADV	adverb
C	common (gender)
CARD	cardinal numeral
COLL	collective
COMP	complementizer
COND	conditional
CONJ	conjunction
COP	copula
DEM	demonstrative pronoun
DET	determiner/article
DOM	differential object marker
DU	dual
ENCL	enclitic
EXST	existential
F	feminine
HI	Hifil/הִפְעִיל
HIT	Hitpael/הִתְפַּעֵל
HO	Hofal/הָפְעַל
I, II, or III	designates Hebrew letter position in the triconsonantal שֹׁרֶשׁ
IMPF	Imperfect
IMPV	imperative
INF	infinitive
INTER	interrogative
INTJ	interjection
LOC	locative
M	masculine
NI	Nifal/נִפְעַל
NIS	נִסְמָךְ/bound/clitic form
NOUN	noun
NP	noun phrase
ORD	ordinal numeral
P	plural
PASS	passive
PERF	Perfect
PI	Piel/פִּעֵל
PN	proper noun

PP	prepositional phrase
PREP	preposition
PRON	pronoun
PTCP	participle
PU	Pual/פֻּעַל
Q	Qal/קַל
$R_{1,2,3}$	first, second, or third root consonant
S	singular
TAM	tense-aspect-mood
VB	verb
VP	verb phrase
W.	with
X/Y	unspecified word
XP/YP	phrase X / phrase Y (i.e., unspecified type of phrase)

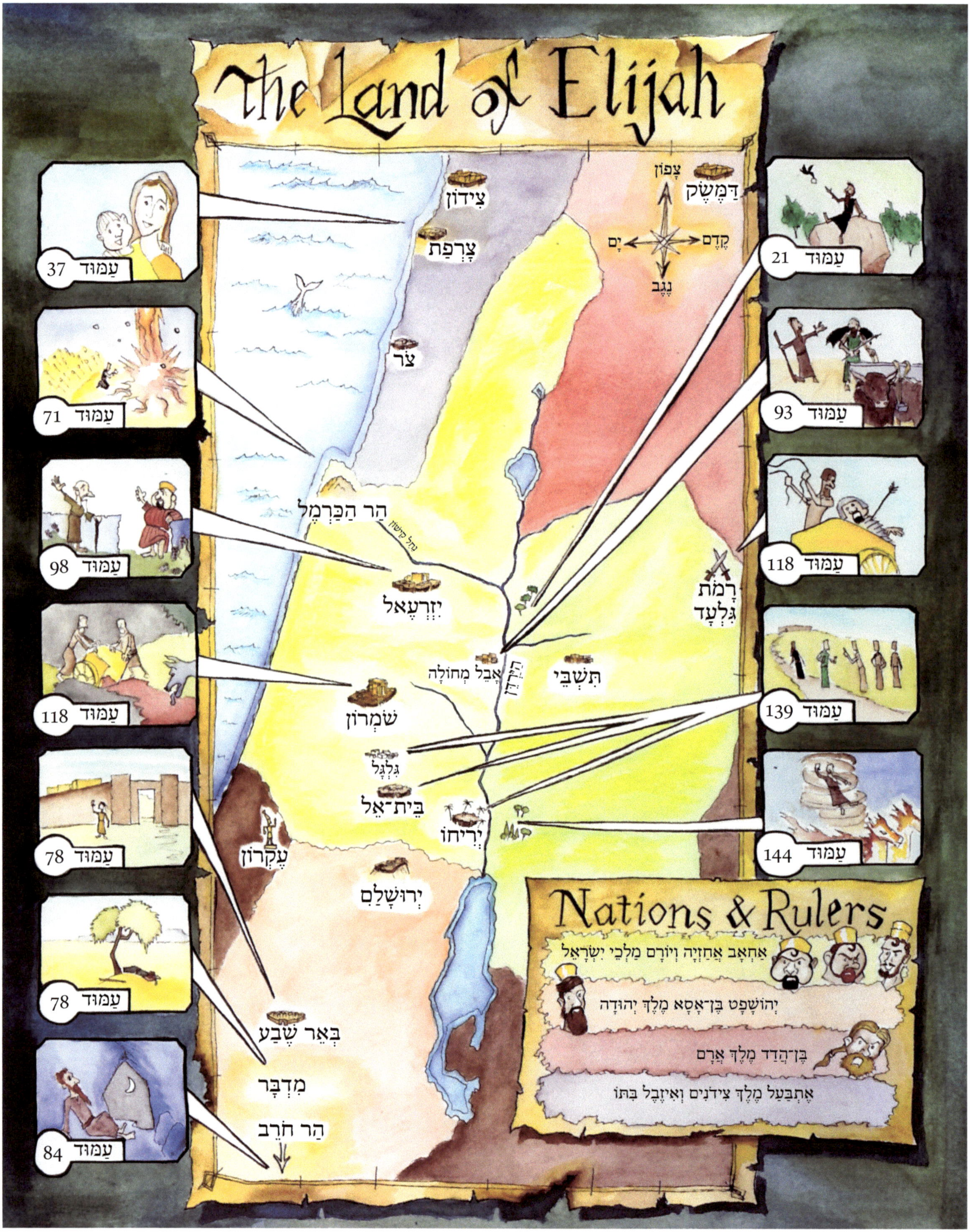

The Land of Elijah
צָפוֹן
קֶדֶם
יָם
נֶגֶב
דַּמֶּשֶׂק
צִידוֹן
צָרְפַת
צֹר
הַר הַכַּרְמֶל
נַחַל קִישׁוֹן
יִזְרְעֶאל
רָמֹת גִּלְעָד
אָבֵל מְחוֹלָה
הַיַּרְדֵּן
תִּשְׁבִּי
שֹׁמְרוֹן
גִּלְגָּל
בֵּית־אֵל
יְרִיחוֹ
עֶקְרוֹן
יְרוּשָׁלַ͏ִם
בְּאֵר שֶׁבַע
מִדְבָּר
הַר חֹרֵב
עַמּוּד 37
עַמּוּד 71
עַמּוּד 98
עַמּוּד 118
עַמּוּד 78
עַמּוּד 78
עַמּוּד 84
עַמּוּד 21
עַמּוּד 93
עַמּוּד 118
עַמּוּד 139
עַמּוּד 144
Nations & Rulers
אַחְאָב אֲחַזְיָה וְיוֹרָם מַלְכֵי יִשְׂרָאֵל
יְהוֹשָׁפָט בֶּן־אָסָא מֶלֶךְ יְהוּדָה
בֶּן־הֲדַד מֶלֶךְ אֲרָם
אֶתְבַּעַל מֶלֶךְ צִידֹנִים וְאִיזֶבֶל בִּתּוֹ

Readings

מלכים א
טז, כט-לג
בֵּית בַּעַל
כט וְאַחְאָ֣ב בֶּן־עָמְרִ֗י מָלַךְ֙ עַל־
יִשְׂרָאֵ֔ל בִּשְׁנַ֙ת שְׁלֹשִׁ֤ים
וּשְׁמֹנֶה֙ שָׁנָ֔ה לְאָסָ֖א מֶ֣לֶךְ
יְהוּדָ֑ה וַֽיִּמְלֹ֙ךְ אַחְאָ֣ב בֶּן־
עָמְרִ֗י עַל־יִשְׂרָאֵל֙ בְּשֹׁ֣מְר֔וֹן
עֶשְׂרִ֥ים וּשְׁתַּ֖יִם שָׁנָֽה׃ ל וַיַּ֜עַשׂ
אַחְאָ֧ב בֶּן־עָמְרִ֛י הָרַ֖ע בְּעֵינֵ֣י
יְהוָ֑ה מִכֹּ֖ל אֲשֶׁ֥ר לְפָנָֽיו׃
לא וַיְהִי֙ הֲנָקֵ֣ל לֶכְתּ֔וֹ בְּחַטֹּ֖אות
יָרָבְעָ֣ם בֶּן־נְבָ֑ט וַיִּקַּ֣ח אִשָּׁ֗ה
אֶת־אִיזֶ֙בֶל֙ בַּת־אֶתְבַּ֙עַל֙
מֶ֣לֶךְ צִידֹנִ֔ים וַיֵּ֙לֶךְ֙ וַיַּעֲבֹ֣ד
אֶת־הַבַּ֔עַל וַיִּשְׁתַּ֖חוּ לֽוֹ׃
לב וַיָּ֥קֶם מִזְבֵּ֖חַ לַבָּ֑עַל בֵּ֣ית
הַבַּ֔עַל אֲשֶׁ֥ר בָּנָ֖ה בְּשֹׁמְרֽוֹן׃
לג וַיַּ֥עַשׂ אַחְאָ֖ב אֶת־הָאֲשֵׁרָ֑ה
וַיּ֣וֹסֶף אַחְאָ֗ב לַעֲשׂ֙וֹת
לְהַכְעִיס֙ אֶת־יְהוָה֙ אֱלֹהֵ֣י
יִשְׂרָאֵ֔ל מִכֹּל֙ מַלְכֵ֣י יִשְׂרָאֵ֔ל
אֲשֶׁ֥ר הָי֖וּ לְפָנָֽיו׃

Reading 1

מלכים א טז:כט–לג

Words to Learn

אֲשֵׁרָה NOUN F ______________; PN ______________

(___ ___ ___) הִכְעִיס VB HI ______________

(___ ___ ___) הִשְׁתַּחֲוָה VB HISHTAFEL ____________________

(___ ___ ___) נָקֵל VB NI ______________

שְׁמֹנֶה ORD ______________

Going Deeper with Grammar

סְמִיכוּת

One of the most common strategies for modifying nouns in Hebrew is the סְמִיכוּת, or bound relationship. In this relationship, the first noun X "leans" on the second, the host noun Y. The result is analogous to "of" in English, that is, "X of Y." Unlike English, this grammatical construction does not use a preposition like "of" but is enabled by the fact that Hebrew nouns have two forms: a סוֹמֵךְ (free) form, which is the form listed in the lexicon and typically learned in word lists, and a נִסְמָךְ (bound) form, which often has a different ending and vowel pattern than the סוֹמֵךְ form.

For example, the סוֹמֵךְ form of the word *queen* is מַלְכָּה, whereas the נִסְמָךְ form is מַלְכַּת. Note the ת ending instead of the ה of the סוֹמֵךְ form as well as the slightly different vocalization.

The vowel changes are due to the phonological binding (cliticization) of the נִסְמָךְ (supported) noun to the following סוֹמֵךְ (supporting) noun, so that they function as a compound with a single word stress. Hyphenation in English has the same effect of joining two words in a compound with a single phonological stress. In fact, Hebrew bound forms frequently appear with a connecting מַקֵּף (similar to an English hyphen) between them.

The meaning of the סְמִיכוּת "of" construction is a product of the relationship between the bound and host nouns. Is the host noun the agent/possessor, the complement of implied action, or a quality of the bound noun? The examples below illustrate each basic type. The host noun is underlined in the English gloss in each of the examples.

- *Agent/possessor*: host noun is agent/subject or possessor of bound noun

  דְּבַר יְהוָה

  the word of <u>YHWH</u> ≈ the word that <u>YHWH</u> spoke (מלכים א יח:לא)

עֵינֵי יְהוָה
the eyes of YHWH ≈ YHWH's eyes (מלכים א טז:ל)

- *Complement*: host noun is verbal complement of action implied by bound noun

יִרְאַת אֱלֹהִים
the fear of God ≈ fearing God (בראשית כ:יא)

- *Quality*: host noun provides a quality describing bound noun

אֵזוֹר עוֹר
belt of leather ≈ a leather belt (מלכים ב א:ח)

וּבִגְדֵי הַקֹּדֶשׁ
and the clothes of holiness ≈ the holy clothes (שמות כט:כט)

The סְמִיכוּת relationship can have more than one נִסְמָךְ noun in a row, both leaning on a single host noun. Note how the definiteness of the host noun is assumed for the nouns bound to it.

קוֹל הֲמוֹן הַגָּשֶׁם
the sound of the roar of rain (מלכים א יח:מא)

The סְמִיכוּת relationship can also have a single נִסְמָךְ noun related to coordinated סוֹמֵךְ nouns.

בְּעֵינֵי אֱלֹהִים וְאָדָם
in the eyes of God and man (משלי ג:ד)

Often, however, the bound noun is repeated in two coordinated סְמִיכוּת phrases.

אֱלֹהֵי הַשָּׁמַיִם וֵאלֹהֵי הָאָרֶץ
the God of heaven and the God of earth (בראשית כד:ג)

Find three נִסְמָךְ (bound) forms in this reading, and list their סוֹמֵךְ (free) forms.

Constituency

Constituents are the basic building blocks of syntax. Constituents are words or groups of words that function as a grammatical unit, such as a noun phrase (NP), verb phrase (VP), adjective phrase (ADJP), or prepositional phrase (PP). As constituents relate to each other syntactically, they combine to form successively larger constituents. For example, in the sequence of words אֶת־אִיזֶבֶל בַּת־אֶתְבַּעַל מֶלֶךְ צִידֹנִים (מלכים א טז:לא), the noun מֶלֶךְ is combined with the noun צִידֹנִים to form the larger NP, מֶלֶךְ צִידֹנִים. Similarly, the noun בַּת is combined with the noun אֶתְבַּעַל to form the larger

NP בַּת־אֶתְבַּעַל, to which is then added the NP מֶלֶךְ צִידֹנִים by apposition. The resulting large NP בַּת־אֶתְבַּעַל מֶלֶךְ צִידֹנִים is then combined (appositionally) with the noun אִיזֶבֶל to create the even larger NP. And so the principle of constituency applies to successively larger groups of words until the desired phrase or clause is achieved. The largest constituent is the clause, which consists of smaller constituents relating to each other to form a *subject* and a *predicate* (which we may also call the VP).

Many constituents are intuitively easy to identify: nouns, verbs, prepositions—these constituents begin with a word class and build from there. However, the null constituent is a type of constituent that is rarely recognized in Hebrew grammar, though it is both syntactically critical and nearly omnipresent. Null constituents lack a phonological shape and yet have a syntactic reality. The most obvious use of null constituents in Hebrew is when a verbal subject or complement is "missing"; the missing constituent is marked below in the Hebrew with a blank line and in the English glosses with the null sign, ø.

וַיִּשְׂאוּ ___ לָהֶם נָשִׁים מֹאֲבִיּוֹת

And ø (they) [= Mahlon and Kilyon] took Moabite wives for themselves. (רות א:ד)

וַתֵּלֶךְ ___ לָקַחַת ___

And ø (she) went to get ø (it) [= a container of water requested in the previous verse]. (מלכים א יז:יא)

For finite verbs, as in the first example, the subject can be overt and the agreement features (person-gender-number) match the overt subject when it is present. This strongly suggests that the agreement features when an overt subject is not present still match a syntactic subject, but one that is covert. Similarly, in cases like the second example, the valency (see glossary) of the verb is not met by any overt constituent, but there is a previously mentioned constituent in the context to which a covert pronominal complement refers.

Null constituents are allowed within a discourse because their reference is easily recoverable. That is, it is typically easy to determine what a null subject or complement refers to because those constituents have been overtly used in the preceding discourse. Consider the null complements below:

וַתִּקַּח ___ מִפִּרְיוֹ וַתֹּאכַל ___ ___ וַתִּתֵּן ___ ___ גַּם־לְאִישָׁהּ עִמָּהּ וַיֹּאכַל ___ ___

And ø (Eve) took some of its fruit and ø (she) ate ø (it) and ø (she) gave ø (it) also to her husband who was with her and ø (he) ate ø (it). (בראשית ג:ו)

In the example, the antecedent of the null complement pronoun (פְּרִי, fruit) is explicitly identified in the preceding discourse.

Identify the subject and predicate in the two clauses of verse כט.

Within each predicate of verse כט, identify the verb and each smaller constituent that combines with the verb to form the VP (predicate). For example, in the first clause of verse ל, the verb וַיַּעַשׂ, one NP (הָרַע), and two PPs (בְּעֵינֵי יְהוָה and מִכֹּל אֲשֶׁר לְפָנָיו) combine to form the VP.

Find four examples of a null constituent in the passage.

Challenge

What the ה Is Going On?

הֲנָקֵל לֶכְתּוֹ בְּחַטֹּאות יָרָבְעָם (מלכים א טז:לא)

What is the הֲ at the beginning of the clause, and what is its function?

What is the subject of the clause? (Trick question: there are two clauses and two subjects!)

Reading Insights

Idiomatic Phrases

Semantics (*BBH* §50) concerns not just the meanings of words in isolation (i.e., a lexical definition) or the meanings of combinations of words (i.e., the compositional meaning of a noun and its modifying adjective) but also the meanings of phrases that go beyond the sum of the parts, that is, idiomatic meanings.

While the meaning of many verbs does not change depending on the NPs or PPs used as their complements, sometimes the combination results in an idiom. The use of אִשָּׁה with the verb לקח is one of those cases. The phrase לקח אִשָּׁה means "to take a wife," never "to take (as) a wife" (so NRSV). Thus the phrase וַיִּקַּח אִשָּׁה אֶת־אִיזֶבֶל (מלכים א טז:לא) cannot mean "he took (as) a wife Jezebel" but "he took a wife, Jezebel."

What is the function of Jezebel in this analysis?

Geography

Where is שֹׁמְרוֹן on the map of Israel at the front of the book? What does the association with שֹׁמְרוֹן tell you about אַחְאָב?

Review

Find every Past Narrative verb in the passage (*BBH* §35), and identify the שֹׁרֶשׁ and בִּנְיָן for each.

Find all the הִפְעִיל verbs in the passage (*BBH* §29), and identify which ones make sense as a causative verb and which ones do not (that is, those whose meaning must simply be memorized).

אוַיֹּאמֶר אֵלִיָּהוּ הַתִּשְׁבִּי
מִתֹּשָׁבֵי גִלְעָד אֶל־אַחְאָב
חַי־יְהוָה אֱלֹהֵי יִשְׂרָאֵל
אֲשֶׁר עָמַדְתִּי לְפָנָיו אִם־יִהְיֶה
הַשָּׁנִים הָאֵלֶּה טַל וּמָטָר כִּי
אִם־לְפִי דְבָרִי׃ ס
בוַיְהִי דְבַר־יְהוָה
אֵלָיו לֵאמֹר׃
גלֵךְ מִזֶּה וּפָנִיתָ לְּךָ קֵדְמָה
וְנִסְתַּרְתָּ בְּנַחַל כְּרִית אֲשֶׁר
עַל־פְּנֵי הַיַּרְדֵּן׃ דוְהָיָה מֵהַנַּחַל
תִּשְׁתֶּה וְאֶת־הָעֹרְבִים צִוִּיתִי
לְכַלְכֶּלְךָ שָׁם׃
הוַיֵּלֶךְ וַיַּעַשׂ כִּדְבַר יְהוָה וַיֵּלֶךְ וַיֵּשֶׁב
בְּנַחַל כְּרִית אֲשֶׁר עַל־פְּנֵי הַיַּרְדֵּן׃
מלכים א
יז, א-ט
ווְהָעֹרְבִים מְבִיאִים לוֹ
לֶחֶם וּבָשָׂר בַּבֹּקֶר
וְלֶחֶם וּבָשָׂר בָּעָרֶב
וּמִן־הַנַּחַל יִשְׁתֶּה׃
זוַיְהִי מִקֵּץ יָמִים וַיִּיבַשׁ הַנָּחַל כִּי לֹא־הָיָה
גֶשֶׁם בָּאָרֶץ׃ ס חוַיְהִי דְבַר־יְהוָה אֵלָיו לֵאמֹר׃
טקוּם לֵךְ צָרְפַתָה אֲשֶׁר
לְצִידוֹן וְיָשַׁבְתָּ שָׁם הִנֵּה
צִוִּיתִי שָׁם אִשָּׁה
אַלְמָנָה לְכַלְכְּלֶךָ׃

Reading 2

מלכים א יז:א–ט

Words to Learn

אַלְמָנָה NOUN F ______________

גֶּ֫שֶׁם NOUN M ______________

טַל NOUN M ______________

יָבֵשׁ VB Q ______________

כִּלְכֵּל (___ ___) VB PILPEL ______________

מָטָר NOUN F ______________

נַ֫חַל NOUN M ______________

נִסְתַּר (___ ___) VB NI ______________

עֶ֫רֶב NOUN M ______________

עֹרֵב NOUN M ______________

פָּנָה VB Q ______________

קֶ֫דֶם NOUN M ______________

קֵץ NOUN M ______________

תּוֹשָׁב NOUN M ______________

Going Deeper with Grammar

The Article

The article has a basic form הַ attached to the front of a word and a דָּגֵשׁ חָזָק in the first letter, as in הַדָּבָר. But there are variant forms of the article depending on the host word (*BBH* appendix A.5).

Stressed qamets	Unstressed qamets				
			ר	הָ	הָרֹאשׁ
			א	הָ	הָאָב
הָעָז	הֶעָפָר	←	ע	הָ	הָעִיר
הָהָר	הֶהָרִים	←	ה	הַ	הַהֵיכָל
הֶחָ֫יִל	הֶחָכָם	←	ח	הַ	הַחֹ֫דֶשׁ

There are also a few nouns whose first vowel changes when the article is added:

הַ• + אֶ֫רֶץ ← הָאָ֫רֶץ	the earth
הַ• + גַן ← הַגָּן	the garden
הַ• + עַם ← הָעָם	the people

Explain the הָ in הָעֹרְבִים found in verse ד (*BBH* appendix A.5).

Why does the בָּ in בָּאָ֫רֶץ in verse ז have a qamets and not a sheva (בְּ)?

Find two more examples of a non-basic form of the article in the passage.

Demonstratives

Demonstratives are deictic (pointing) words (*BBH* §33). As such, their properties are closely related to definiteness, which often has to do with identifiability of referents. Pointing to referents is one way to identify them. Remember that demonstratives behave like adjectives: both can modify a noun, as in the first example below, and both can substitute for a noun, as in the second example.

נֶפֶשׁ־הַיֶּ֫לֶד הַזֶּה
the life of this boy (מלכים א יז:כא)

עַתָּה זֶה יָדַעְתִּי
Now I know this. (מלכים א יז:כד)

Demonstratives may co-occur with the definite article in order to agree with the definiteness of the noun they modify.

וְיֵדְעוּ הָעָם הַזֶּה
that this people may know (מלכים א יח:לז)

Although it is the common pattern, matching the article of the modified noun is not obligatory.

אָנֹכִי שֹׁמֵעַ אֶת־דִּבְרֵיכֶם רָעִים מֵאֵת כָּל־הָעָם אֵלֶּה
I hear about your evil deeds from all these people. (שמואל א ב:כג)

Demonstratives often have a "near" and a "far" deixis, depending on whether the noun and its demonstrative point to something relatively near or far (in space or time) relative to the speaker (see *BBH* §33). The Hebrew demonstratives זֶה, זאת, and אֵלֶּה have both the near and far use, depending on the stance of the speaker with regard to the position of the item pointed to. The near uses are illustrated by the examples already used; the far uses are illustrated below.

זֹאת אֹמֶרֶת . . . וְזֹאת אֹמֶרֶת

<u>this</u> one is saying . . . and <u>that</u> one is saying (מלכים א ג:כג)

בִּשְׁנַת שֵׁשׁ־מֵאוֹת שָׁנָה לְחַיֵּי־נֹחַ בַּחֹדֶשׁ הַשֵּׁנִי בְּשִׁבְעָה־עָשָׂר יוֹם לַחֹדֶשׁ בַּיּוֹם הַזֶּה

in the six-hundredth year of the life of Noah, in the second month, on the seventeenth day of the month, on <u>that day</u> (בראשית ז:יא)

Hebrew also employs the third-person pronouns in a quasi-demonstrative way.

הָאֲכִילָה הַהִיא

<u>that</u> food (מלכים א יט:ח)

What distinguishes the ז and אֵלֶּה demonstratives from the quasi-demonstrative use of the third-person pronouns is the issue of *deixis* versus *anaphora*. The demonstratives are true deictic words, pointing to something in the sense of "that food [over there]" or "this food [over here]." In contrast, the third-person pronouns, when used similarly, do not point in physical or temporal space, but link the item or concept with a previous mention in the discourse, as in "that food [that we both know about]" or "that wilderness [that we just traveled through]." Since the quasi-demonstrative function of the third-person pronouns is used with nouns that have been previously mentioned in the discourse and are thus specific and identifiable, this use is limited to definite nouns.

Identify and explain any occurrence of a demonstrative in the passage.

Relative Clauses

Relative clauses are one strategy for modifying nouns, along with the סְמִיכוּת construction (chap. 1), apposition (chap. 6), and NP-internal PPs (chap. 11). Relatives simply allow more internal complexity for the modifier, such as containing a verb.

Unlike the clitic forms used in the סְמִיכוּת, the juxtaposition of nouns in apposition, and a preposition for PPs, relative clauses are typically introduced by a relative word such as אֲשֶׁר (or שֶׁ in later Hebrew).

וַיַּעַשׂ אַחְאָב בֶּן־עָמְרִי הָרַע בְּעֵינֵי יְהוָה מִכֹּל אֲשֶׁר לְפָנָיו׃

And Ahab, son of Omri, did evil in the eyes of YHWH more than all <u>who</u> were before him. (מלכים א טז:ל)

Like most types of modification, relative clauses fall into two semantic categories: *restrictive* and *nonrestrictive*. The example above is restrictive—the relative clause provides information critical for identifying the referent of the head of the relative. Without the אֲשֶׁר relative, whom the כֹּל referred to would be entirely ambiguous.

In contrast, many relative clauses do not restrict or define the relative head, but simply provide additional information about the referent's characteristics or behavior.

Proper nouns in particular are inherently identifiable, so any relative clause modifying a proper noun is very likely a nonrestrictive relative.

> Identify every relative clause in the passage, and indicate whether it is restrictive or nonrestrictive.

Discourse וְהָיָה

The קַל 3MS Past Narrative form of the lexical copula הָיָה, namely וַיְהִי, frequently functions with a noncopular sense in narrative (*BBH* §36). This "discourse" וַיְהִי typically comes at the start of a new narrative episode and signals the past-tense time frame of the narrative. The קַל 3MS irreal Perfect form of the copula, וְהָיָה, particularly evident when we move from narrative to other types of discourse (e.g., prophetic speech), has an analogous noncopular "discourse" meaning: it stands at the head of a new speech unit and signals irreal mood. The specific modality of the expression headed by the discourse וְהָיָה may be any of those typically expressed by the irreal Perfect, though it most frequently expresses conditionality or habituality, as illustrated by the examples below.

וְהָיָה אִם־יִקְרָא אֵלֶיךָ וְאָמַרְתָּ דַּבֵּר יְהוָה כִּי שֹׁמֵעַ עַבְדֶּךָ
[Irreal] If he calls to you, then you should say, "Speak, YHWH, for your servant is listening." (שמואל א ג:ט)

וְהָיָה בִּהְיוֹת רוּחַ־אֱלֹהִים אֶל־שָׁאוּל וְלָקַח דָּוִד אֶת־הַכִּנּוֹר וְנִגֵּן בְּיָדוֹ
[Irreal] Whenever the spirit of God would come upon Saul, David would take a lyre and play with his hand. (שמואל א טז:כג)

> Find the discourse וְהָיָה in the passage, and identify the modality of the expression that it heads.

Challenge

הַתִּשְׁבִּי

Nouns exist in two basic subtypes: common and proper. Common nouns refer to general concepts or types of entities, whereas proper nouns are names of individual people or specific entities. As a type of common noun, some adjectives and some participles may also be used substantivally (i.e., like nouns) to refer to individuals whose appearance, character, or behavior is typified by the quality or action indicated by the substantive adjective (e.g., צַדִּיק, righteous [person]) or participle (שׁוֹמֵר, guarding [person] > guard).

An additional type of common noun is the gentilic noun. Gentilic nouns are marked by an additional suffix (ִי) and refer to a place of origin. Elijah is often identified as הַתִּשְׁבִּי (the Tishbite), apparently referring to a place that might have been called תִּשְׁבֵּ, although this location is never mentioned apart from the gentilic.

Find three proper nouns (besides יְהוָה and יִשְׂרָאֵל) and three common nouns in the passage. What is one prominent *grammatical* difference between these two types of nouns (*BBH* §20)?

Find three other place names (besides תִּשְׁבֵּי) in the passage, and create a gentilic for each.

לְכַלְכֶּלְךָ

Among the בִּנְיָנִים, the קַל, הִפְעִיל, פִּעֵל, and נִפְעַל are, in that order, the most commonly used in the Hebrew Bible. The other three primary בִּנְיָנִים, the הִתְפַּעֵל, פֻּעַל, and הָפְעַל occur much less often. Beyond the seven primary בִּנְיָנִים, there are a number of secondarily derived בִּנְיָנִים (mostly associated with פִּעֵל) as well as specific weak verb types (the II-ו and the II-III [the middle and final letters of the verb's שֹׁרֶשׁ are identical]). In the text above, the infinitive לְכַלְכֶּלְךָ is one such secondary בִּנְיָן, which, like the primary בִּנְיָן, are named according to their shape (e.g., פִּעֵל reflects the i-e pattern of the root פ-ע-ל). לְכַלְכֶּלְךָ is a פִּלְפֵּל and is associated with the פִּעֵל בִּנְיָן.

Based on the בִּנְיָן (פִּלְפֵּל), what is the likely root of לְכַלְכֶּלְךָ in verse ט?

Reading Insights

Difficult Prepositions

It may seem like some Hebrew prepositions have many unrelated meanings. While most of this is simply due to the inexact correspondence between Hebrew prepositions and whatever modern counterparts we use to understand them (e.g., English prepositions), there are indeed cases where the use of a preposition or preposition combination is unexpected.

Twice in the passage for this chapter, the compound preposition עַל פְּנֵי is used differently than we might expect. In some places, this combination is not idiomatic and simply means "upon the surface of [the water, etc.]." But here and in a small number of other texts, the combination idiomatically means "in front of," "before," "opposite," or even "east of."

Which use of עַל פְּנֵי makes the best sense in this passage?

Similarly, the preposition מִן may have the expected spatial meaning of "from" (for both movement and origin), the comparative meaning of "more than," or the partitive meaning of "some of." But in this passage, מִן is used temporally as "after" in the phrase מִקֵּץ יָמִים (v. ז). Note that the indefinite יָמִים is also idiomatically used for "some" or "an unspecified number of days."

Finally, the ל preposition has both spatial ("to, toward") and possessive ("[belongs] to") uses, but in the passage above (יז:ג), another use is introduced in the phrase וּפָנִיתָ לְךָ. This use of the ל is difficult to translate in English and is sometimes called the ל of interest. This is better understood as the use of ל to indicate reflexivity when the verb itself does not (e.g., a נִפְעַל or הִתְפַּעֵל verb is not used). The reflexive ל indicates that the subject of the verbal action is also affected by the action.

Find and explain all the examples of ל in the passage.

Geography

Where is תִּשְׁבֵּי on the map? Is אֵלִיָּהוּ from the North (יִשְׂרָאֵל) or South (יְהוּדָה)?

Where are צָרְפַת and צִידוֹן? Why would YHWH send his prophet there?

Review

What is וַיְהִי (*BBH* §36)? How does it function in the phrase וַיְהִי דְבַר־יְהוָה אֵלָיו (יז:ב)?

What is לֵאמֹר (יז:ב) and how does it function (*BBH* §36)?

Find every occurrence of a III-ה verb (the final letter of the verb's שֹׁרֶשׁ is ה) in the passage. Identify the שֹׁרֶשׁ, the בִּנְיָן, and the person-gender-number (or list the matching subject pronoun).

Aleppo Codex

To review the passages of chapters 1 and 2, turn to the first page of the Aleppo Codex, and read from the seventh line of the second column (i.e., the new "paragraph," וְאַחְאָב בֶּן־עָמְרִי) to the first two words on the second page (i.e., אַלְמָנָה לְכַלְכְּלֵךְ).

י וַיָּ֣קָם ׀ וַיֵּ֣לֶךְ צָֽרְפַ֗תָה וַיָּבֹא֙ אֶל־פֶּ֣תַח הָעִ֔יר
וְהִנֵּה־שָׁ֛ם אִשָּׁ֥ה אַלְמָנָ֖ה מְקֹשֶׁ֣שֶׁת עֵצִ֑ים וַיִּקְרָ֨א אֵלֶ֜יהָ וַיֹּאמַ֗ר
קְחִי־נָ֨א לִ֧י מְעַט־מַ֛יִם בַּכְּלִ֖י וְאֶשְׁתֶּֽה׃
יא וַתֵּ֖לֶךְ לָקַ֑חַת וַיִּקְרָ֤א אֵלֶ֙יהָ֙ וַיֹּאמַ֔ר
לִֽקְחִי־נָ֥א לִ֛י פַּת־לֶ֖חֶם בְּיָדֵֽךְ׃
יב וַתֹּ֗אמֶר
חַי־יְהוָ֤ה אֱלֹהֶ֙יךָ֙ אִם־יֶשׁ־לִ֣י מָע֔וֹג כִּ֣י אִם־מְלֹ֤א כַף־קֶ֙מַח֙ בַּכַּ֔ד וּמְעַט־שֶׁ֖מֶן בַּצַּפָּ֑חַת וְהִנְנִ֤י מְקֹשֶׁ֙שֶׁת֙ שְׁנַ֣יִם עֵצִ֔ים וּבָ֙אתִי֙ וַעֲשִׂיתִ֙יהוּ֙ לִ֣י וְלִבְנִ֔י וַאֲכַלְנֻ֖הוּ וָמָֽתְנוּ׃
מלכים א
יז, י־טו
יג וַיֹּ֨אמֶר אֵלֶ֜יהָ אֵלִיָּ֗הוּ
אַל־תִּ֣ירְאִ֔י בֹּ֖אִי עֲשִׂ֣י כִדְבָרֵ֑ךְ אַ֣ךְ עֲשִׂי־לִ֣י מִ֠שָּׁם עֻגָ֨ה קְטַנָּ֤ה בָרִאשֹׁנָה֙ וְהוֹצֵ֣את לִ֔י וְלָ֣ךְ וְלִבְנֵ֔ךְ תַּעֲשִׂ֖י בָּאַחֲרֹנָֽה׃ ס
יד כִּ֣י כֹה֩ אָמַ֨ר יְהוָ֜ה אֱלֹהֵ֣י יִשְׂרָאֵ֗ל כַּ֤ד הַקֶּ֙מַח֙ לֹ֣א תִכְלָ֔ה וְצַפַּ֥חַת הַשֶּׁ֖מֶן לֹ֣א תֶחְסָ֑ר עַ֠ד י֛וֹם תֵּת* יְהוָ֥ה גֶּ֖שֶׁם עַל־פְּנֵ֥י הָאֲדָמָֽה׃
טו וַתֵּ֥לֶךְ וַתַּעֲשֶׂ֖ה כִּדְבַ֣ר אֵלִיָּ֑הוּ וַתֹּ֧אכַל הוּא־וָהִ֛יא* וּבֵיתָ֖הּ יָמִֽים׃
*Ketiv: הוא־והיא
Qere: הִיא־וָה֛וּא
*Ketiv: תתן
Qere: תֵּת

Reading 3

מלכים א יז:י–טו

Words to Learn

אַחֲרוֹן	ADJ ______________
אַךְ	ADV ______________
חָסֵר	VB Q ______________
יֵשׁ	COP ______________; EXST ______________
כַּד	NOUN F ______________
כַּף	NOUN F ______________
מְלֹא	NOUN M ______________
מָעוֹג	NOUN M ______________
מְעַט	ADJ ______________
עֻגָה	NOUN F ______________
פַּת	NOUN M ______________
פֶּתַח	NOUN M ______________
צַפַּחַת	NOUN F ______________
קָטָן	ADJ ______________
קֶמַח	NOUN M ______________
(___ ___) קֹשֵׁשׁ	VB POEL ______________
רִאשׁוֹן	ADJ ______________
שֶׁמֶן	NOUN M ______________

Going Deeper with Grammar

Definiteness

Definiteness is a grammatical category (like gender, number, or tense) that represents a noun's identifiability. When a noun is definite, the item to which it refers is identifiable by a reader/listener. Consider the English example below:

I want to buy the book.

In the clause given, the definite NP "the book" signals to the reader that the real-world referent (i.e., the precise book) should be identifiable to the reader/listener. However, when a NP is not definite (as below), its referent (e.g., that of the phrase "a book") is unidentifiable until it is identified by sight, description, etc.

> I want to buy a book.

Languages express and use definiteness differently. For example, in some languages NPs referring to specific but unidentifiable items are often definite, whereas in other languages, such specific, unidentifiable NPs are indefinite. For example, read עמוס ה:יט below:

> כַּאֲשֶׁר יָנוּס אִישׁ מִפְּנֵי הָאֲרִי וּפְגָעוֹ הַדֹּב
> וּבָא הַבַּיִת וְסָמַךְ יָדוֹ עַל־הַקִּיר וּנְשָׁכוֹ הַנָּחָשׁ׃

> just as a man flees from the lion
> and the bear meets him
> and he enters the house
> and leans his hand upon the wall
> and the snake bites him

In this verse, the NPs "the lion," "the bear," "the house," "the wall," and "the snake" denote an arbitrary member of the class described by each (e.g., an arbitrary member of the class "bear"). In Hebrew, such NPs are often definite; whereas in English, such NPs are overwhelmingly indefinite. Compare the translation given above for this verse with its translation in the NRSV:

> as if someone fled from a lion,
> and was met by a bear;
> or went into the house and rested a hand against the wall,
> and was bitten by a snake.

While definiteness in Hebrew and definiteness in English often correspond, this is not always the case.

Definiteness, like other grammatical categories such as gender, number, tense, and aspect, often takes on a morphological form in languages. This is accomplished by means of grammatical words referred to as definite and indefinite articles. Some languages have both a definite and an indefinite article (so English: *the* versus *a*/*an*), while many others have just one or the other.

Hebrew marks definiteness by a definite article (•הַ) as well as by other means, such as cliticization to a definite noun (i.e., סְמִיכוּת) or an enclitic possessive pronoun. Most proper nouns are inherently definite. However, if a common noun (e.g., גִּבְעָה, hill) is drawn into service as a proper noun (הַגִּבְעָה, the hill > Gibeah), it may still appear with the article. (On how Hebrew may use a substitute for an indefinite article, see chap. 11, below.)

Why is the chapter 2 word מֵהַנַּחַל in verse ד definite?

Why is the chapter 2 word הַתִּשְׁבִּי in verse א definite?

Why does the chapter 2 word הַיַּרְדֵּן in verse ג have the article?

Directive and Volitive Verbs

Imperative and jussive verbs (*BBH* §39) together form a subsystem of irreal mood that conveys directive (commands) and volitive (wishes) modalities. That these two conjugations function as a system is evident from their complementary distribution. The imperative is restricted to second-person positive expressions, while the jussive covers all persons. But in the second person, the jussive is limited to negative expressions (using אַל). Semantically the system is unified by its constant reference to the speaker's will: the forms consistently express a speaker's command (directive) or wish (volitive).

The Hebrew Directive-Volitive Irreal Mood Subsystem

	Prefix Pattern		
	Positive	*Negative*	
First person	jussive	(rare)	mostly volitive
Second person	imperative	אַל + jussive	mostly directive
Third person	jussive	אַל + jussive	directive and volitive

From John A. Cook, *Time and the Biblical Hebrew Verb: The Expression of Tense, Aspect, and Modality in Biblical Hebrew*, Linguistic Studies in Ancient West Semitic 7 (Winona Lake, IN: Eisenbrauns, 2012), 245.

The semantic attachment of the imperative-jussive forms to the speaker's will is the distinguishing feature of the subsystem of irreal mood from the rest of the irreal expressions.

The Expression of Irreal Mood in Biblical Hebrew

Modalities	Directive-Volitive	Irreal Imperfect	Irreal Perfect
directive	✓ (subjective)	✓	✓ (procedural)
volitive	✓	✓ (merger with directives)	
epistemic		✓	
dynamic		✓	
contingent		✓ (more lexically marked)	✓ (less lexically marked)
habitual		✓	✓ (procedural)

Adapted from John A. Cook, *Time and the Biblical Hebrew Verb: The Expression of Tense, Aspect, and Modality in Biblical Hebrew*, Linguistic Studies in Ancient West Semitic 7 (Winona Lake, IN: Eisenbrauns, 2012), 255.

If we examine the imperative-jussive system alongside the Imperfect and Perfect verbs used to express irreal mood (*BBH* §§21, 23), we see both overlap and complementary distribution.

The imperative-jussive system is confined to speaker-originating directive and volitive expressions.

שְׁמַע בְּנִי מוּסַר אָבִיךָ וְאַל־תִּטֹּשׁ תּוֹרַת אִמֶּךָ׃

Hear, my son, the instruction of your father and do not abandon the teaching of your mother. (משלי א:ח)

The irreal Imperfect can express directives that originate either with the speaker or with someone else (implied or left ambiguous).

יַעֲשֶׂה פַרְעֹה וְיַפְקֵד פְּקִדִים עַל־הָאָרֶץ

Pharaoh should act and appoint overseers over the land. (בראשית מא:לד)

The irreal Perfect is common in procedural directives.

וּלְקַחְתֶּם אֶת־אֲרוֹן יְהוָה וּנְתַתֶּם אֹתוֹ אֶל־הָעֲגָלָה . . . וְשִׁלַּחְתֶּם אֹתוֹ

You should take the ark of YHWH and place it into the cart . . . and send it away. (שמואל א ו:ח)

The Imperfect is the most broadly used irreal verb, in part because it merges with jussives, from which it is only sometimes morphologically distinct. It is the dominant form for morphologically (versus lexically) expressing epistemic modality (probability of a situation) and dynamic modality (potential of a situation).

וָאֹמַר אֶל־אֲדֹנִי אֻלַי לֹא־תֵלֵךְ הָאִשָּׁה אַחֲרָי׃

And I said to my master, "Perhaps the woman will not follow after me." (בראשית כד:לט)

אֵיכָה אֶשָּׂא לְבַדִּי טָרְחֲכֶם וּמַשַּׂאֲכֶם וְרִיבְכֶם׃

How can I bear alone your trouble and your burden and your bickering? (דברים א:יב)

The irreal Imperfect and irreal Perfect overlap to a greater degree in expressions of habituality (regularity of situations rather than actual situations) and contingency (situations whose actualization is dependent on the actualization of another). Nevertheless, some differences are evident, such as the preference of irreal Perfect for procedural habitual actions. In the example below, the habitual event is introduced by discourse וְהָיָה and a temporal expression followed by an irreal Imperfect. When the habitual event becomes a procedure, the verbs switch to irreal Perfects.

וְהָיָה כְּצֵאת מֹשֶׁה אֶל־הָאֹהֶל יָקוּמוּ כָּל־הָעָם וְנִצְּבוּ אִישׁ פֶּתַח אָהֳלוֹ
וְהִבִּיטוּ אַחֲרֵי מֹשֶׁה עַד־בֹּאוֹ הָאֹהֱלָה׃

[Irreal] Whenever Moses went out to the tent of meeting, all the people would arise [IMPF] and would stand [PERF], each at the door of his tent, and they would watch [PERF] after Moses until he entered into the tent. (שמות לג:ח)

In contingent expressions (e.g., conditional, purpose/result), the irreal Imperfect is more frequently headed by a subordinating conjunction, whereas the irreal Perfect (usually prefixed with the phrase-marking ו conjunction) more frequently appears without a subordinating conjunction expressing these meanings.

וְעָשִׂיתָ הַיָּשָׁר וְהַטּוֹב בְּעֵינֵי יְהוָה לְמַעַן יִיטַב לָךְ וּבָאתָ וְיָרַשְׁתָּ אֶת־הָאָרֶץ הַטֹּבָה אֲשֶׁר־נִשְׁבַּע יְהוָה לַאֲבֹתֶיךָ׃

You should do (what is) right and good in the eyes of YHWH, so that it might go well [IMPF] for you; that you might enter [PERF] and you might take possession [PERF] of the good land that YHWH promised to your ancestors. (דברים ו:יח)

וְנָתַן מַלְכֵיהֶם בְּיָדֶךָ וְהַאֲבַדְתָּ אֶת־שְׁמָם מִתַּחַת הַשָּׁמָיִם

When he [YHWH] places [PERF] their kings in your hand, you should destroy [PERF] their name from under the heavens. (דברים ז:כד)

Identify any sequence of an imperative followed by an irreal Imperfect in the passage.

Identify any sequence of an imperative followed by an irreal Perfect in the passage.

What difference in meaning between the two sequences can you identify?

The Directional ה

Adpositions are relational words that head noun complements and signal location, direction, means, manner, time, possession, as well as mark some nouns as the complements of multivalent verbs. Hebrew solely employs prepositions, the type of adposition that precedes (and is often attached directly to) its noun, *with one exception*: the postposition ָ-ה. This adposition is attached to the end of its complement noun (hence, *post*position) and indicates direction for verbs of motion.

Find the directional ה in the passage.

Challenge

Qere-Ketiv

In the last two panels (verses יד–טו in the text), the Masoretic text contains two cases of textual variants, typically known as *Qere-Ketiv* (read vs. written). Though the later tradition seems to have taken the variants as cases where the variant in the margins (the *Qere*) was preferred over the variant in the text (the *Ketiv*), it is more likely that the variants simply represent the preservation of differences in the manuscript traditions. Thus the critical reader must decide which variant makes better sense of the text. The two sets of variants in the passage above are given again below (with the *Qere* in brackets).

עַד יוֹם תִּתֶּן־[תֵּת־]יְהוָה גֶּשֶׁם עַל־פְּנֵי הָאֲדָמָה׃

תֹּאכַל הוּא־וָהִיא [הִיא־וָהוּא] וּבֵיתָהּ יָמִים׃

In the first verse (יד), what is the difference between the two forms? Does one make better grammatical sense?

In the second verse (טו), does the switched order of pronouns make a difference? Why or why not?

לִקְחִי

The verb לקח is a unique verb, whose first root consonant is a ל. Why is it unique? It is the only I-ל verb to behave like the I-נ weak verbs. The ל assimilates to the ק in many Imperfect forms and drops out entirely in the infinitive and imperative (see appendix B.3). That said, both לקח and many I-נ verbs have rare variants in which the ל or נ does not assimilate or disappear. This passage gives us one of those rare cases for לקח.

Out of 111 occurrences of the קַל imperative of לקח in the Bible, it appears with the initial ל only four times. It is unclear why the ל is included in these four cases. Particularly surprising is the current case of לִקְחִי, since it follows the more usual form קְחִי in an immediately preceding speech and it is out of the mouth of the same character, Elijah, addressed to the same character, the widow.

Besides the imperative קְחִי (v. י), find the one other case of לקח in which the ל drops out.

Find the one case of a I-נ verb in which the נ assimilates or drops out.

Reading Insights

Narrative Economy and Null Constituents

Hebrew storytelling is often highly economical, avoiding repetition when possible, sometimes by eliding the repetitive element. Thus when Elijah says קְחִי־נָא לִי מְעַט־מַיִם בַּכְּלִי וְאֶשְׁתֶּה (v. י), the widow's response (v. יא) is narrated simply as וַתֵּלֶךְ לָקַחַת. It is assumed that the listener or reader can fill in the complement (מְעַט־מַיִם), the means (בַּכְּלִי), and the reason (יִשְׁתֶּה) and so these syntactic constituents are not repeated. Technically, a linguistic analysis does not see "missing" constituents, but "null" constituents (*BBH* §§18, 48), constituents that are syntactically real and so complete the grammar of the verb but are phonologically empty. Such null constituents fulfill grammaticality while also allowing what the speaker says and the listener hears to be less complicated.

Find another example of a null, or unexpressed, complement in the passage.

Lack of Full Subject-Verb Agreement and the Narrator's Subtle Cues

Did you notice something syntactically strange about the last clause of the passage? What person-gender-number is the verb תֹּאכַל? What person-gender-number is the subject הִיא־וָהוּא וּבֵיתָהּ יָמִים? This kind of number and/or gender mismatch is fairly common in Hebrew narrative. While it complicates the grammar, since the subject and verb ought to match in their features, it is a literary device by which the author signals which among multiple agents (or patients) of the verb is the primary one in view.

Who is signaled as the primary agent of the last clause? Why would this be?

Review

How does the particle נָא add to the meaning in the passage (*BBH* §39)?

Does the order of words in Yhwh's statement in verse יד (כַּד הַקֶּמַח לֹא תִכְלָה וְצַפַּחַת הַשֶּׁמֶן לֹא תֶחְסָר) reflect basic subject-verb order (*BBH* §18)? If not, what is the grammatical reason for the word order and how does it affect the meaning (*BBH* §46)?

Find every occurrence of a II-ו/י verb (the middle letter of the verb's שֹׁרֶשׁ is ו or י). Identify the שֹׁרֶשׁ, the בִּנְיָן, and the person-gender-number (or list the matching subject pronoun).

מלכים א
יז, טז-יט
טזכַּ֣ד הַקֶּ֙מַח֙ לֹ֣א כָלָ֔תָה וְצַפַּ֥חַת הַשֶּׁ֖מֶן לֹ֣א חָסֵ֑ר
כִּדְבַ֣ר יְהוָ֔ה אֲשֶׁ֥ר דִּבֶּ֖ר בְּיַ֥ד אֵלִיָּֽהוּ׃ פ
יזוַיְהִ֗י אַחַר֙ הַדְּבָרִ֣ים הָאֵ֔לֶּה
חָלָ֕ה בֶּן־הָאִשָּׁ֖ה בַּעֲלַ֣ת הַבָּ֑יִת
וַיְהִ֤י חָלְיוֹ֙ חָזָ֣ק מְאֹ֔ד
עַ֛ד אֲשֶׁ֥ר לֹא־נֽוֹתְרָה־בּ֖וֹ נְשָׁמָֽה׃
יחוַתֹּ֙אמֶר֙ אֶל־אֵ֣לִיָּ֔הוּ
מַה־לִּ֥י וָלָ֖ךְ אִ֣ישׁ
הָאֱלֹהִ֑ים בָּ֧אתָ אֵלַ֛י
לְהַזְכִּ֥יר אֶת־עֲוֺנִ֖י
וּלְהָמִ֥ית אֶת־בְּנִֽי׃
יטוַיֹּ֥אמֶר אֵלֶ֖יהָ
תְּנִֽי־לִ֣י
אֶת־בְּנֵ֑ךְ
וַיִּקָּחֵ֣הוּ מֵחֵיקָ֗הּ וַֽיַּעֲלֵ֙הוּ֙ אֶל־
הָעֲלִיָּ֗ה אֲשֶׁר־הוּא֙ יֹשֵׁ֣ב שָׁ֔ם
וַיַּשְׁכִּבֵ֖הוּ עַל־מִטָּתֽוֹ׃

מלכים א
יז, כ-כד
כ וַיִּקְרָ֥א אֶל־יְהוָ֖ה וַיֹּאמַ֑ר
יְהוָ֣ה אֱלֹהָ֔י הֲ֠גַם עַל־הָאַלְמָנָ֞ה אֲשֶׁר־אֲנִ֨י מִתְגּוֹרֵ֥ר עִמָּ֛הּ הֲרֵע֖וֹתָ לְהָמִ֥ית אֶת־בְּנָֽהּ׃
כא וַיִּתְמֹדֵ֤ד עַל־הַיֶּ֙לֶד֙ שָׁלֹ֣שׁ פְּעָמִ֔ים וַיִּקְרָ֥א אֶל־יְהוָ֖ה
וַיֹּאמַ֑ר
יְהוָ֣ה אֱלֹהָ֔י תָּ֥שָׁב נָ֛א נֶֽפֶשׁ־הַיֶּ֥לֶד הַזֶּ֖ה עַל־קִרְבּֽוֹ׃
כב וַיִּשְׁמַ֥ע יְהוָ֖ה בְּק֣וֹל אֵלִיָּ֑הוּ וַתָּ֧שָׁב נֶֽפֶשׁ־הַיֶּ֛לֶד עַל־קִרְבּ֖וֹ וַיֶּֽחִי׃
כג וַיִּקַּ֨ח אֵלִיָּ֜הוּ אֶת־הַיֶּ֗לֶד וַיֹּרִדֵ֤הוּ מִן־הָֽעֲלִיָּה֙ הַבַּ֔יְתָה וַֽיִּתְּנֵ֖הוּ לְאִמּ֑וֹ וַיֹּ֙אמֶר֙ אֵֽלִיָּ֔הוּ
רְאִ֖י חַ֥י בְּנֵֽךְ׃
כד וַתֹּ֤אמֶר הָֽאִשָּׁה֙ אֶל־אֵ֣לִיָּ֔הוּ
עַתָּה֙ זֶ֣ה יָדַ֔עְתִּי כִּ֛י אִ֥ישׁ אֱלֹהִ֖ים אָ֑תָּה וּדְבַר־יְהוָ֥ה בְּפִ֖יךָ אֱמֶֽת׃ פ

Reading 4

מלכים א יז:טז–כד

Words to Learn

אֱמֶת NOUN F ______________

בַּעֲלָה NOUN F ______________

הֵרַע (___) VB HI ______________

הִתְגֹּרֵר (___) VB HITPOLEL ______________

הִתְמֹדֵד (___) VB HITPOEL ______________

חָזָק ADJ ______________

חֵיק NOUN M ______________

חָלָה VB Q ______________

חֳלִי NOUN M ______________

יֶלֶד NOUN M ______________

מִטָּה NOUN F ______________

נוֹתַר (___) VB NI ______________

נְשָׁמָה NOUN F ______________

עֲלִיָּה NOUN F ______________

פַּעַם NOUN M ______________

Going Deeper with Grammar

Copular Clauses and Null Copulas

Copular clauses are those in which a subject and copular complement are linked in a semantic (propositional) relationship. Unlike lexical verbs, copulas have minimal semantic content but simply link a subject and a predicate (hence *copula*, which is derived from Latin meaning "fasten together"). Copulas are typically found in equative clauses (the first example below) or predicative clauses (the second through fourth examples).

David is the king.
[equative]

David is a king.
[predicative]

David is righteous.
 [predicative]

David is in the palace.
 [predicative]

In the equative example, the copular subject (David) is *equated with* the definite/specific copular complement NP (the king). An intuitive (i.e., nontheoretical) way to describe what these clauses do is "who-ness": they provide information not about the subject but tell who the subject is. In contrast to these equative clauses stand the predicative copular clauses. In the first of the three examples, the clause asserts that the indefinite and nonspecific copular complement NP (a king) is a property of the subject NP. Similarly, the adjective "righteous" and the PP "in the place" are properties of character and location, respectively. The intuitive descriptor for these clauses is "about-ness": they provide information about the subject.

Copular clauses are expressed in four ways in Hebrew: with an overt copular verb (הָיָה), with a null copula, with יֵשׁ or אֵין, and with a pronominal copula. All four types are used in the Elijah narrative and will be discussed as they arise (see chaps. 5, 6, 8, and 10).

The passage above provides an opportunity to discuss null copulas. Clauses without a lexical copula—indeed, without any overt verb—are analyzed as null copula clauses. That is, the verb is syntactically and semantically real and present (otherwise, the subject and predicate would not be linked in a meaningful way) but phonologically empty (which is why the clause seems "verbless").

וְשֵׁם הָאִישׁ ___ אֱלִימֶלֶךְ
And the name of the man ø (was) Elimelek. (רות א:ב)

The tense/aspect/modality (TAM) of the null copula is determined by the extraclausal context. In isolation, a null copula clause would default to the present tense (e.g., "the name of the man (is) Elimelek"), but following the initial *wayyiqtol* clauses in רות א:א–ב, the TAM of the null copula is contextually determined in the past temporal frame, reflected in the translation using "was."

Null copula clauses may also have a null subject, resulting in a clause with only one overt constituent. This is rare in main clauses but more common within relative clauses.

אֲשֶׁר ___ ___ לְצִידוֹן
which ø (it) ø (belongs) to Sidon (מלכים א יז:ט)

Find any null copula clause in the passage.

Basic and Derived Word Order

Hebrew has a basic subject-verb word order, like English. Unlike English, however, Hebrew exhibits a great deal of derived word order. For instance, many grammatical words—such as subordinators, interrogatives, and negatives—trigger an inversion from subject-verb word order to verb-subject word order with finite verbs (*BBH* §18). That is, the verb "moves" (or "raises") from its normal place to a place in front of the subject.

Hebrew word order also interacts with verbal semantics, so that irreal mood also triggers verb-raising, hence verb-subject order (*BBH* §21). However, null copulas never automatically trigger verb-raising. Similarly, the discourse-pragmatic features associated with topic and focus (see the Linguistics Glossary and also *BBH* §41) typically result in verb-subject order. Thus Hebrew word order can be summarized as follows:

- Hebrew has a basic (i.e., unmarked) word order of subject-verb (whether the verb is an overt finite verb or null copula).
- Inversion of the basic word order due to verb-raising is triggered at three levels of the language:
    1. *Syntactically*, in clauses with a finite verb, most grammatical or "function" words: subordinators, interrogatives, negative words (this list notably excludes ו, עַתָּה, and הִנֵּה), and the "underspecified" function word in Past Narrative (i.e., the function word that became the gemination in the prefix between the ו and the verb) will trigger inverted verb-subject order. Note that syntax triggering does not occur with null copulas.
    2. *Semantically*, irreal mood: irreal Perfect and irreal Imperfect are distinct from their real counterparts by this triggered word order, and the imperative-jussive modal system shows this irreal mood inversion.
    3. *Pragmatically*, moving any item to the first position in the clause (i.e., for focus or topic) triggers inverted verb-subject order (including in null copula and participial clauses).

Explain the word order in the following examples from the passage:

(יז:טז) כַּד הַקֶּמַח לֹא כָלָתָה וְצַפַּחַת הַשֶּׁמֶן לֹא חָסֵר

(יז:יז) אַחַר הַדְּבָרִים הָאֵלֶּה חָלָה בֶּן־הָאִשָּׁה

(יז:כב) וַתָּשָׁב נֶפֶשׁ־הַיֶּלֶד עַל־קִרְבּוֹ

Identify at least one case of pragmatically induced fronting in a null copula clause in the passage.

Constituents, Syntactic Roles, and Valency

Within the verb phrase (VP), the nonverbal elements are treated in traditional, Latinate-based grammar discussions in terms of word/phrase class (e.g., prepositional phrase, noun phrase) and case (e.g., accusative and dative). These categories can be problematic when applied to Hebrew because morphologically marked case is a lost feature. Instead, Hebrew verb-argument relationships are better described in terms of valency, which provides a structural description of grammaticality (*BBH* §48).

A verb's valency concerns what type and number of constituents a verb licenses (i.e., specifies and limits) to produce a well-formed clause. The two types of licensed syntactic constituents are the subject and the complement. The subject is, of course, the agent doing the (active) verbal activity or the patient experiencing the (passive or stative) activity. The complement (which has some overlap with the traditional "object" [direct and indirect]) is the constituent that is affected by the verbal activity or event and is thus semantically and syntactically integral to the activity. Both types of licensed constituents may be phonologically null (see chaps. 1 and 3).

The examples below illustrate the basic patterns.

Avalent: no subject or complement

תַּשְׁלֵג בְּצַלְמוֹן
snowing on Zalmon (תהלים סח:טו)

Monovalent: subject licensed; no complement licensed

לָכֵן שָׂמַח לִבִּי
Therefore my heart rejoices. (תהלים טז:ט)

Bivalent: subject licensed; one complement licensed

יְהוָה תְּפִלָּתִי יִקָּח
YHWH will accept my prayer. (תהלים ו:י)

Trivalent: subject licensed; two complements licensed

מִי יַשְׁקֵנִי מַיִם
Who will give me a drink of water? (שמואל ב כג:טו)

The avalent pattern is rarer than the other three and mostly restricted to meteorological events such as שָׁלַג (to snow). English requires the dummy pronoun *it*, which is so termed because it has no semantic role to fill, such as agent; for this reason, "it" is a *syntactic* subject but not a semantic one. Trivalent verbs such as נָתַן, הִשְׁקָה, שִׂים, and שִׁית constitute a small set of verbs (though used frequently). Monovalent verbs such as שָׂמַח and bivalent verbs such as לָקַח predominate.

Since a verb licenses just one subject, multiple subject candidates are interpreted as a compound subject constituent. Similarly, if multiple candidates appear for a single complement role, they are interpreted as a compound, such as with the patient complement *coat and hat* in *The lady took her coat and hat*.

By contrast, adjuncts are unlicensed modifiers. That is, they are neither specified nor limited by the verb. In *The lady hurriedly took her coat and hat outside into the rain*, the adjuncts *hurriedly, outside*, and *into the rain* are just a few of the (theoretically) unlimited adjunct modifiers that could be added to the clause.

Based on the passage, what is the valency of the following verbs: כָּלָה, יָשַׁב, and הִשְׁכִּיב?

Challenge

Difficult Prepositions (Again)

The preposition ב is used ubiquitously but also has multiple nuances, some of which are not transparently related. Most of the meanings fall into either a basic spatial or temporal category, though the full variety in which ב is used is impressive. To illustrate this, consider the list of meanings given in *DCH* (2:82):

> 1. בְּ of place/time; 2. בְּ of accompaniment; 3. בְּ of cause; 4. בְּ of instrument; 5. בְּ of agent; 6. בְּ partitive; 7. בְּ of essence; 8. בְּ of comparison; 9. בְּ *according to*; 10. בְּ *at the cost of*; 11. בְּ *despite*; 12. בְּ *in respect of*; 13. בְּ *against*; 14. בְּ *over*; 15. בְּ *from*; 16. בְּ *after*; 17. בְּ *to, with*; 18. introducing [complement].

Only time and much reading can conquer multivalent prepositions such as ב, which, thankfully, are a small set of words (though they are used frequently).

Find the occurrence of the שמע בקול idiom in the passage, and use the context to provide an educated guess about the idiomatic meaning.

There are two more occurrences of ב in the passage; locate each and identify its meaning.

Reading Insights

Idiomatic Phrases (Again)

This passage provides another idiom (see chap. 1) using the interrogative מָה. When "what" is followed by the preposition ל, it typically carries an idiomatic meaning, though pinning down the meaning can prove difficult. Sometimes מָה ל refers to owning something (e.g., מַה־לָּךְ, what do you have?, שפטים א:יד). The sense of possession or ownership can be abstract (e.g., מַה־לְּךָ לְסַפֵּר חֻקָּי, what right do you have to recite my rules?, תהלים נ:טז). And sometimes the idiom is more elliptical and blunt (e.g., מַה־לְּךָ, what's the matter with you?!, יונה א:ו).

Identify the idiomatic phrase with מָה in the passage and use the context to provide an educated guess at the idiomatic meaning.

The Masoretic טְעָמִים (Accents)

The Masoretic טְעָמִים (accents) are a medieval layer of the textual history representing a complex history that may have originated as a notation related to the natural (storytelling) recitation of the biblical text and then later became associated with liturgical chanting (see appendix C). As a prosodic layer likely associated with reading the text in natural contours, the טְעָמִים provide access to the Masoretic interpretation of the text, since recitation inherently includes interpretation in the pauses, the highs, and the lows of the speaking-reading patterns.

In verses יח–כ of the text, explain how the טְעָמִים aid in identifying the beginning of reported speech from the narrative frame.

Review

There are two occurrences of וַיְהִי in the passage (*BBH* §36). How does each function?

What function do the two infinitives, לְהַזְכִּיר and לְהָמִית, have (*BBH* §24)?

What verbal conjugation is used in this phrase: תְּשָׁב נָא? What are the clues that tell you what kind of verb it is?

Find every occurrence of a II-III verb (the middle and final letters of the verb's שֹׁרֶשׁ are identical). Identify the שֹׁרֶשׁ, the בִּנְיָן, and the person-gender-number (or list the matching subject pronoun).

א וַיְהִי֙ יָמִ֣ים רַבִּ֔ים וּדְבַר־יְהוָ֗ה הָיָה֙
אֶל־אֵ֣לִיָּ֔הוּ בַּשָּׁנָ֥ה הַשְּׁלִישִׁ֖ית לֵאמֹ֑ר
לֵ֚ךְ הֵרָאֵ֣ה אֶל־אַחְאָ֔ב
וְאֶתְּנָ֥ה מָטָ֖ר עַל־פְּנֵ֥י
הָאֲדָמָֽה׃
מלכים א
יח, א-ז
ב וַיֵּ֙לֶךְ֙ אֵלִיָּ֔הוּ לְהֵרָא֖וֹת
אֶל־אַחְאָ֑ב וְהָרָעָ֖ב
חָזָ֥ק בְּשֹׁמְרֽוֹן׃
ג וַיִּקְרָ֣א אַחְאָ֔ב אֶל־עֹבַדְיָ֖הוּ אֲשֶׁ֣ר עַל־
הַבָּ֑יִת וְעֹבַדְיָ֗הוּ הָיָ֛ה יָרֵ֥א אֶת־יְהוָ֖ה מְאֹֽד׃
ה וַיֹּ֤אמֶר אַחְאָב֙
אֶל־עֹ֣בַדְיָ֔הוּ
לֵ֤ךְ בָּאָ֙רֶץ֙ אֶל־כָּל־מַעְיְנֵ֣י הַמַּ֔יִם וְאֶ֖ל
כָּל־הַנְּחָלִ֑ים אוּלַ֣י ׀ נִמְצָ֣א חָצִ֗יר וּנְחַיֶּה֙
ס֣וּס וָפֶ֔רֶד וְל֥וֹא נַכְרִ֖ית מֵהַבְּהֵמָֽה׃
ד וַיְהִ֗י בְּהַכְרִ֤ית אִיזֶ֙בֶל֙ אֵ֚ת נְבִיאֵ֣י יְהוָ֔ה וַיִּקַּ֨ח עֹבַדְיָ֜הוּ מֵאָ֣ה
נְבִאִ֗ים וַֽיַּחְבִּיאֵ֞ם חֲמִשִּׁ֥ים אִישׁ֙ בַּמְּעָרָ֔ה וְכִלְכְּלָ֖ם לֶ֥חֶם וָמָֽיִם׃
ו וַיְחַלְּק֥וּ לָהֶ֛ם אֶת־הָאָ֖רֶץ לַעֲבָר־בָּ֑הּ אַחְאָ֞ב הָלַ֨ךְ
בְּדֶ֤רֶךְ אֶחָד֙ לְבַדּ֔וֹ וְעֹבַדְיָ֛הוּ הָלַ֥ךְ בְּדֶֽרֶךְ־אֶחָ֖ד לְבַדּֽוֹ׃
ז וַיְהִ֤י עֹבַדְיָ֙הוּ֙ בַּדֶּ֔רֶךְ וְהִנֵּ֥ה
אֵלִיָּ֖הוּ לִקְרָאת֑וֹ וַיַּכִּרֵ֔הוּ

Reading 5

מלכים א יח:א–ז

Words to Learn

אוּלַי ADV ______________

בַּד NOUN M (WITH לְ) ______________

בְּהֵמָה NOUN F ______________

(___ ___ ___) הֶחְבִּיא VB HI ______________

(___ ___ ___) חִלֵּק VB PI ______________

חָצִיר NOUN M ______________

יָרֵא ADJ ______________

מַעְיָן NOUN M ______________

מְעָרָה NOUN F ______________

סוּס NOUN M ______________

פֶּ֫רֶד NOUN M ______________

רָעָב NOUN M ______________

שְׁלִישִׁי ORD ______________

Going Deeper with Grammar

Foreground and Background

Narratives typically present events in the order in which they occur. That timeline of key events that each lead to the next is referred to as the foreground of the narrative. In Hebrew, the Past Narrative is the preferred (though not exclusively used) conjugation to express foregrounded events (see *BBH* §43).

Various "supporting" events that help the reader to understand the progression of the narrative (i.e., the foreground) are set apart by departures from the typical foreground pattern of Past Narrative verbs. Background events are often events that occurred before the current time in the narrative, and explain the foregrounded actions, such as the reference to Rachel's previous stealing of her father's household idols in בראשית לא:לב.

וְלֹא־יָדַע יַעֲקֹב כִּי רָחֵל גְּנָבָתַם

But Jacob did not know that Rachel <u>had stolen them</u>.

Other background events set the scene of what is going on concurrently with the foregrounded events, as in the example from the Joseph story.

וַיָּשָׁב רְאוּבֵן אֶל־הַבּוֹר וְהִנֵּה אֵין־יוֹסֵף בַּבּוֹר וַיִּקְרַע אֶת־בְּגָדָיו׃
Reuben returned to the pit, and, hey!, Joseph was not in the pit, and he tore his garments. (בראשית לז:כט)

The presentative הִנֵּה highlights the cruciality of the background scene for the foregrounded actions. Without the report of Joseph's absence, Reuben's return to the pit followed by tearing his garments would make no sense.

Identify any case of backgrounded information in the passage and describe how it functions.

Copular Clauses and the Overt Lexical Copula היה

Copular clauses and null copulas were described in chapter 4. Hebrew has a lexical copula, הָיָה, which also has a noncopular meaning. Though rare, the verb הָיָה may signal an existential semantic meaning instead of its much more common copular function. When הָיָה is existential, it is necessarily monovalent and thus takes no VP complements.

וַיְהִי־אוֹר
And light existed. (בראשית א:ג)

When copular (just linking, with no lexical content), the verb הָיָה is bivalent. Its VP complement is often a PP, which may be, for example, locative (first two examples below), temporal (third and fourth examples), or a result of a status change (fifth example).

וַיִּהְיוּ־שָׁם
And they were there. (רות א:ב)

הַנְּפִלִים הָיוּ בָאָרֶץ בַּיָּמִים הָהֵם
The Nephilim were in the land in those days. (בראשית ו:ד)

הָרָעָב הָרִאשׁוֹן אֲשֶׁר הָיָה בִּימֵי אַבְרָהָם
the first famine, which was in the days of Abraham (בראשית כו:א)

וְהַשֹּׁפְטִים אֲשֶׁר יִהְיוּ בַּיָּמִים הָהֵם
and the judges who will be in those days (דברים יט:יז)

וַתְּהִי־לוֹ לְאִשָּׁה
And (she) became for him [for] a wife. (רות ד:יג)

There are also cases of nominal complements, which may be a NP or ADJP.

כִּי הִוא הָיְתָה אֵם כָּל־חָי
because she was the mother of all living (בראשית ג:כ)

וּתְהִי מַשְׂכֻּרְתֵּךְ שְׁלֵמָה מֵעִם יְהוָה
And may your wage be complete from YHWH. (רות ב:יב)

And finally, copular הָיָה occurs with participial complements.

וְהָיִיתָ מְמַשֵּׁשׁ בַּצָּהֳרַיִם כַּאֲשֶׁר יְמַשֵּׁשׁ הָעִוֵּר בָּאֲפֵלָה
And you shall be groping about at noon like the blind person gropes in the darkness. (דברים כח:כט)

Overt subjects certainly may occur with the copular verb, but this is not the majority pattern.

וַיְהִי רָעָב בָּאָרֶץ
And a famine was in the land. (רות א:א)

Many copula clauses have a null subject, which is typically linked to an overt noun (the antecedent) in the preceding discourse.

וְהָיוּ לָכֶם לַאֲחֻזָּה
And ø (they) shall become for you a possession. (ויקרא כה:מה)

The discourse וַיְהִי and וְהָיָה are avalent, since they have neither a VP complement nor any semantic role (e.g., agent, etc.) for a subject. The form serves the discourse function of reasserting the past reference time, often at the beginning of a new narrative episode.

וַיְהִי מִקֵּץ יָמִים וַיָּבֵא קַיִן מִפְּרִי הָאֲדָמָה מִנְחָה לַיהוָה׃
[Past] At the end of so many days, Cain brought some of the fruit of the ground (as) a gift to YHWH. (בראשית ד:ג)

Find and identify all the uses of היה in the passage.

Challenge

To Be a Verb or Not to Be a Verb: Adjective or Stative Verb?

With some stative verbs (i.e., verbs that describe a state or condition), the form of the 3MS קַל Perfect conjugation is identical to the MS adjective. Thus, הוּא כָּבֵד could be "he is heavy" (adjective) or "he is heavy" (Perfect); only in the other inflected forms does the ambiguity disappear: הֵם כְּבֵדִים (they [are] heavy; adjective) versus הֵם כָּבְדוּ (they are heavy; Perfect).

Making matters more complex is that some of the stative adjectives shifted over time to take on verbal characteristics. For example, the adjective קָרֵב in the clause אַתֶּם קְרֵבִים הַיּוֹם לַמִּלְחָמָה (you are drawing near today to war, דברים כ:ג) is clearly adjectival in form, but the meaning is verbal (i.e., not a property but a progressive activity) and it has a locative complement, לַמִּלְחָמָה.

Identify the stative adjective/verb in the passage, and determine whether it is adjectival or verbal.

Reading Insights

Nonspecific Quantification

In Hebrew storytelling, indications of time can be very specific (on X day, of Y month, in Z year) but also nonspecific (after so many days). For example, the plural noun יָמִים (days) by itself can reference "so many days," as in the clause תֵּשֵׁב הַנַּעֲרָ אִתָּנוּ יָמִים אוֹ עָשׂוֹר (let the girl stay with us [a few] days, or ten [days], בראשית כד:נה). The connotation "few" in this example is contextually derived, since it is contrasted with "ten" (presumably the high end of the scale).

Hebrew provides a grammatical means to force a small ("few") or large ("many") nonspecific reading. For the former, Hebrew uses the plural of אֶחָד.

וַיִּהְיוּ בְעֵינָיו כְּיָמִים אֲחָדִים בְּאַהֲבָתוֹ אֹתָהּ
And [the seven years] were like a few days in his eyes because he loved her. (בראשית כט:כ)

Can you identify in the passage the means for forcing a nonspecific large ("many") reading of יָמִים?

Review

If the וַיְהִי at the start of verse א is a discourse וַיְהִי (*BBH* §36), where does יָמִים רַבִּים fit syntactically?

Explain the sequence of verbs in לֵךְ הֵרָאֵה אֶל־אַחְאָב וְאֶתְּנָה (v. א).

Identify every non-קַל verb in the passage, its שֹׁרֶשׁ, and its בִּנְיָן.

Aleppo Codex

To review the passages of chapters 3–5, turn to the second page of the Aleppo Codex, and read from the third word of the first line (i.e., וַיָּקָם) to the first word on the fourth line of the third page (i.e., אֵלִיָּהוּ).

מלכים א
יח, ז-יט
ז וַיִּפֹּל עַל־פָּנָיו וַיֹּאמֶר
הַאַתָּה זֶה אֲדֹנִי אֵלִיָּהוּ׃
ח וַיֹּאמֶר לוֹ
אָנִי לֵךְ אֱמֹר לַאדֹנֶיךָ הִנֵּה אֵלִיָּהוּ׃
ט וַיֹּאמֶר
מֶה חָטָאתִי כִּי־אַתָּה נֹתֵן אֶת־עַבְדְּךָ בְּיַד־אַחְאָב לַהֲמִיתֵנִי׃ י חַי ׀ יְהוָה אֱלֹהֶיךָ אִם־יֶשׁ־גּוֹי וּמַמְלָכָה אֲשֶׁר לֹא־שָׁלַח אֲדֹנִי שָׁם לְבַקֶּשְׁךָ וְאָמְרוּ אָיִן וְהִשְׁבִּיעַ אֶת־הַמַּמְלָכָה וְאֶת־הַגּוֹי כִּי לֹא יִמְצָאֶכָּה׃
יא וְעַתָּה אַתָּה אֹמֵר לֵךְ אֱמֹר לַאדֹנֶיךָ הִנֵּה אֵלִיָּהוּ׃ יב וְהָיָה אֲנִי ׀ אֵלֵךְ מֵאִתָּךְ וְרוּחַ יְהוָה ׀ יִשָּׂאֲךָ עַל אֲשֶׁר לֹא־אֵדָע
וּבָאתִי לְהַגִּיד לְאַחְאָב וְלֹא יִמְצָאֲךָ וַהֲרָגָנִי וְעַבְדְּךָ יָרֵא אֶת־יְהוָה מִנְּעֻרָי׃
יג הֲלֹא־הֻגַּד לַאדֹנִי אֵת אֲשֶׁר־עָשִׂיתִי בַּהֲרֹג אִיזֶבֶל אֵת נְבִיאֵי יְהוָה וָאַחְבִּא מִנְּבִיאֵי יְהוָה מֵאָה אִישׁ חֲמִשִּׁים חֲמִשִּׁים אִישׁ בַּמְּעָרָה וָאֲכַלְכְּלֵם לֶחֶם וָמָיִם׃
יד וְעַתָּה אַתָּה אֹמֵר לֵךְ אֱמֹר לַאדֹנֶיךָ הִנֵּה אֵלִיָּהוּ וַהֲרָגָנִי׃ ס
טו וַיֹּאמֶר אֵלִיָּהוּ
חַי יְהוָה צְבָאוֹת אֲשֶׁר עָמַדְתִּי לְפָנָיו כִּי הַיּוֹם אֵרָאֶה אֵלָיו׃
טז וַיֵּלֶךְ עֹבַדְיָהוּ לִקְרַאת אַחְאָב וַיַּגֶּד־לוֹ וַיֵּלֶךְ אַחְאָב לִקְרַאת אֵלִיָּהוּ׃ יז וַיְהִי כִּרְאוֹת אַחְאָב אֶת־אֵלִיָּהוּ וַיֹּאמֶר אַחְאָב אֵלָיו
הַאַתָּה זֶה עֹכֵר יִשְׂרָאֵל׃
יח וַיֹּאמֶר
לֹא עָכַרְתִּי אֶת־יִשְׂרָאֵל כִּי אִם־אַתָּה וּבֵית אָבִיךָ בַּעֲזָבְכֶם אֶת־מִצְוֺת יְהוָה וַתֵּלֶךְ אַחֲרֵי הַבְּעָלִים׃ יט וְעַתָּה שְׁלַח קְבֹץ אֵלַי אֶת־כָּל־יִשְׂרָאֵל אֶל־הַר הַכַּרְמֶל וְאֶת־נְבִיאֵי הַבַּעַל אַרְבַּע מֵאוֹת וַחֲמִשִּׁים וּנְבִיאֵי הָאֲשֵׁרָה אַרְבַּע מֵאוֹת אֹכְלֵי שֻׁלְחַן אִיזָבֶל׃

Reading 6

מלכים א יח:ז–יט

Words to Learn

הִכִּיר (__ __ __) VB HI ________________

הָרַג VB Q ________________

הִשְׁבִּיעַ (__ __ __) VB HI ________________

מַמְלָכָה NOUN F ________________

מִצְוָה NOUN F ________________

נְעוּרִים NOUN MP ________________

עָבַר VB Q ________________

קָבַץ VB Q ________________

שֻׁלְחָן NOUN M ________________

Going Deeper with Grammar

Apposition

Apposition is typically the modification of one constituent (the anchor) by a second constituent (the appositive) standing in juxtaposition with the first. Apposition is common for noun modification and stands between the סְמִיכוּת construction (see chap. 1), on the one hand, and more complex types of modification (e.g., relative clauses; see chap. 2), on the other. An appositive noun is not in a bound relationship with the anchor noun, which distinguishes it from the סְמִיכוּת construction, and yet it is the same category as the noun it modifies (i.e., both are nouns), which distinguishes it from adjectives. Below, the NP בֶּן־עָמְרִי modifies the PN אַחְאָב appositively.

וְאַחְאָב בֶּן־עָמְרִי מָלַךְ עַל־יִשְׂרָאֵל

And Ahab, son of Omri, ruled over Israel. (מלכים א טז:כט)

Apposition is also used for other constituents: PPs, verbs, and even clauses may be modified by appositives of the same constituent type.

וַיָּבֹאוּ אֶל־נֹחַ אֶל־הַתֵּבָה

And they came to Noah, to the ark. (בראשית ז:טו)

וְאַבְרָהָם וְשָׂרָה זְקֵנִים בָּאִים בַּיָּמִים
And Abraham and Sarah (were) old, advanced in years. (בראשית יח:יא)

וּמִבְצַר מִשְׂגַּב חוֹמֹתֶיךָ הֵשַׁח הִשְׁפִּיל הִגִּיעַ לָאָרֶץ עַד־עָפָר׃
And the fortress of the stronghold of your walls he has thrown down, brought low, thrown to the ground, to the dirt. (ישעיהו כה:יב)

As with relative clauses, apposition falls into two semantic types: restrictive and nonrestrictive. Restrictive apposition is used when the appositive is necessary to define the anchor. This occurs primarily when numerals are anchors (*BBH* §45).

עֲשָׂרָה אֲנָשִׁים
ten, men > ten men (רות ד:ב)

Without the appositive אֲנָשִׁים, the referent of the numeral עֲשָׂרָה would be unclear.

A nonrestrictive appositive is not necessary for the identification of the anchor, but provides further information about the anchor's characteristics or features by specifying, rewording, or reformulating the anchor. Thus when a numeral is the appositive, the referent of the anchor is clear enough to identify it, and the numeral provides only its quantity.

יָמִים שְׁלוֹשָׁה
days, three > three days (דברי הימים א יב:מ)

Clausal apposition is used only nonrestrictively and appears mostly in poetry, where it is the grammatical construction that underlies the traditional notion of parallelism.

לָמָּה רָגְשׁוּ גוֹיִם וּלְאֻמִּים יֶהְגּוּ־רִיק
Why do the nations rage, that is, the nations plot emptiness? (תהלים ב:א)

Note how the appositive clause restates the essential idea of the anchor clause and adds one feature, the notion that the activity is רִיק.

Identify at least four cases of nonclausal apposition, and explain the type of apposition.

There are two cases of clausal apposition in the passage; see if you can find them.

Nonverbal Copulas with זֶה

The demonstrative is used as a nonverbal copula (see chap. 4) in a relatively small set of examples (just sixteen times, in fact). Either the demonstrative-as-copula strategy was marginal (perhaps it seemed strange to most listeners) and never quite caught on, or there is a pragmatic nuance to the use that we cannot discern. Regardless of the small number of examples, the grammar is clear (and is attested in other languages too). The demonstrative copula is labeled as DEM in the example below.

וַיֹּאמֶר יִצְחָק אֶל־יַעֲקֹב גְּשָׁה־נָּא וַאֲמֻשְׁךָ בְּנִי הַאַתָּה זֶה בְּנִי עֵשָׂו אִם־לֹא׃

And Isaac said to Jacob, "Draw near and let me feel you, my son. You DEM (are) my son Esau, or not?" (i.e., Are you my son Esau or not?) (בראשית כז:כא)

וַיִּפֶן אַבְנֵר אַחֲרָיו וַיֹּאמֶר הַאַתָּה זֶה עֲשָׂהאֵל וַיֹּאמֶר אָנֹכִי׃

And Abner turned behind him and said, "You DEM (are) Asahel?" And he said, "I am." (שמואל ב ב:כ)

> Find the cases of the copular זֶה in the passage.

Oath Making

There was a full oath formula in ancient Hebrew that was usually truncated. The full formula is represented in שמואל א ג:יז.

כֹּה יַעֲשֶׂה־לְּךָ אֱלֹהִים וְכֹה יוֹסִיף אִם־תְּכַחֵד מִמֶּנִּי דָּבָר

Thus may God do to you and thus may he add if you hide something from me.

This oath formula utilizes a conditional subordinate clause (*BBH* §30), which is introduced by אִם.

The syntactic complication about the oath formula is that the full form is rarely used even though אִם is used in contexts that are both clearly oath-like and clearly not straightforward conditional clauses. It seems that the truncation of the full oath formula led to the re-analysis of אִם and the corresponding negative אִם לֹא as strong adverbs: in oath contexts, אִם typically becomes a strong negative adverb (surely not) and אִם לֹא typically becomes a strong positive adverb (surely, certainly).

Further complicating the shortened oath statement is the introduction of the oath statement by an exclamative phrase, such as חַי יְהוָה ([by] the life of YHWH) followed by the re-analyzed אִם or אִם לֹא component.

> Where is the oath formula in the text above? Is it the full form or truncated? How must you understand אִם?

Challenge

Relatives without Heads?

Though it sounds like a horror movie or Halloween theme, headless relatives are also a common feature in Hebrew grammar. For many relative clauses, the noun that is modified (the relative head) is an overt noun, as with הָאָדָם in the clause וַיָּשֶׂם שָׁם אֶת־הָאָדָם אֲשֶׁר יָצָר (and [YHWH] put there the man that he created, בראשית ב:ח). And yet, since Hebrew allows the use of null constituents (see chap. 1), the use of a null noun as the head of a relative clause is commonplace. In such cases, the content of the null noun can be reconstructed from the information provided in the relative clause. For example, in כַּאֲשֶׁר צִוָּה אֱלֹהִים אֶת־נֹחַ (בראשית ז:ט), what is missing is the content of what God commanded Noah. Thus there is a null relative head noun between the preposition כ and the relative אֲשֶׁר (like [the instruction] that God commanded Noah).

> Find the two occurrences of a null head relative clause in the passage; explain how you identified them as null relative clauses and the content you can reconstruct for the null head.

Finding the כִּי*: Time, Cause, or Condition?*

Like some of the more notorious prepositions (e.g., ב), the subordinator כִּי exhibits many uses in Hebrew. Most grammars assign it a host of functions, from introducing complement, causal, temporal, conditional, consecutive, concessive, and adversative clauses to serving as an exclamative ("indeed!").

Unfortunately, no compelling analysis of כִּי that shortens this list of supposed uses has been proposed, and we must live without a key to a unified כִּי.

> Find all the cases of כִּי in the passage, and propose a reasonable, context-based function.

Reading Insights

Distribution

A sense of distribution, in which each individual item of a class (and not the class as a whole) is referred to—"each X" or "X by X"—is expressed in Hebrew by the appositional repetition of a noun. Thus שָׁנָה שָׁנָה can mean "year by year" or "each year," and שִׁבְעָה שִׁבְעָה in the flood story (בראשית ו–ח) refers to the "seven each" of animal kinds that Noah was to bring along.

> Find the distributive phrase in the passage and explain its use.

אֵת on the Subject

The majority of cases of אֵת in Hebrew mark a type of NP complement. However, there are a handful of clauses in which the אֵת precedes a NP that is the subject of a passive verb.

וַיִּוָּלֵד לַחֲנוֹךְ אֶת־עִירָד
And Irad was born to Enoch. (בראשית ד:יח)

וְלֹא־יִקָּרֵא עוֹד אֶת־שִׁמְךָ אַבְרָם
And your name shall no longer be called Abram. (בראשית יז:ה)

Though not common, keep an eye out for these, and do not let them confuse you.

Find the example of אֶת introducing the subject in the passage.

Review

Explain the use of זֶה in the clause הַאַתָּה זֶה אֲדֹנִי אֵלִיָּהוּ (v. ז).

Find the discourse וְהָיָה in the passage, and explain the modality of the expression (see chap. 2).

Find every verb with an attached complement pronoun. Identify the שֹׁרֶשׁ, בִּנְיָן, and conjugation, and the person-gender-number of the attached pronoun (or the corresponding subject pronoun).

מלכים א
יח, כ-כד
כ וַיִּשְׁלַח אַחְאָב בְּכָל־בְּנֵי יִשְׂרָאֵל
וַיִּקְבֹּץ אֶת־הַנְּבִיאִים אֶל־הַר הַכַּרְמֶל:
כא וַיִּגַּשׁ אֵלִיָּהוּ אֶל־כָּל־הָעָם וַיֹּאמֶר
עַד־מָתַי אַתֶּם פֹּסְחִים עַל־שְׁתֵּי הַסְּעִפִּים אִם־יְהוָה הָאֱלֹהִים לְכוּ אַחֲרָיו וְאִם־הַבַּעַל לְכוּ אַחֲרָיו
וְלֹא־עָנוּ הָעָם אֹתוֹ דָּבָר:
כב וַיֹּאמֶר אֵלִיָּהוּ אֶל־הָעָם
אֲנִי נוֹתַרְתִּי נָבִיא לַיהוָה לְבַדִּי וּנְבִיאֵי הַבַּעַל אַרְבַּע־מֵאוֹת וַחֲמִשִּׁים אִישׁ:
כג וְיִתְּנוּ־לָנוּ שְׁנַיִם פָּרִים וְיִבְחֲרוּ לָהֶם הַפָּר הָאֶחָד וִינַתְּחֻהוּ וְיָשִׂימוּ עַל־הָעֵצִים וְאֵשׁ לֹא יָשִׂימוּ וַאֲנִי אֶעֱשֶׂה ׀ אֶת־הַפָּר הָאֶחָד וְנָתַתִּי עַל־הָעֵצִים וְאֵשׁ לֹא אָשִׂים: כד וּקְרָאתֶם בְּשֵׁם אֱלֹהֵיכֶם וַאֲנִי אֶקְרָא בְשֵׁם־יְהוָה וְהָיָה הָאֱלֹהִים אֲשֶׁר־יַעֲנֶה בָאֵשׁ הוּא הָאֱלֹהִים
וַיַּעַן כָּל־הָעָם וַיֹּאמְרוּ
טוֹב הַדָּבָר:

Reading 7

מלכים א יח:כ–כד

Words to Learn

בָּחַר	VB Q ______________
מָתַי	INTER ______________
נָגַשׁ	VB Q ______________
(___ ___ ___) נִתַּח	VB PI ______________
סְעִפִּים	NOUN FP ______________
פָּסַח	VB Q ______________
פַּר	NOUN M ______________

Going Deeper with Grammar

The Participle, Irreal Imperfect, and Irreal Perfect Used for Habitual Events

Habitual events are those that occur regularly; thus they have a sort of plurality to them as well as the character of irreal mood. That is, the event is portrayed not as actually occurring but as potentiality regularly occurring. Because of these characteristics, Biblical Hebrew can choose to express habitual events as either a progressive event, using the participle (see *BBH* §42), or as an irreal mood event, using the Imperfect (*BBH* §§23, 27) or Perfect (see *BBH* §21).

In the following example, each generation comes and goes in its turn, but those comings and goings are described as ongoing (progressive) events.

דּוֹר הֹלֵךְ וְדוֹר בָּא וְהָאָרֶץ לְעוֹלָם עֹמָדֶת

A generation comes and a generation goes but the earth stands forever. (קהלת א:ד)

In the example below, Elkanah's yearly trips to Shiloh are reported not as actually happening but as something that happened on a regular basis, reinforced by the PPs מִיָּמִים יָמִימָה.

וְעָלָה הָאִישׁ הַהוּא מֵעִירוֹ מִיָּמִים יָמִימָה לְהִשְׁתַּחֲוֹת וְלִזְבֹּחַ לַיהוָה צְבָאוֹת בְּשִׁלֹה

That man would go up from his city periodically (lit., from days to days) to worship and to sacrifice to Yhwh of Hosts in Shiloh. (שמואל א א:ג)

Isolated habitual expressions are often made clear by the addition of temporal expressions such as מִיָּמִים יָמִימָה in the preceding example and כָּל־הַיָּמִים in the following example. The meaning of the Imperfect verb in the description of Job's sacrificing is clarified by the addition of the final temporal expression, stating that Job did this regularly (habitually).

כָּכָה יַעֲשֶׂה אִיּוֹב כָּל־הַיָּמִים
Like thus Job would do all the time. (איוב א:ה)

Identify any participle, Imperfect, or Perfect used for habitual action in the passage.

Dislocations

Casus pendens, Latin for "hanging case" (also sometimes called nominative absolute), refers to the construction in many European morphological case languages in which a constituent stands at the front edge of a clause and is resumed within the clause by a different constituent in a different case. Since Hebrew does not exhibit morphological case, this term is descriptively inaccurate. The term current in linguistics for these items that hang on the edges of a clause is *dislocation*. The Hebrew form of this is illustrated below.

מִקְנֵהֶם וְקִנְיָנָם וְכָל־בְּהֶמְתָּם הֲלוֹא לָנוּ הֵם
Their cattle and their property and all their beasts—are they not ours? (בראשית לד:כג)

In the example, the initial compound NP מִקְנֵהֶם וְקִנְיָנָם וְכָל־בְּהֶמְתָּם cannot be a formal syntactic part of the null copula clause, which already has a subject (הֵם) and a complement of the null copula (לָנוּ). Moreover, the initial NP is separated from the clause proper by the interrogative הֲ, which has a fixed position at the front edge of a clause. The pronoun הֵם within the clause refers back (i.e., it is "anaphoric") to the syntactically hanging or dislocated NP at the front edge of the clause. This is an example of "left" dislocation.[1]

Hebrew also allows dislocations at the final edge of the clause—that is, "right" dislocation—as below.

וַתְּגָרֶשׁ אוֹתָם מִפְּנֵיכֶם שְׁנֵי מַלְכֵי הָאֱמֹרִי
And it [the hornet] drove them out from before you—the two Amorite kings. (יהושע כד:יב)

In right dislocation, the core clause contains a cataphoric or "presumptive" element. This element is אוֹתָם in the above example. This cataphoric pronoun is coreferential with the constituent that resides on the "right" (or ending) edge of the clause, שְׁנֵי מַלְכֵי הָאֱמֹרִי. The dislocated NP (שְׁנֵי מַלְכֵי הָאֱמֹרִי) has no other syntactic link to the clause besides the cataphoric pronoun, in this case אוֹתָם.

1. The term originates from the study of English and other languages that are written left-to-right; for Hebrew, a left-dislocated constituent actually occurs at the right, at the front of the clause.

Dislocations are used to force particular pragmatic readings of the information. Each type of dislocation forces a topic and focus reading of the dislocated item and the resumed item (see *BBH* §41). In left dislocation, the hanging item orients the reader to what the rest of the clause will be about (topic), which then marks that same item for focus by the resumption (e.g., the cattle [topic]—are *they* [focus] not ours?). Right dislocation is similar, except that the focus comes first and the topic is clarifying (not orienting): "it drove *them* [focus] out from before you—the two kings [topic]."

Identify the case of dislocation in the passage, and explain the meaning.

Challenge

Ellipsis

The omission of one or more constituents from a clause is known as ellipsis. Some familiar examples of ellipsis include omitted, or "null," copulas (*BBH* §6); null subjects (*BBH* §18); and null complements (*BBH* §48). Biblical Hebrew poetry employs ellipsis quite frequently for poetic effect, whereby the omitted part of a clause is "recovered" from an element in an adjacent clause. Ellipsis of the verb or VP is common in Biblical Hebrew poetry.

רְעָדָה אֲחָזָתַם שָׁם חִיל כַּיּוֹלֵדָה
Trembling seized them there;
pain [seized them] like a woman in labor. (תהלים מח:ז)

Though less frequent, verb or VP ellipsis can occur in coordinate clauses in prose as well, where it seems to be an economizing device.

בַיּוֹם אֲכָלַנִי חֹרֶב וְקֶרַח בַּלָּיְלָה
By day heat consumed me, and cold by night [consumed me]. (בראשית לא:מ)

Find the elliptical structure in the text.

Case Relations and ל Preposition

The preposition ל, like ב (chap. 4), has a wide range of uses (chap. 2). Most of these involve marking the complement or adjunct of the verb (*BBH* §48). The ל can also indicate an attributive case relation in a NP (*BBH* §49), a function more commonly expressed by the סְמִיכוּת, or bound, structure (chap. 1). In contrast to the wide range of meanings expressed by the סְמִיכוּת, the ל preposition expresses possession when marking an attributive case relation (e.g., מִזְמוֹר לְדָוִד, a psalm of David, i.e., one of David's psalms), just as it frequently does when it introduces a copular complement (e.g., לִי־הֵם, they [are] mine [בראשית מח:ה]) (*BBH* §9).

Find each ל preposition in the passage. Identify what constituent it modifies and the case relation it indicates.

Reading Insights

Syntax and Lexical Semantics

The particular nuance of a lexical item is frequently signaled by the particular structure it occurs in. The verb קָרָא appears in a wide range of structures, including in a bivalent structure with a לְ-PP complement (the first example below) and a trivalent "naming" structure (the second example below).

וַיִּקְרָא פַרְעֹה לְאַבְרָם
Pharaoh summoned Abram. (בראשית יב:יח)

וַתִּקְרָא אֶת־שְׁמוֹ שֵׁת
She named him Seth. (בראשית ד:כה)

Another particular nuance of קָרָא occurs with the complement בְּשֵׁם (on the name), always bound to the name of a deity.

וַיִּקְרָא בְּשֵׁם יְהוָה
He called on the name of YHWH. (בראשית יב:ח)

Frequently the context is cultic, so that this particular syntagm indicates a cultic calling on deity (i.e., praying or petitioning the deity).

Find an occurrence of קָרָא בְּשֵׁם without יהוה in the text.

Idiomatic Phrases

Certain combinations of words can produce an idiomatic phrase, one that is more than the sum of its parts (chap. 1). Other phrases arrive at an idiomatic meaning by metaphorically employing certain images. One such instance is פֹּסְחִים עַל־שְׁתֵּי הַסְּעִפִּים (v. כא), which scholars have suggested may portray the image of birds hopping among the branches of a tree. The "two branches" in the context metaphorically refer to following Baal and following YHWH.

Explain the meaning of this idiom in the text, and suggest an appropriate idiomatic translation of the expression.

Review

Find the וְהָיָה in this passage, and identify whether it is a copula verb or a discourse marker of irreal mood.

Find all the numerals in the text, and explain their grammatical construction (*BBH* §45).

Find every occurrence of a I-נ verb (the first letter of the verb's שֹׁרֶשׁ is נ). Identify the שֹׁרֶשׁ, the בִּנְיָן, and the person-gender-number (or list the matching subject pronoun).

כה וַיֹּאמֶר אֵלִיָּהוּ לִנְבִיאֵי הַבַּעַל
בַּחֲרוּ לָכֶם הַפָּר הָאֶחָד וַעֲשׂוּ
רִאשֹׁנָה כִּי אַתֶּם הָרַבִּים וְקִרְאוּ
בְּשֵׁם אֱלֹהֵיכֶם וְאֵשׁ לֹא תָשִׂימוּ׃
כו וַיִּקְחוּ אֶת־הַפָּר אֲשֶׁר־נָתַן לָהֶם וַיַּעֲשׂוּ
וַיִּקְרְאוּ בְשֵׁם־הַבַּעַל מֵהַבֹּקֶר
וְעַד־הַצָּהֳרַיִם לֵאמֹר
הַבַּעַל עֲנֵנוּ
וְאֵין קוֹל וְאֵין עֹנֶה וַיְפַסְּחוּ
עַל־הַמִּזְבֵּחַ אֲשֶׁר עָשָׂה׃
כז וַיְהִי בַצָּהֳרַיִם וַיְהַתֵּל
בָּהֶם אֵלִיָּהוּ
וַיֹּאמֶר
קִרְאוּ בְקוֹל־גָּדוֹל כִּי־אֱלֹהִים
הוּא כִּי שִׂיחַ וְכִי־שִׂיג לוֹ וְכִי־
דֶרֶךְ לוֹ אוּלַי יָשֵׁן הוּא וְיִקָץ׃
כח וַיִּקְרְאוּ בְּקוֹל גָּדוֹל וַיִּתְגֹּדְדוּ
כְּמִשְׁפָּטָם בַּחֲרָבוֹת וּבָרְמָחִים
עַד־שְׁפָךְ־דָּם עֲלֵיהֶם׃
כט וַיְהִי כַּעֲבֹר הַצָּהֳרַיִם
וַיִּתְנַבְּאוּ עַד לַעֲלוֹת הַמִּנְחָה
וְאֵין־קוֹל וְאֵין־עֹנֶה וְאֵין קָשֶׁב׃
מלכים א
יח, כה-כט

Reading 8

מלכים א יח:כה–כט

Words to Learn

הִתְגֹּדֵד (__ __ __) VB HITPOEL _______________

הִתֵּל (__ __ __) VB PI _______________

הִתְנַבֵּא (__ __ __) VB HIT _______________

יָקַץ VB Q _______________

יָשֵׁן ADJ _______________

פִּסֵּחַ (__ __ __) VB PI _______________

צָהֳרַ֫יִם NOUN M DU _______________

קֶ֫שֶׁב NOUN M _______________

רֹ֫מַח NOUN M _______________

שִׂיג NOUN M _______________

שִׂיחַ NOUN M _______________

שָׁפַךְ VB Q _______________

Going Deeper with Grammar

Adjectives and Participles

Hebrew adjectives are typically divided into two categories of usage: attributive and predicative. The attributive category refers to adjectives that, in Hebrew, follow a noun and provide an attribute or property of that noun (e.g., the invisible God). The predicative category refers to adjectives used within a predicative statement about a noun (e.g., God is invisible).

Predicative adjectives occur either with a null copula or the overt copula היה; as such, these adjectives are the copular complements.

וְהָרָעָב חָזָק בְּשֹׁמְרוֹן
The famine (was) severe in Samaria. (מלכים א יח:ב)

וַיְהִי חָלְיוֹ חָזָק מְאֹד
His sickness was very severe. (מלכים א יז:יז)

A few adjectives can even take their own complements and so exhibit a degree of verb-like valency.

וְעֹבַדְיָהוּ הָיָה יָרֵא אֶת־יְהוָה מְאֹד
Obadiah was very <u>reverent of YHWH</u>. (מלכים א יח:ג)

The adjective יָרֵא is not bound to the complement את יהוה, which means that the two constituents must be related differently. Moreover, את יהוה also conveniently has the את, making its status as the adjectival complement quite clear. Thus when the adjective יָרֵא describes some attribute of the noun it modifies (in this case, predicatively), it may license its own complement to further specify the description.

In their semantic role as noun modifiers, adjectives exist on a continuum of noun modification strategies that includes PPs, appositives, and relative clauses (*BBH* §32).

אִישׁ צַדִּיק
a man (who is) <u>righteous</u> ≈ a <u>righteous</u> man (בראשית ו:ט)

Already in the 1600s a group of grammarians were analyzing sentences such as *The <u>invisible</u> God created the <u>visible</u> world* as *The God <u>who is invisible</u> created the world <u>that is visible</u>*. Such an analysis is particularly appropriate for Hebrew, which allows for null heads of relative clauses.

הֲלֹא־הֻגַּד לַאדֹנִי אֵת אֲשֶׁר־עָשִׂיתִי
Has it not been told to my master <u>ø (the thing)</u> that I did? (מלכים א יח:יג)

Similarly, adjectives modifying nouns (i.e., attributive adjectives) can be analyzed as a variety of null copula relative clauses.

קִרְאוּ בְקוֹל־גָּדוֹל
call out in a voice [that is] <u>loud</u> / a <u>loud</u> voice (מלכים א יח:כז)

Along those same lines, adjectives used as noun substitutes (i.e., substantival adjectives) can be analyzed as relatives that have both a null head and a null copula.

וַיַּעַשׂ אַחְאָב בֶּן־עָמְרִי הָרַע בְּעֵינֵי יְהוָה
Ahab, son of Omri, did [the thing that is] <u>evil</u> in the eyes of YHWH. (מלכים א טז:ל)

Analyzing attributive adjectives as the complement within a relative clause structure simplifies the overall view of the adjective by eliminating attributive-predicative distinction. *All adjectives exist in a predicative relationship with the noun they describe.*

Participles constitute a special type of adjective: they are adjectives that encode event predicates (as opposed to the typical adjectives that express properties, as described above). Unlike most predicate adjectives (excepting rare cases, such as יָרֵא), participles exhibit verb-like valency, which means they license complements and may be modified by adverbial type adjuncts. Otherwise they function in all the same ways that adjectives do: they can modify a head noun, substitute for a noun, or serve as a complement of a verb.

When employed as the main predicate of a clause, the participle is always supported by a copula, which is usually null.

הָעַלְמָה הַיֹּצֵאת לִשְׁאֹב

the woman who (is) coming out to draw water (בראשית כד:מג)

לְעֵת צֵאת הַשֹּׁאֲבֹת

at the time of the coming out of (those) who (were) drawing water (בראשית כד:יא)

הוּא יֹשֵׁב שָׁם

he (was) living there (מלכים א יז:יט)

Find and explain the grammar of any adjective in the passage.

Find and explain the grammar of any participle in the passage.

Nonverbal Copulas with אֵין *and* יֵשׁ

Copular clauses have been discussed in chapters 4, 5, and 6 (and will appear again in chap. 10). The words יֵשׁ (positive) and אֵין (negative), which are polarized opposites, are similar to the verb הָיָה in that they sometimes present copular statements (X is Y) but at other times are uninflected predicators of existence (X exists).

כִּי אֵין יְהוָה בְּקִרְבְּכֶם

because YHWH is not in your midst (במדבר יד:מב)

וְגַם יֵשׁ גֹּאֵל קָרוֹב מִמֶּנִּי

And also a redeemer closer than me exists. (רות ג:יב)

Null subjects with יֵשׁ clauses (translated by the English expletive subject "there") are not frequent, although they do occur. In contrast, null subjects are common with אֵין clauses, whereas an overt subject with אֵין appears much less frequently.

Identify any אֵין or יֵשׁ in the passage and explain its function.

Challenge

Infinitives with Prepositions

The infinitive frequently appears with a proclitic ל, often expressing purpose/result, or with כ or ב with a temporal meaning (*BBH* §24). The infinitive may also be the complement of other prepositions, with meanings appropriate to each preposition.

אַחֲרֵי שׁוּבוֹ מֵהַכּוֹת אֶת־כְּדָר־לָעֹמֶר וְאֶת־הַמְּלָכִים
after he returned from striking Chedorlaomer and the kings (בראשית יד:יז)

עַד־שׁוּב אַף־אָחִיךָ מִמְּךָ
until your brother's anger turns back from you (בראשית כז:מה)

Find all the infinitives in the passage that are complements of a preposition, and identify the meaning of the construction.

Reading Insights

Biblical Hebrew Sarcasm

Elijah's sarcastic mockery of the prophets of Baal can be difficult to grasp because the meanings of some of the terms are uncertain and the syntax is difficult. To begin with, כִּי throughout is asseverative. In the first instance (כִּי־אֱלֹהִים הוּא, מלכים א יח:כז), Elijah ironically affirms that Baal is a real god. In the other כִּי clauses, he mockingly affirms that some distraction or other has kept Baal from answering his prophets: "surely he must have a ______." Further, scholars debate whether the hapax legomenon שִׂיג (i.e., occuring only here in the Hebrew Bible) and/or שִׂיחַ might be intended here as euphemisms for bathroom business.

Review

Find every וַיְהִי in the passage, and identify it as a copula or discourse marker (*BBH* §36).

Aleppo Codex

To review the passages of chapters 6–8, turn to the third page of the Aleppo Codex, and read from the remaining words of the fourth line (i.e., וַיֹּאמֶר לוֹ אֲנִי לֵךְ) through the tenth line of the fourth page (i.e., ending with קָשֶׁב).

לוַיֹּ֨אמֶר אֵלִיָּ֤הוּ לְכָל־הָעָם֙
גְּשׁ֣וּ אֵלַ֔י
וַיִּגְּשׁ֥וּ כָל־הָעָ֖ם אֵלָ֑יו וַיְרַפֵּ֛א
אֶת־מִזְבַּ֥ח יְהוָ֖ה הֶהָרֽוּס׃
לאוַיִּקַּ֣ח אֵלִיָּ֗הוּ שְׁתֵּ֤ים עֶשְׂרֵה֙ אֲבָנִ֔ים כְּמִסְפַּ֖ר שִׁבְטֵ֣י
בְנֵֽי־יַעֲקֹ֑ב אֲשֶׁ֨ר הָיָ֤ה דְבַר־יְהוָה֙ אֵלָיו֙ לֵאמֹ֔ר יִשְׂרָאֵ֖ל
יִהְיֶ֥ה שְׁמֶֽךָ׃ לבוַיִּבְנֶ֧ה אֶת־הָאֲבָנִ֛ים מִזְבֵּ֖חַ בְּשֵׁ֣ם יְהוָ֑ה
וַיַּ֣עַשׂ תְּעָלָ֗ה כְּבֵית֙ סָאתַ֣יִם זֶ֔רַע סָבִ֖יב לַמִּזְבֵּֽחַ׃
לגוַיַּעֲרֹ֖ךְ אֶת־הָעֵצִ֑ים וַיְנַתַּח֙ אֶת־הַפָּ֔ר וַיָּ֖שֶׂם עַל־הָעֵצִֽים׃
לדוַיֹּ֗אמֶר
מִלְא֨וּ אַרְבָּעָ֤ה כַדִּים֙
מַ֔יִם וְיִצְק֥וּ עַל־הָעֹלָ֖ה
וְעַל־הָעֵצִ֑ים
וַיֹּ֣אמֶר
שְׁנוּ֙
וַיִּשְׁנ֔וּ וַיֹּ֣אמֶר
שַׁלֵּ֖שׁוּ
וַיְשַׁלֵּֽשׁוּ׃
להוַיֵּלְכ֣וּ הַמַּ֔יִם סָבִ֖יב לַמִּזְבֵּ֑חַ
וְגַ֥ם אֶת־הַתְּעָלָ֖ה מִלֵּא־מָֽיִם׃
לווַיְהִ֣י ׀ בַּעֲל֣וֹת הַמִּנְחָ֗ה וַיִּגַּ֞שׁ
אֵלִיָּ֣הוּ הַנָּבִיא֮ וַיֹּאמַר֒
יְהוָ֗ה אֱלֹהֵי֙ אַבְרָהָם֙ יִצְחָ֣ק וְיִשְׂרָאֵ֔ל הַיּ֣וֹם יִוָּדַ֗ע
כִּֽי־אַתָּ֤ה אֱלֹהִים֙ בְּיִשְׂרָאֵ֔ל וַאֲנִ֖י עַבְדֶּ֑ךָ וּבדברך*
עָשִׂ֔יתִי אֵ֥ת כָּל־הַדְּבָרִ֖ים הָאֵֽלֶּה׃ לזעֲנֵ֤נִי יְהוָה֙ עֲנֵ֔נִי
וְיֵֽדְעוּ֙ הָעָ֣ם הַזֶּ֔ה כִּֽי־אַתָּ֥ה יְהוָ֖ה הָאֱלֹהִ֑ים וְאַתָּ֛ה
הֲסִבֹּ֥תָ אֶת־לִבָּ֖ם אֲחֹרַנִּֽית׃
*Ketiv: ובדבריך
Qere: וּבִדְבָרְךָ֖
מלכים א
יח, ל-לז

Reading 9

מלכים א יח:ל–לז

Words to Learn

אַחֲרַנִית ADV ______________

(___) הֵסֵב VB HI ______________

הָרַס VB Q ______________

יָצַק VB Q ______________

מִסְפָּר NOUN M ______________

סְאָה NOUN F ______________

עָרַךְ VB Q ______________

עֶשֶׂר CARD ______________

(___) רִפֵּא VB PI ______________

שֵׁבֶט NOUN M ______________

(___) שִׁלֵּשׁ VB PI ______________

שָׁנָה VB Q ______________

שְׁנַיִם CARD ______________

תְּעָלָה NOUN F ______________

Going Deeper with Grammar

ה-Relatives (BBH §42)

In chapter 8 we identified attributive and substantival adjectives and participles as a variety of relative clause. Though relatives are often signaled by the relative word אֲשֶׁר or, in later Hebrew, שֶׁ (chap. 2), one relative word that is often missed is ה. Besides functioning as the definite article, ה also signals that an adjective or participle is modifying a noun (whether overt or null) as a relative.

וְאֶעֱשֶׂה־שָּׁם מִזְבֵּחַ לָאֵל הָעֹנֶה אֹתִי בְּיוֹם צָרָתִי
and I will make there an altar to the god who answers me on the day of my distress (בראשית לה:ג)

Relative clauses with finite verbs or null copulas with a NP or PP complement are typically introduced with אֲשֶׁר, whereas relative clauses with a null copula and adjectival or participial complement are often introduced with ה. In both cases, the overt relative word may be omitted, sometimes making identifying relative clauses a challenge.

Identify all the relative clauses in the passage, noting in particular any ה-relatives.

Numerals (BBH §45)

Numeral syntax falls into two basic patterns: סְמִיכוּת (chap. 1) and apposition (chap. 6). Combining these two patterns with the two possible orders—noun-numeral and numeral-noun—results in four options, all of which appear in Biblical Hebrew:

bound noun + numeral

וּבִשְׁנַת שְׁמֹנֶה עֶשְׂרֵה לַמֶּלֶךְ יָרָבְעָם
and in the eighteenth year of King Jeroboam (מלכים א טו:א)

bound numeral + noun

כִּי שֵׁשֶׁת חֳדָשִׁים יָשַׁב־שָׁם יוֹאָב וְכָל־יִשְׂרָאֵל
because six months Joab and all Israel stayed there (מלכים א יא:טז)

free noun + numeral

לֹא־נָפַל דָּבָר אֶחָד מִכֹּל דְּבָרוֹ הַטּוֹב
One word did not fail from his every good word. (מלכים א ח:נו)

free numeral + noun

מָלַךְ עָמְרִי עַל־יִשְׂרָאֵל שְׁתֵּים עֶשְׂרֵה שָׁנָה
Omri ruled over Israel twelve years. (מלכים א טז:כג)

Identify every use of a numeral in the passage, and explain the syntax.

Challenge

וַיִּבְנֶה

The Past Narrative form, like the second- and third-person jussive, generally has a somewhat different vocalization than the Imperfect form with certain weak verbs (*BBH* §39). One of those weak verb types is the III-ה verb, which has a "shortened" form without the final ה (see appendix B.5): e.g., וַיֵּשְׁתְּ, he drank (√שתה). At other times, the Past Narrative form of these III-ה verbs retains the ה: e.g., וַיִּשְׁתֶּה, he drank.

Find all the III-ה verbs in the passage, and parse them.

מלא

Some verbs may show a consistent valency pattern, such as licensing just a subject or a subject and complement, and so on (*BBH* §49). Other verbs show variations and even overlapping valency structures among the same root in different בִּנְיָנִים. This is the case for מָלֵא and מִלֵּא. The subject of the קַל verb is sometimes that which is filled:

מָלְאָה הָאָרֶץ חָמָס
The earth has filled with violence. (בראשית ו:יג)

At other times, the subject is that which fills something:

וּכְבוֹד יְהוָה מָלֵא אֶת־הַמִּשְׁכָּן
And the glory of YHWH filled the tabernacle. (שמות מ:לד)

And at still other times, the subject is the agent that fills something with something else:

מָלְאוּ אֶת־הָאָרֶץ חָמָס
They have filled the land with violence. (יחזקאל ח:יז)

By contrast, the פִּעֵל form only ever expresses the agent that does the filling as the subject, either with an implicit "filling" item:

וַתְּמַלֵּא כַדָּהּ
She filled her jug. (בראשית כד:טז)

or with an overt one:

וַתְּמַלֵּא אֶת־הַחֵמֶת מַיִם
She filled the skin with water. (בראשית כא:יט)

Find the מלא verbs in the passage, parse them, and describe their syntax.

Reading Insights

Lost Shared Knowledge

One of the challenges in reading ancient texts is that some knowledge shared by the writer and earliest readers is now lost to us. This is the case for the phrase כְּבֵית סָאתַיִם זֶרַע (מלכים א יח:לב) in the text. The bound word בֵּית is used in a generalized sense to refer to the capacity or size of the trench. The dual סָאתַיִם is a measure of uncertain capacity, used for (among other things) seed, given the appositive זֶרַע. *HALOT* 737–38 states that סָאתַיִם is equivalent to 15 liters (each סְאָה equivalent to 7.5 liters); *DCH* 6:103 gives the size as 12 liters. In either case, the size of the trench was enough to require twelve jars (also of undetermined size) to fill it with water.

Turning Back Where?

In his petition of Yhwh, Elijah includes the following: וְאַתָּה הֲסִבֹּתָ אֶת־לִבָּם אֲחֹרַנִּית (יח:לז). But what does Elijah want God to let the people know? Scholars have interpreted this expression as either referring to the people's waywardness (e.g., סַרְתֶּם מֵחֻקַּי, you have turned away from my statutes, מלאכי ג:ז) or to their turning back to Yhwh (e.g., שׁוּבוּ בָנִים שׁוֹבָבִים, turn back, rebellious children! ירמיהו ג:יד). Some have rejected the latter understanding because a Perfect verb does not suit the necessary future meaning required in the context. However, a future Perfect understanding works well: "you (will) have turned them back around."

Review

Locate any null complements in the passage, and identify their antecedents.

Explain how סביב and the ל are functioning in the phrase סָבִיב לַמִּזְבֵּחַ (hint: סביב can be a noun, an adverb, or a preposition).

מלכים א
יח, לח
לח וַתִּפֹּל אֵשׁ־יְהוָה וַתֹּאכַל אֶת־הָעֹלָה וְאֶת־
הָעֵצִים וְאֶת־הָאֲבָנִים וְאֶת־הֶעָפָר וְאֶת־
הַמַּיִם אֲשֶׁר־בַּתְּעָלָה לִחֵכָה׃

מלכים א
יח, לט-מב
לט וַיַּרְא֙ כָּל־הָעָ֔ם וַֽיִּפְּל֖וּ עַל־פְּנֵיהֶ֑ם וַיֹּ֣אמְר֔וּ
יְהוָה֙ ה֣וּא הָאֱלֹהִ֔ים יְהוָ֖ה ה֥וּא הָאֱלֹהִֽים׃
מ וַיֹּאמֶר֩ אֵלִיָּ֨הוּ לָהֶ֜ם
תִּפְשׂ֣וּ ׀ אֶת־נְבִיאֵ֣י הַבַּ֗עַל אִ֛ישׁ אַל־יִמָּלֵ֥ט מֵהֶ֖ם
וַֽיִּתְפְּשׂ֔וּם וַיּוֹרִדֵ֤ם אֵלִיָּ֙הוּ֙ אֶל־נַ֣חַל קִישׁ֔וֹן וַיִּשְׁחָטֵ֖ם שָֽׁם׃
מא וַיֹּ֤אמֶר אֵלִיָּ֙הוּ֙ לְאַחְאָ֔ב
עֲלֵ֖ה אֱכֹ֣ל וּשְׁתֵ֑ה כִּי־ק֖וֹל הֲמ֥וֹן הַגָּֽשֶׁם׃
מב וַיַּעֲלֶ֥ה אַחְאָ֖ב לֶאֱכֹ֣ל וְלִשְׁתּ֑וֹת
וְאֵלִיָּ֗הוּ עָלָ֞ה אֶל־רֹ֤אשׁ הַכַּרְמֶל֙ וַיִּגְהַ֣ר אַ֔רְצָה וַיָּ֥שֶׂם פָּנָ֖יו בֵּ֥ין בִּרְכָּֽיו*׃
*Ketiv: ברכו
Qere: בִּרְכָּֽיו

Reading 10

מלכים א יח:לח–מב

Words to Learn

בֶּ֫רֶךְ	NOUN F	______________
גָּהַר	VB Q	______________
הָמוֹן	NOUN M	______________
לִחַךְ (____)	VB PI	______________
נִמְלַט (____)	VB NI	______________
עָפָר	NOUN M	______________
שָׁחַט	VB Q	______________
תָּפַשׂ	VB Q	______________

Going Deeper with Grammar

Compounds

When multiple constituents appear with the same semantic role or function in a clause, they are interpreted as compounds—that is, a constituent composed of a number of conjoined constituents.

וַיְכֻלּוּ הַשָּׁמַיִם וְהָאָרֶץ וְכָל־צְבָאָם
The heavens and the earth and all their host were completed. (**בראשית ב:א**)

> Find any compounds in the passage.

Nonverbal Copulas with הוּא

Like the limited use of זֶה as a copula (see chaps. 4, 5, 6, and 8), Hebrew occasionally employs the third-person pronoun as a nonverbal copula (*BBH* §6). In such cases, the pronoun is an uninflected nonverbal copula (i.e., simply a phonological placeholder for TAM features). The pronominal copula is labeled as PRON in the examples below.

אִשֵּׁי יְהוָה אֱלֹהֵי יִשְׂרָאֵל הוּא נַחֲלָתוֹ
The fire-offerings of YHWH, the God of Israel, are [PRON] its inheritance. (**יהושע יג:יד**)

The distribution of the copular PRON closely parallels the verbal copula הָיָה. Like הָיָה, the PRON הוּא (and the plural הֵם) may appear with nominal, prepositional, and adjectival copular complements.

אֵלֶּה הֵם מִשְׁפְּחֹת הַלֵּוִי
These are [PRON] the families of the Levites. (במדבר ג:כ)

הָאָשָׁם הוּא לַכֹּהֵן
The guilt offering belongs [PRON] to the priest. (ויקרא יד:יג)

צַדִּיק הוּא יְהוָה
YHWH is [PRON] righteous. (איכה א:יח)

The one syntactic feature that distinguishes the pronominal copula from the verbal copula היה is the strict placement of the PRON: it must intervene between the subject and the complement. By contrast, the verbal copula היה exhibits the full range of movement associated with finite verbs (see chap. 4).

The lack of person agreement in some examples unambiguously points to the pronoun as copula. Other cases are ambiguous between a pronominal copula analysis and a dislocated structure (chap. 7). In such cases, the decision relies on determining whether or not there is a suitable topic or focus function in the context for the constituent that would be dislocated in such an analysis.

אַתָּה־הוּא הָאֱלֹהִים לְבַדְּךָ
You are [PRON] the God, you alone. (מלכים ב יט:טו)

וְהַקֶּרֶן הַגְּדוֹלָה אֲשֶׁר בֵּין־עֵינָיו הוּא הַמֶּלֶךְ הָרִאשׁוֹן
And the great horn that (is) between its eyes is [PRON] the first king.
or And as for the great horn that (is) between its eyes [TOPIC], it [PRON] (is) the first king. (דניאל ח:כא)

> Find the pronominal copula candidate in the passage, decide whether a pronominal copular analysis or a dislocated structure analysis is preferable, and explain why.

Challenge

I-א Verbs

Most verbs with an א as the first root letter behave like I-guttural verbs (see *BBH* appendix C.3a), but five verbs have a unique vocalization in the קל Imperfect and Past Narrative. These are classified as I-א verbs (see appendix B.1).

> Find the I-א verb in the passage and explain how its vocalization is different from I-gutturals.

What are the other four I-א verbs?

Directional Verbs

Verbs that express motion in a certain direction (יָרַד, שׁוּב, etc.) license directional PP complements:

וַיֵּרֶד אַבְרָם מִצְרַיְמָה

Abram went down to Egypt. (בראשית יב:י)

However, frequently the complement is implicit or null because either the location is unspecified (implicit) or is known from the context (null):

וַתְּהִי־עוֹד מִלְחָמָה לַפְּלִשְׁתִּים אֶת־יִשְׂרָאֵל וַיֵּרֶד דָּוִד וַעֲבָדָיו עִמּוֹ וַיִּלָּחֲמוּ אֶת־פְּלִשְׁתִּים

The Philistines had a war again with Israel. So David and his men with him went down and fought with the Philistines. (שמואל ב כא:טו)

אֵרְדָה־נָּא

I will go down (there) [= Sodom and Gomorrah]. (בראשית יח:כא)

Find all the directional verbs in the passage, and determine whether they have overt, null, or implicit PP complements.

Reading Insights

The Masoretic טְעָמִים (Accents) and Syntax

The system of accents marks off prosodic units in the text (chap. 4; appendix C) and not syntax. However, syntax and prosody often coincide, making the accents useful for sorting out otherwise ambiguous constructions.

Describe how the accents help decide which complements go with which verbs in the passage.

Qere-Ketiv

The marginal textual readings are sometimes a matter of simple spelling variation, as in the case of [בִּרְכָּיו] בִּרְכָּו in the passage (v. מב). The preceding בֵּין preposition makes it clear that the noun must be plural. The most frequent spelling of this pronoun is preserved in the *Qere*, בִּרְכָּיו.

The *Ketiv* form has a singular noun. What is the expected vocalization of this pronoun on a singular noun?

Review

What gender must אֵשׁ (v. לח) be in light of the agreement features of the verb for which it is the subject?

Give the שֹׁ֫רֶשׁ and בִּנְיָן of וַיַּ֫רְא. What would the same form of יָרֵא look like?

Find all the verbs in the passage with attached pronouns.

מלכים א
יח, מג-מו
מג וַיֹּ֨אמֶר אֶל־נַעֲר֜וֹ
עֲלֵה־נָא֙ הַבֵּ֣ט דֶּרֶךְ־יָ֔ם
וַיַּ֙עַל֙ וַיַּבֵּ֔ט וַיֹּ֖אמֶר
אֵ֣ין מְא֑וּמָה
וַיֹּ֕אמֶר
שֻׁ֖ב שֶׁ֥בַע פְּעָמִֽים׃
מד וַיְהִי֙ בַּשְּׁבִעִ֔ית וַיֹּ֕אמֶר
הִנֵּה־עָ֛ב קְטַנָּ֥ה כְּכַף־אִ֖ישׁ עֹלָ֣ה מִיָּ֑ם
וַיֹּ֗אמֶר
עֲלֵ֨ה אֱמֹ֤ר אֶל־אַחְאָב֙ אֱסֹ֣ר וָרֵ֔ד וְלֹ֥א יַעַצָרְכָ֖ה הַגָּֽשֶׁם׃
מה וַיְהִ֣י ׀ עַד־כֹּ֣ה וְעַד־כֹּ֗ה וְהַשָּׁמַ֙יִם֙ הִתְקַדְּרוּ֙ עָבִ֣ים וְר֔וּחַ וַיְהִ֖י גֶּ֣שֶׁם גָּד֑וֹל וַיִּרְכַּ֥ב אַחְאָ֖ב וַיֵּ֥לֶךְ יִזְרְעֶֽאלָה׃
מו וְיַד־יְהוָ֗ה הָֽיְתָה֙ אֶל־אֵ֣לִיָּ֔הוּ וַיְשַׁנֵּ֖ס מָתְנָ֑יו וַיָּ֙רָץ֙ לִפְנֵ֣י אַחְאָ֔ב עַד־בֹּאֲכָ֖ה יִזְרְעֶֽאלָה׃

מלכים א
יט, א-ה
אוַיַּגֵּ֤ד אַחְאָב֙ לְאִיזֶ֔בֶל אֵ֛ת כָּל־אֲשֶׁ֥ר עָשָׂ֖ה אֵלִיָּ֑הוּ
וְאֵ֨ת כָּל־אֲשֶׁ֥ר הָרַ֛ג אֶת־כָּל־הַנְּבִיאִ֖ים בֶּחָֽרֶב׃
בוַתִּשְׁלַ֤ח אִיזֶ֙בֶל֙ מַלְאָ֔ךְ אֶל־אֵלִיָּ֖הוּ לֵאמֹ֑ר
כֹּֽה־יַעֲשׂ֤וּן אֱלֹהִים֙ וְכֹ֣ה יוֹסִפ֔וּן כִּֽי־כָעֵ֣ת
מָחָ֗ר אָשִׂים֙ אֶֽת־נַפְשְׁךָ֔ כְּנֶ֖פֶשׁ אַחַ֥ד מֵהֶֽם׃
גוַיַּ֗רְא וַיָּ֙קָם֙ וַיֵּ֣לֶךְ אֶל־נַפְשׁ֔וֹ
וַיָּבֹ֕א בְּאֵ֥ר שֶׁ֖בַע אֲשֶׁ֣ר לִיהוּדָ֑ה וַיַּנַּ֥ח אֶֽת־נַעֲר֖וֹ שָֽׁם׃
דוְהֽוּא־הָלַ֤ךְ בַּמִּדְבָּר֙ דֶּ֣רֶךְ י֔וֹם וַיָּבֹ֕א וַיֵּ֕שֶׁב תַּ֖חַת
רֹ֣תֶם אֶחָ֑ד* וַיִּשְׁאַ֤ל אֶת־נַפְשׁוֹ֙ לָמ֔וּת וַיֹּ֣אמֶר ׀
*Ketiv: אחת
Qere: אֶחָ֑ד
רַ֗ב עַתָּ֤ה יְהוָה֙ קַ֣ח נַפְשִׁ֔י
כִּֽי־לֹא־ט֥וֹב אָנֹכִ֖י מֵאֲבֹתָֽי׃
הוַיִּשְׁכַּב֙ וַיִּישַׁ֔ן תַּ֖חַת רֹ֣תֶם אֶחָ֑ד

Reading 11

מלכים א יח:מג–יט:ה

Words to Learn

אָסַר VB Q ______________

(____) הִבִּיט VB HI ______________

(____) הִתְקַדֵּר VB HIT ______________

יָשֵׁן VB Q ______________

מְאוּמָה PRON ______________

מָחָר NOUN M ______________

מָתְנַיִם NOUN DU ______________

נוּחַ VB Q ______________; HI ______________

עָב NOUN F ______________

עָצַר VB Q ______________

רוּץ VB Q ______________

רָכַב VB Q ______________

רֹתֶם NOUN M ______________

שָׁאַל VB Q ______________

שְׁבִיעִי ORD ______________

(____) שִׁנֵּס VB PI ______________

Going Deeper with Grammar

Negation

Biblical Hebrew has several different negative words, including לֹא, אַל, אַיִן, and בִּלְתִּי. The choice of negative word in a passage is an important clue to the grammar of the passage. For example, בִּלְתִּי is typically used in an infinitive clause, and אַל belongs to the directive-volitive irreal subsystem (see chap. 3).

רַק חֲזַק לְבִלְתִּי אֲכֹל הַדָּם

Only take care not to eat the blood. (דברים יב:כג)

The negative אַיִן can serve as either a negative copula or an uninflected existential particle. The difference can be syntactically determined by whether or not there is a copular complement (chap. 8).

> Find the negative words in the text, and identify the grammatical context in which they appear.

NP-Internal PP Modifiers

The majority of PPs in Biblical Hebrew modify a verbal head. That is, they appear as adjuncts or complements in the VP of a clause. Less recognized is that PPs also modify nominal heads within NPs. NP-internal PPs function as restrictive modifiers of the nominal head. A common NP-internal PP is the partitive מִן PP. Typically it has a null nominal head, though it may also have an overt one.

וַיִּקַּח מֵאַבְנֵי הַמָּקוֹם
He took (one) of the stones of the place. (בראשית כח:יא)

וַיִּקַּח אַחַת מִצַּלְעֹתָיו
He took one of his ribs. (בראשית ב:כא)

> Find all the NP-internal PPs in the passage.

Indefinite Article

Biblical Hebrew has a definite article, but it does not have a corresponding indefinite one (cf. English *the* vs. *a*/*an*). Unless the noun is definite in some other way (chap. 2), the lack of an article suffices to indicate an expression as indefinite.

Sometimes an indefinite noun appears with the numeral אחד/אחת. In such cases, the result is a specific but nonidentifiable referent, "a certain X." In other words, in contrast to a nonspecific referent ("an X" or "any old X"), the referent in question is one specific item whose precise identity is irrelevant to the discourse. This use of the numeral is generally recognizable because the more usual numeric meaning does not fit the context well.

> Find and explain whether אחד/אחת is used in the passage as a numeral or indefinite marker.

Challenge

Spelling of the 2MS Enclitic Pronoun

The 2MS enclitic pronoun is usually quite distinctive in Biblical Hebrew, spelled with the final form of the ך and a קָמֵץ vowel (ךָ). Sometimes, however, the קָמֵץ vowel is followed by the ה vowel letter, which appears after this vowel in so many other forms (e.g., feminine nouns such as מַלְכָּה).

Find all the 2MS enclitic pronouns in the passage.

Valency Alternation with Motion Verbs

Motion verbs typically have a locative PP complement. Some such verbs allow for unsystematic alternation between a PP complement and a NP or pronoun one (e.g., *They climbed up the mountain* versus *They climbed the mountain*). Compare the following examples:

וַיֵּלֶךְ יְהוֹשֻׁעַ אֵלָיו
Joshua went to him. (יהושע ה:יג)

וַנֵּלֶךְ אֵת כָּל־הַמִּדְבָּר הַגָּדוֹל וְהַנּוֹרָא הַהוּא
We went (through) all that great and awesome wilderness. (דברים א:יט)

Such alternations form part of the lexical information of a verb.

Find a motion verb with a NP complement in the passage.

ב Instrumental

Of the many meanings the preposition ב may have, one of the more frequent ones is to mark an instrumental adjunct, the item with which or by which something is accomplished.

הַסְּנֶה בֹּעֵר בָּאֵשׁ
The bush was burning with fire. (שמות ג:ב)

Find the instrumental ב in the passage.

Reading Insights

Contextual Idioms

In this passage the PP עַד־כֹּה is repeated. The expression without repetition elsewhere has a locative sense:

וַאֲנִי וְהַנַּעַר נֵלְכָה עַד־כֹּה
I and the boy will go over there. (בראשית כב:ה)

Or it can have a temporal sense:

וְהִנֵּה לֹא־שָׁמַעְתָּ עַד־כֹּה
Look, you have not listened so far. (שמות ז:טז)

The repetition of the PP can convey a sense of locative distribution ("here and there") or temporal gradualness ("little by little").

Make a case from the context as to how this expression should be interpreted in the passage.

נֶפֶשׁ as Life and Self

The noun נֶפֶשׁ refers to the vital life force that constitutes a person. With this basic meaning, the noun may appear with an enclitic pronoun either with reference to "one's life" or as a reflexive expression "oneself." Sometimes these two senses can ambiguously appear in a passage.

וְנָתְנוּ אִישׁ כֹּפֶר נַפְשׁוֹ לַיהוָה
Each of them must provide a ransom to YHWH for his life/himself. (שמות ל:יב)

Locate and explain the meaning of each נֶפֶשׁ in the passage.

Comparative מן

Hebrew does not have any comparative or superlative adjectives (cf. English *better*, *best*). Instead, these senses are expressed syntactically. The superlative degree is typically expressed by a סְמִיכוּת relationship consisting of an identical noun.

שִׁיר הַשִּׁירִים
song of songs > the best song (שיר השירים א:א)

The comparative degree is typically constructed using a מן-PP.

צָדְקָה מִמֶּנִּי
[She is] more righteous than me. (בראשית לח:כו)

With the addition of the quantifier כל superlative statements may also be constructed using a מן-PP.

גָּבֹהַּ מִכָּל־הָעָם
[He was] taller than all the people. > [He was] the tallest of the people. (שמואל א ט:ב)

Find and explain the מן PPs in the passage.

Review

Identify how each הָיָה verb is functioning in the text—whether as a discourse marker, a copula, or an existential predicator.

Find all the examples of the locative postposition ה.

Describe the typical valency for הִגִּיד, and identify the structural constituents in the passage.

Describe how oath clauses are typically constructed, illustrating from the passage.

Aleppo Codex

To review the passages of chapters 9–11, turn to the fourth page of the Aleppo Codex, and read from the eleventh line (i.e., וַיֹּאמֶר אֵלִיָּהוּ לְכָל־הָעָם) through the tenth line of the fifth page (i.e., ending with אֱכוֹל).

מלכים א
יט, ה-יא
ה וְהִנֵּה־זֶה מַלְאָךְ נֹגֵעַ בּוֹ וַיֹּאמֶר לוֹ
קוּם אֱכוֹל׃
ו וַיַּבֵּט וְהִנֵּה מְרַאֲשֹׁתָיו עֻגַת רְצָפִים וְצַפַּחַת מָיִם
וַיֹּאכַל וַיֵּשְׁתְּ וַיָּשָׁב וַיִּשְׁכָּב׃
ז וַיָּשָׁב מַלְאַךְ יְהוָה ׀ שֵׁנִית וַיִּגַּע־בּוֹ וַיֹּאמֶר
קוּם אֱכֹל כִּי רַב מִמְּךָ הַדָּרֶךְ׃
ח וַיָּקָם וַיֹּאכַל וַיִּשְׁתֶּה
וַיֵּלֶךְ בְּכֹחַ ׀ הָאֲכִילָה הַהִיא אַרְבָּעִים יוֹם וְאַרְבָּעִים לַיְלָה עַד הַר הָאֱלֹהִים חֹרֵב׃
ט וַיָּבֹא־שָׁם אֶל־הַמְּעָרָה וַיָּלֶן שָׁם
וְהִנֵּה דְבַר־יְהוָה אֵלָיו וַיֹּאמֶר לוֹ
מַה־לְּךָ פֹה אֵלִיָּהוּ׃
י וַיֹּאמֶר
קַנֹּא קִנֵּאתִי לַיהוָה ׀ אֱלֹהֵי צְבָאוֹת כִּי־עָזְבוּ בְרִיתְךָ בְּנֵי יִשְׂרָאֵל אֶת־מִזְבְּחֹתֶיךָ הָרָסוּ וְאֶת־נְבִיאֶיךָ הָרְגוּ בֶחָרֶב וָאִוָּתֵר אֲנִי לְבַדִּי וַיְבַקְשׁוּ אֶת־נַפְשִׁי לְקַחְתָּהּ׃
יא וַיֹּאמֶר
צֵא וְעָמַדְתָּ בָהָר לִפְנֵי יְהוָה
וְהִנֵּה יְהוָה עֹבֵר וְרוּחַ גְּדוֹלָה וְחָזָק מְפָרֵק הָרִים
וּמְשַׁבֵּר סְלָעִים לִפְנֵי יְהוָה לֹא בָרוּחַ יְהוָה

Reading 12

מלכים א יט:ה–יא

Words to Learn

אֲכִילָה NOUN F ______________

כֹּחַ NOUN M ______________

לִין VB Q ______________

מְרַאֲשׁוֹת NOUN FP ______________

נָגַע VB Q ______________

סֶלַע NOUN M ______________

פֹּה ADV ______________

(___) פֵּרֵק VB PI ______________

(___) קִנֵּא VB PI ______________

רִצְפָּה NOUN F ______________

(___) שִׁבֵּר VB PI ______________

שֵׁנִי ORD ______________

Going Deeper with Grammar

Participles in Narrative

In chapter 7 we discussed the use of the irreal Imperfect, irreal Perfect, and the participle to express habitual events. The other central function of the participle in narrative discourse is to express events that are ongoing or progressive at the point or time of their description. As with all predicatively used participles, as a progressive predicate the participle is the complement of an overt or (more often) null copula.

Often the purpose of using a progressive participle in narrative is to express overlapping events. That is, another event occurs during the time that the progressive event is happening. In the following example, Laban comes to the spring at the time when the servant of Abraham is standing beside the camels and the spring.

וַיָּבֹא אֶל־הָאִישׁ וְהִנֵּה עֹמֵד עַל־הַגְּמַלִּים עַל־הָעָיִן

He came to the man and—hey!—(he) <u>(was) standing</u> beside the camels beside the spring. (בראשית כד:ל)

A second purpose is to dramatically slow or pause the narrative, thus highlighting the event in some way. This may occur at some sort of climactic point in the story, such as when Dathan and Abiram and their families come out and stand at the entrances of their tents just before the ground opens and swallows them.

וְדָתָן וַאֲבִירָם יָצְאוּ נִצָּבִים פֶּתַח אָהֳלֵיהֶם

Dathan and Abiram came out; they (were) standing at the entrance of their tents. (במדבר טז:כז)

Find all the participles in the passage, and explain how they are functioning.

!הִנֵּה

The word הִנֵּה is traditionally translated in English by the archaic imperative "behold," but this provides little insight into the nature of הִנֵּה. The word's Semitic etymology is unclear, so we must rely on its form and pattern of use in the Bible to triangulate its function.

First, it clearly does not have the morphology of an imperative verb (compare רְאֵה, look!), alerting us immediately that it is not even in the same word class as the English "behold." Second, הִנֵּה occasionally occurs in the middle of a clause that already has a verb. This suggests that הִנֵּה belongs to a class of particles called interjections, which may be inserted at almost any phrase edge, whether at the beginning of the clause or between a verb and its complement NP.

As an interjection, הִנֵּה is both deictic and presentative, meaning that it directs the addressee (whether a character in the narrative or the audience) to turn attention to new and imminent discourse information. הִנֵּה sometimes carries an exclamatory force, which means that the information following is unexpected or surprising. Though colloquial, the English "hey!" is probably a better gloss for הִנֵּה than "behold" or the more modern "look" or "see."

Explain the uses of הִנֵּה in the passage.

Challenge

Agreement of Adjectives

Generally adjectives agree in both gender and number with the noun head they modify. However, masculine gender has priority grammatically. This is manifested in the preference of masculine gender when the adjective modifies two nouns, one feminine and the other masculine.

חֻקִּים וּמִצְוֹת טוֹבִים

good [M] statutes [M] and commandments [F] (נחמיה ט:יג)

This masculine priority also accounts for the rare cases in which multiple adjectives modify a single feminine noun and only the first of the adjectives agrees in gender with the noun.

בְּאֶרֶץ־צִיָּה וְעָיֵף
in a dry [F] and weary [M] land [F] (תהלים סג:ב)

Find the adjectives in the text and identify their agreement features.

Play It Again

Hebrew can express the idea of "again" with an adverb.

וַיֵּדַע אָדָם עוֹד אֶת־אִשְׁתּוֹ
Adam knew his wife again. (בראשית ד:כה)

Another common strategy is to employ a form of the verbs שׁוּב or הוֹסִיף with another verb to form a verbal hendiadys (i.e., two verbs expressing the equivalent of a verb and an adverb):

וַיֹּסֶף וַיִּקַּח
[he] took again (בראשית כה:א)

שֻׁבוּ שִׁבְרוּ
buy grain again (בראשית מג:ב)

Find the occurrences of שׁוּב in the passage, and identify whether or not they are being used to express "again."

Reading Insights

Narrative Economy and Null Constituents

In chapter 3 we pointed out the economy of Hebrew storytelling. A phrase or idea may be elided rather than repeated in subsequent occurrences in the story. Thus when Elijah says קְחִי־נָא לִי מְעַט־מַיִם בַּכְּלִי וְאֶשְׁתֶּה (מלכים א יז:י), the widow's response is narrated simply as וַתֵּלֶךְ לָקַחַת (יז:יא). The reader is able to fill in the missing or non-overt elements such as the complement (מַיִם), the means (בַּכְּלִי), and the reason (יִשְׁתֶּה), and so these syntactic constituents are not repeated. Elements that have an antecedent and are licensed by the verb will be understood not as actually "missing" but as "null" constituents (*BBH* §§18, 48). That is, they are syntactically real but phonologically empty or null. Such null constituents fulfill grammaticality while also allowing what the speaker says and the listener hears to be less complicated.

Find all the examples of null, or unexpressed, complements in the passage.

Review

Review I-ו/י verbs (see appendix B.4), and identify and parse any I-ו/י verbs in the passage.

Find and explain the use of any adverbial infinitives in the passage (*BBH* §25).

מלכים א
יט, יא-יח
יאוְאַחַר הָרוּחַ רַעַשׁ
לֹא בָרַעַשׁ יְהוָה׃
יבוְאַחַר הָרַעַשׁ אֵשׁ
לֹא בָאֵשׁ יְהוָה
וְאַחַר הָאֵשׁ קוֹל דְּמָמָה דַקָּה׃
מַה־לְּךָ פֹה אֵלִיָּהוּ׃
ידוַיֹּאמֶר
קַנֹּא קִנֵּאתִי לַיהוָה | אֱלֹהֵי צְבָאוֹת כִּי־עָזְבוּ בְרִיתְךָ בְּנֵי יִשְׂרָאֵל אֶת־מִזְבְּחֹתֶיךָ הָרָסוּ וְאֶת־נְבִיאֶיךָ הָרְגוּ בֶחָרֶב וָאִוָּתֵר אֲנִי לְבַדִּי וַיְבַקְשׁוּ אֶת־נַפְשִׁי לְקַחְתָּהּ׃ ס
יגוַיְהִי | כִּשְׁמֹעַ אֵלִיָּהוּ וַיָּלֶט פָּנָיו בְּאַדַּרְתּוֹ וַיֵּצֵא וַיַּעֲמֹד פֶּתַח הַמְּעָרָה וְהִנֵּה אֵלָיו קוֹל וַיֹּאמֶר
טווַיֹּאמֶר יְהוָה אֵלָיו
לֵךְ שׁוּב לְדַרְכְּךָ מִדְבַּרָה דַמָּשֶׂק וּבָאתָ וּמָשַׁחְתָּ אֶת־חֲזָאֵל לְמֶלֶךְ עַל־אֲרָם׃
טזוְאֵת יֵהוּא בֶן־נִמְשִׁי תִּמְשַׁח לְמֶלֶךְ עַל־יִשְׂרָאֵל וְאֶת־אֱלִישָׁע בֶּן־שָׁפָט מֵאָבֵל מְחוֹלָה תִּמְשַׁח לְנָבִיא תַּחְתֶּיךָ׃
יזוְהָיָה הַנִּמְלָט מֵחֶרֶב חֲזָאֵל יָמִית יֵהוּא וְהַנִּמְלָט מֵחֶרֶב יֵהוּא יָמִית אֱלִישָׁע׃ יחוְהִשְׁאַרְתִּי בְיִשְׂרָאֵל שִׁבְעַת אֲלָפִים כָּל־הַבִּרְכַּיִם אֲשֶׁר לֹא־כָרְעוּ לַבַּעַל וְכָל־הַפֶּה אֲשֶׁר לֹא־נָשַׁק לוֹ׃

Reading 13

מלכים א יט:יא–יח

Words to Learn

אַדֶּ֫רֶת NOUN F ______________
דְּמָמָה NOUN F ______________
דַּק ADJ ______________
(___ ___ ___) הִלְוִיט VB HI ______________
(___ ___ ___) הִשְׁאִיר VB HI ______________
כָּרַע VB Q ______________
מָשַׁח VB Q ______________
נָשַׁק VB Q ______________
רַ֫עַשׁ NOUN M ______________

Going Deeper with Grammar

Irreal Perfect and Irreal Imperfect in Discourse

The irreal Perfect and irreal Imperfect verbs overlap in significant ways. Syntactically they both show verb-subject inverted order, and semantically they overlap in terms of the modalities they may express, such as habitual and directive modalities (chap. 3). However, aside from the lack of full semantic overlap (e.g., only the irreal Imperfect is used for epistemic modality), they complement each other in directive and habitual discourse. The irreal Perfect is the default verb for procedural directives and habitual expressions, in which each described event occurs or should occur in the order in which it is described (as is the default narrative order of events). By contrast, the irreal Imperfect in these contexts does not express procedural actions. Instead, it expresses unordered events that may be related in various unordered ways to the procedures in the discourse. In the first example below, the irreal Imperfect expresses an unordered event that relates to the preceding event somewhat like two sides of a coin. In the second example, the habitual event is summarized by the irreal Imperfect before being procedurally described by the irreal Perfect forms.

וְצִפִּיתָ אֹתוֹ זָהָב טָהוֹר מִבַּיִת וּמִחוּץ תְּצַפֶּנּוּ

You should overlay [PERF] it with pure gold inside, and outside you should overlay it [IMPF]. (שמות כה:יא)

כִּי מִן־הַבְּאֵר הַהִוא יַשְׁקוּ הָעֲדָרִים . . . וְנֶאֶסְפוּ־שָׁמָּה כָל־הָעֲדָרִים וְגָלְלוּ
אֶת־הָאֶבֶן מֵעַל פִּי הַבְּאֵר וְהִשְׁקוּ אֶת־הַצֹּאן

Because from that well they would water [IMPF] the flocks. . . . All the flocks would gather [PERF] there, and [then] they would roll [PERF] the stone from upon the mouth of the well, and [then] they would water [PERF] the sheep. (בראשית כט:ב–ג)

Find the irreal Perfect and irreal Imperfect verbs in the passage, and describe how they are functioning.

Word Order and Focus

In chapter 4 we associated the pragmatic operation "focus" with verb-subject inversion. In chapter 7 we saw that focus is associated with both left and right dislocation. In stripped-down terms, focus isolates an item in the discourse from a set of items to which it belongs; this set can be based on the shared cultural assumptions behind the text (e.g,. sun, moon, stars) or based on a set explicitly established in the discourse (e.g., Cain and Abel). Once the item is isolated, focus requires that the proposition made in the given clause applies *only* to the item in focus, not the other members of its set. A classic example of the use of focus is the dialogue between the man, the woman, and God after they disobeyed in the garden of Eden.

וַיֹּאמֶר הָאָדָם הָאִשָּׁה אֲשֶׁר נָתַתָּה עִמָּדִי הִוא נָתְנָה־לִּי מִן־הָעֵץ . . . וַתֹּאמֶר
הָאִשָּׁה הַנָּחָשׁ הִשִּׁיאַנִי . . . וַיֹּאמֶר יְהוָה אֱלֹהִים אֶל־הַנָּחָשׁ . . . אָרוּר אַתָּה

And the man said: the woman that you put with me—*she* gave me [something] from the tree. . . . And the woman said: *the serpent* deceived me! And YHWH God said to the serpent: . . . *cursed* are you! (בראשית ג:יב–יד)

The membership set in this example is established in the immediate discourse context: man, woman, serpent. In the first two examples, the characters use focus to isolate an agent outside themselves for blame, and in the third example YHWH uses focus to isolate the agent to whom he assigns primary blame for the way the episode unfolded.

Identify any examples of focus in the passage.

Challenge

ל of Result

The ל preposition has a lot of different functions, including expressing possession or interest (see chap. 2). Another of its uses is to express the result or goal of a status change.

וַתִּתֶּן אֹתָהּ לְיַעֲקֹב לְאִשָּׁה

[She] gave her to Jacob [for] a wife. (בראשית ל:ט)

The literal translation of this function is awkward in English, which more naturally employs "as" for such expressions.

Find and identify the function of each לְ PP in the passage.

Directional ה (Again)

The postposition ה functions just like a preposition, except it follows its complement instead of preceding it (chap. 3). Potentially confusing is its ability to occur in the middle of its complement phrase. This occurs when it has a bound phrase complement: אַ֫רְצָה כְּנַ֫עַן, toward the land of Canaan (בראשית יא:לא).

Find the directional ה in the passage, and identify its complement.

Reading Insights

Copula in Motion

The copula (null or overt) can have a number of different types of complements (see chap. 4). One of the less immediately recognizable ones is the אל-PP, which is most frequent in the divine word formula: וַיְהִי דְּבַר־יְהוָה אֶל־שְׁמוּאֵל, the word of YHWH <u>was</u> to Samuel (שמואל א טו:י). In these sorts of expressions, the אל-PP marks the recipient of the divine word, which may be less awkwardly rendered in English by "came": "the word of YHWH <u>came</u> to Samuel."

Identify the copulas (null and overt) in the passage, and describe the type of complement each has.

Review

Find all the occurrences of וַיְהִי and וְהָיָה in the passage, and identify how they are functioning (i.e., copula, existential, or discourse).

Find all the occurrences of כִּי in the passage, and explain the most appropriate function for each.

מלכים א
יט, יט-כא
יט וַיֵּ֣לֶךְ מִ֠שָּׁם וַיִּמְצָ֞א אֶת־אֱלִישָׁ֤ע בֶּן־
שָׁפָט֙ וְה֣וּא חֹרֵ֔שׁ שְׁנֵים־עָשָׂ֤ר צְמָדִים֙
לְפָנָ֔יו וְה֖וּא בִּשְׁנֵ֣ים הֶעָשָׂ֑ר
וַיַּעֲבֹ֤ר אֵלִיָּ֙הוּ֙ אֵלָ֔יו
וַיַּשְׁלֵ֥ךְ אַדַּרְתּ֖וֹ אֵלָֽיו׃
כ וַיַּעֲזֹ֣ב אֶת־הַבָּקָ֗ר וַיָּ֙רָץ֙ אַחֲרֵ֣י
אֵֽלִיָּ֔הוּ וַיֹּ֗אמֶר
אֶשְּׁקָה־נָּא֙
לְאָבִ֣י וּלְאִמִּ֔י
וְאֵלְכָ֖ה אַחֲרֶ֑יךָ
וַיֹּ֤אמֶר לוֹ֙
לֵ֣ךְ שׁ֔וּב
כִּ֥י מֶה־עָשִׂ֖יתִי
לָֽךְ׃
כא וַיָּ֨שָׁב מֵאַחֲרָ֜יו וַיִּקַּ֣ח אֶת־צֶ֧מֶד
הַבָּקָ֣ר וַיִּזְבָּחֵ֗הוּ וּבִכְלִ֤י הַבָּקָר֙ בִּשְּׁלָ֣ם
הַבָּשָׂ֔ר וַיִּתֵּ֥ן לָעָ֖ם וַיֹּאכֵ֑לוּ
וַיָּ֗קָם וַיֵּ֛לֶךְ אַחֲרֵ֥י אֵלִיָּ֖הוּ וַיְשָׁרְתֵֽהוּ׃ פ

Reading 14

מלכים א יט:יט–כא

Words to Learn

בָּקָר NOUN M ______________

(___) בִּשֵּׁל VB PI ______________

(___) הִשְׁלִיךְ VB HI ______________

זָבַח VB Q, PI ______________

חָרַשׁ VB Q ______________

צֶמֶד NOUN M ______________

(___) שֵׁרֵת VB PI ______________

Going Deeper with Grammar

Modalities of the Directive-Volitive Verbs

The directive-volitive subsystem of irreal mood can be used for a wide range of different modalities (chap. 3), including commands, granting permission, petitioning, expressing intent, wishes, and desires. While some of these modal distinctions are expressed by intonation in spoken language—e.g., the difference between the directive *GO* (*now*)*!* and permissive *Go* (*on*)—grammatical and contextual clues must be employed to distinguish among possible modalities in Biblical Hebrew.

Grammatically *person* is a significant indicator of the type of modality expressed by the imperative and jussive forms. We can think of the directive and volitive meanings on a continuum based on the tendencies (not rules!) of each verb to express certain modalities.

directive ◄	———————————	► **volitive**
second-person	third-person	first-person

At the one end, second-person forms (positive imperative and negative jussive) are predominantly used for directives (commands).

עֲשֵׂה לְךָ תֵּבַת עֲצֵי־גֹפֶר

Make for yourself an ark of gopher wood. (בראשית ו:יד)

וְאַל־תַּעַשׂ לוֹ מְאוּמָה רָע
Do not do to him anything bad. (ירמיהו לט:יב)

At the other end of the continuum, the first-person jussive forms frequently express volitive modality (intents and wishes).

וְאֶתְּנָה בְרִיתִי בֵּינִי וּבֵינֶךָ
I will place my covenant between me and between you. (בראשית יז:ב)

וְאֶשְׁמְרָה תוֹרָתְךָ תָמִיד לְעוֹלָם וָעֶד
I desire to keep your torah continually forever and ever. (תהלים קיט:מד)

In between these two extremes are the third-person jussives, which regularly express directive or volitive modality.

אַל־יֵשְׂטְ אֶל־דְּרָכֶיהָ לִבֶּךָ
Do not let your heart turn to her ways. (משלי ז:כה)

הַיּוֹם הַהוּא יְהִי חֹשֶׁךְ
May that day be darkness! (איוב ג:ד)

Contextually the *status* of the speaker and addressee distinguishes among nuances of directive and volitive modalities. For example, the difference between a command and a request or petition depends on the social status of the speaker and the addressee. Similarly, a wish is appropriate of a soliloquy, but it becomes a request when spoken to a superior.

קוּמָה יְהוָה הוֹשִׁיעֵנִי
Rise up, Yhwh; save me! (תהלים ג:ח)

אֶעְבְּרָה־נָּא וְאֶרְאֶה אֶת־הָאָרֶץ הַטּוֹבָה
Allow me, please, to cross over and see the good land. (דברים ג:כה)

Find the imperatives and jussives in the passage, and identify the most appropriate modal interpretation for each.

Null Subjects

Clauses require subjects (chap. 1). When a subject is not overt, the reader recovers it based on clues in the text. The most common clue is verb agreement features, enabling the reader to supply the correct person-gender-number pronoun. But the reader must also discern the antecedent of the appropriate pronoun. Most often this is done by looking to a preceding clause. When multiple clauses have the same subject, the subject will usually be overt in only the first clause, and the continuity of subject will enable the reader to trace the antecedent back to the beginning of the string of clauses.

וַתַּהַר לֵאָה וַתֵּלֶד בֵּן וַתִּקְרָא שְׁמוֹ רְאוּבֵן

Leah conceived and ø (she) [= Leah] bore a son and ø (she) [= Leah] named him Reuben. (בראשית כט:לב)

Find any null subjects in the passage.

Challenge

A Missing ב?

We have already highlighted the multivalency of the preposition ב (chap. 4). And chapter 11 highlighted the instrumental use of ב. Related to the passage above, in most texts that use חרשׁ as "to plow," the ב marks the instrument of plowing:

לֹא־תַחֲרֹשׁ בְּשׁוֹר־וּבַחֲמֹר יַחְדָּו

Do not plow with an ox and with a donkey together. (דברים כב:י)

So is a ב missing in the reading? Hebrew does allow for NPs to serve adverbially, that is, for a preposition to be missing. And it might be tempting to see a missing ב in the passage here. But the syntax of the following words strongly argues against this analysis.

Can you determine why?

This passage provides two additional examples of ב; find them and identify the function.

Reading Insights

Twelve Yoke of Oxen: Communal Plowing, or a Sign of Wealth?

The description of Elijah's first encounter with Elisha contains an ambiguous description. When the narrator in verse יט depicts Elisha בִּשְׁנֵים הֶעָשָׂר, is it a reference to his position as the twelfth in line during a community plowing event (so some commentators) or as the master of twelve yokes, a sign of family wealth? (Remember that the "teen" numerals do not differ in their cardinal [twelve] or ordinal [twelfth] form.)

If the text references Elisha's position in line, is it engaging a trope that figures prominently in the David story (i.e., choosing the last among the eligible young men)? If the text references Elisha's family wealth, is it establishing a brief backstory detail that sets up the subsequent exchange about kissing his parents farewell? Perhaps the ambiguity is a deliberate narrative choice and the narrator is using both nuances to enrich the narrative.

Elijah's Attitude

When Elijah first encounters Elisha, no dialogue is given before Elijah abruptly casts his cloak on Elisha. This might be intended to set Elijah up as a taciturn and crotchety fellow who knows he is being forcibly retired. Though this may sound speculative, Elijah's response to Elisha's request to see his parents one last time seems to support Elijah's attitude (לֵךְ שׁוּב כִּי מֶה־עָשִׂיתִי לָךְ, v. כ), which only makes sense as a slightly less flippant variant of the modern slang response, "Yeah, whatever." It seems he is invested so little in this passing of the mantle that he essentially denies having done anything to Elisha. It is a strange penultimate episode in a fascinating career.

Review

Find all the null complements in the passage, and identify each of their antecedents.

Aleppo Codex

To review the passages of chapters 12–14, turn to the fifth page of the Aleppo Codex, and read from the eleventh line (i.e., וַיַּבֵּט וְהִנֵּה מְרַאֲשֹׁתָיו עֻגַת) through the twenty-second line of the third column (i.e., until the "paragraph" break near the bottom of that column).

אוַיְהִי אַחַר הַדְּבָרִים הָאֵלֶּה כֶּרֶם הָיָה לְנָבוֹת
הַיִּזְרְעֵאלִי אֲשֶׁר בְּיִזְרְעֶאל אֵצֶל הֵיכַל אַחְאָב
מֶלֶךְ שֹׁמְרוֹן׃ בוַיְדַבֵּר אַחְאָב אֶל־נָבוֹת ׀ לֵאמֹר ׀
תְּנָה־לִּי אֶת־כַּרְמְךָ וִיהִי־לִי לְגַן־יָרָק כִּי הוּא קָרוֹב אֵצֶל בֵּיתִי וְאֶתְּנָה לְךָ תַּחְתָּיו כֶּרֶם טוֹב מִמֶּנּוּ אִם טוֹב בְּעֵינֶיךָ אֶתְּנָה־לְךָ כֶסֶף מְחִיר זֶה׃
גוַיֹּאמֶר נָבוֹת אֶל־אַחְאָב
חָלִילָה לִּי מֵיהוָה מִתִּתִּי אֶת־נַחֲלַת אֲבֹתַי לָךְ׃
מלכים א
כא, א-י
דוַיָּבֹא אַחְאָב אֶל־בֵּיתוֹ סַר וְזָעֵף עַל־הַדָּבָר
אֲשֶׁר־דִּבֶּר אֵלָיו נָבוֹת הַיִּזְרְעֵאלִי וַיֹּאמֶר
לֹא־אֶתֵּן לְךָ אֶת־נַחֲלַת אֲבוֹתָי וַיִּשְׁכַּב
עַל־מִטָּתוֹ וַיַּסֵּב אֶת־פָּנָיו וְלֹא־אָכַל לָחֶם׃
הוַתָּבֹא אֵלָיו אִיזֶבֶל אִשְׁתּוֹ וַתְּדַבֵּר אֵלָיו
מַה־זֶּה רוּחֲךָ סָרָה וְאֵינְךָ אֹכֵל לָחֶם׃
ווַיְדַבֵּר אֵלֶיהָ
כִּי־אֲדַבֵּר אֶל־נָבוֹת הַיִּזְרְעֵאלִי וָאֹמַר לוֹ תְּנָה־לִּי אֶת־כַּרְמְךָ בְּכֶסֶף אוֹ אִם־חָפֵץ אַתָּה אֶתְּנָה־לְךָ כֶרֶם תַּחְתָּיו וַיֹּאמֶר לֹא־אֶתֵּן לְךָ אֶת־כַּרְמִי׃
זוַתֹּאמֶר אֵלָיו אִיזֶבֶל אִשְׁתּוֹ
אַתָּה עַתָּה תַּעֲשֶׂה מְלוּכָה עַל־יִשְׂרָאֵל קוּם אֱכָל־לֶחֶם וְיִטַב לִבֶּךָ אֲנִי אֶתֵּן לְךָ אֶת־כֶּרֶם נָבוֹת הַיִּזְרְעֵאלִי׃
חוַתִּכְתֹּב סְפָרִים בְּשֵׁם אַחְאָב וַתַּחְתֹּם בְּחֹתָמוֹ וַתִּשְׁלַח הַסְפָּרִים* אֶל־הַזְּקֵנִים וְאֶל־הַחֹרִים אֲשֶׁר בְּעִירוֹ הַיֹּשְׁבִים אֶת־נָבוֹת׃ טוַתִּכְתֹּב בַּסְּפָרִים לֵאמֹר
*Ketiv: הספרים
Qere: סְפָרִים
קִרְאוּ־צוֹם וְהוֹשִׁיבוּ אֶת־נָבוֹת בְּרֹאשׁ הָעָם׃ יוְהוֹשִׁיבוּ שְׁנַיִם אֲנָשִׁים בְּנֵי־בְלִיַּעַל נֶגְדּוֹ וִיעִדֻהוּ לֵאמֹר בֵּרַכְתָּ אֱלֹהִים וָמֶלֶךְ וְהוֹצִיאֻהוּ וְסִקְלֻהוּ וְיָמֹת׃

Reading 15

מלכים א כא:א–י

Words to Learn

אֵ֫צֶל	NOUN M ______________; PREP ______________
בְּלִ֫יַּעַל	NOUN M ______________
גַּן	NOUN M ______________
הֵיכָל	NOUN M ______________
הֵעִיד (___)	VB HI ______________
זָעֵף	ADJ ______________
זָקֵן	ADJ ______________
חָלִילָ	INTJ ______________
חָפֵץ	ADJ ______________
חֹר	NOUN M ______________
חָתַם	VB Q ______________
יָטַב	VB Q ______________
יָרָק	NOUN M ______________
מְחִיר	NOUN M ______________
מְלוּכָה	NOUN F ______________
נֶ֫גֶד	ADV, PREP ______________
סֵ֫פֶר	NOUN M ______________
סָקַל	VB Q ______________
סַר	ADJ ______________
צוֹם	NOUN M ______________
קָרוֹב	ADJ ______________

Going Deeper with Grammar

Constituent Movement: Fronting and Extraposition

The movement of constituents from their "normal" positions to other positions in the clause has been introduced in chapter 4, and the concepts of topic and focus have been discussed in chapters 7 and 13. Most cases of constituent movement in Hebrew are types of fronting, that is, the constituent moves toward the front, or left (reading linearly from left-to-right), of the clause.

The table below offers a concise visual summary of the Hebrew clause and the various landing sites for constituent movement, whether for syntactic, semantic, or pragmatic reasons.

Front (Left)			Core Clause	Back (Right)
particle, dislocation, topic XP	focus XP	verb [raised]	subj-[V]-(comp)	extraposed XP, dislocation

Note: XP indicates any type of phrase; the bracketed V indicates the basic position of the verb before it is raised above the subject (verb raising that is triggered by, e.g., a subordinator).

For example, a clause can begin with כִּי, which will trigger the verb to raise in front (or left) of the subject. Additionally, between the כִּי and the raised verb, it is possible to have a NP (say, the complement) that has been raised due to focus. To this, one might even add a right dislocated NP that is linked to the focus-fronted pronominal complement.

The one element in the scheme above that has not yet been introduced is extraposition. Extraposition is the opposite of fronting; that is, a constituent moves to the back (or right) of the clause. Constituents may be extraposed for two basic reasons: (1) the constituent carries what is essentially a delayed focus or (2) the constituent is complex ("heavy") enough that it is easier to process mentally only after smaller ("lighter") constituents. Examples of two types of this "processing" extraposition are given below: heavy NP shift and relative extraposition.

הָאֵמִים לְפָנִים יָשְׁבוּ בָהּ עַם גָּדוֹל וְרַב וָרָם כָּעֲנָקִים׃
The Emim formerly dwelled in it, a people great and numerous and tall like the Anakim. (דברים ב:י)

וְהִנֵּה רִבְקָה יֹצֵאת אֲשֶׁר יֻלְּדָה לִבְתוּאֵל
And look—Rebekah was going out, who was born to Bethuel. (בראשית כד:טו)

Explain the first clause of the passage in light of the possibilities provided by Hebrew constituent movement.

Valency and בִּנְיָנִים

The system of בִּנְיָנִים is a key determiner of the valency of a verb. Although the system is inconsistent, some systematic valency alterations can be seen between verbs of different בִּנְיָנִים but of the same root. For example, הִפְעִיל verbs frequently (but not always!) represent causative-increased valency relative to the קַל of the same root. For example, the קַל יָצָא is bivalent with a locative complement in the first example below, whereas the הִפְעִיל is trivalent with a patient complement in addition to the locative one in the second example.

וַיֵּצֵא קַיִן מִלִּפְנֵי יְהוָה
Cain went out from before YHWH. (בראשית ד:טז)

הוֹצֵאתִיךָ מֵאוּר כַּשְׂדִּים
I brought you out from Ur of the Chaldeans. (בראשית טו:ז)

Similarly, the נִפְעַל is often a passive valency-reducing בִּנְיָן relative to קַל verbs of the same root. The patient of the קַל סָקַל is the VP complement, making the pattern bivalent. By contrast, the נִפְעַל of the same root (נִסְקַל) is monovalent with the patient as subject.

וּסְקַלְתּוֹ בָאֲבָנִים
You should stone him with stones. (דברים יג:יא)

וְהַשּׁוֹר יִסָּקֵל
The ox must be stoned. (שמות כא:לב)

Recognizing these tendencies aids in analyzing argument structure. For example, in a passage with the קַל verb קוּם, we will be expecting a monovalent pattern or perhaps a bivalent with a locative complement, as in the example below. In contrast, if we come across the הִפְעִיל הֵקִים of the same root, we will expect to find not only a possible locative complement but a patient complement as well in the VP, as in the second example below.

וַיָּקָם קַיִן אֶל־הֶבֶל אָחִיו
Cain stood up to/against Abel, his brother. (בראשית ד:ח)

וַהֲקִמֹתִי אֶת־בְּרִיתִי אִתָּךְ
I will set up my covenant with you. (בראשית ו:יח)

Find and parse all the verbs of the same root in different בִּנְיָנִים in the passage. Explain their different argument structures.

Challenge

Anathemas

Like oaths, curses often present grammatical difficulties because their forms have become stylized or reflect the grammaticalization of formulas. Consider the example below with the word חָלִלָה, which appears to mean "profanation":

חָלִלָה לְּךָ מֵעֲשֹׂת | כַּדָּבָר הַזֶּה
Profanation [would be] yours because of doing something like this thing!
(בראשית יח:כה)

The point of the curse is to warn or threaten the object of the adjuration that they would become profane if the situation unfolds as imagined. The מִן PP provides the source of the supposed profanation.

The self curse uttered by Naboth in response to Ahab's proposal to buy his vineyard is a good example of this curse formula, but with a twist:

> How does מֵיְהוָה in the passage provide the source and how does the second מִן PP function (hint: you may need to review chap. 6)?

Null Subjects That Are Not NPs

Null subjects in Hebrew discourse are overwhelmingly tied to a NP antecedent. Thus when a clause is lacking an overt subject, the reader simply looks back a clause or two to find the antecedent that fits the verbal agreement features and the discourse context. This is true of all anaphoric devices (pronouns, demonstratives), whether null or overt. And yet, finding the antecedent in some cases is not so simple. What is the antecedent for the null subject in the clause below?

אִם טוֹב בְּעֵינֶיךָ
if ø (?) is good in your eyes (מלכים א כא:ב)

What is the semantic subject (i.e., the antecedent of the null subject) in this clause? It can only be the entire "deal" that Ahab just presented. Thus the antecedent is not a simple NP but a proposition encapsulating an anticipated event.

Reading Insights

Jezebel: Domineering and Scornful, or Caring and Encouraging?

The dialogue between Jezebel and Ahab is both rich and intriguing. On the one hand, when Jezebel notices Ahab's ill humor, she asks מַה־זֶּה רוּחֲךָ סָרָה וְאֵינְךָ אֹכֵל לָחֶם (v. ה), which sounds like a concerned spouse. On the other hand, after she hears his explanation, her response is אַתָּה עַתָּה תַּעֲשֶׂה מְלוּכָה עַל־יִשְׂרָאֵל (v. ז). Is this an exhortation that Ahab has the power to do what he wants, or does it reflect sarcasm and contempt for a husband she sees as not behaving as he can and should? Either way, she follows up by taking control of the situation entirely, painting a picture of a queen who is in many ways stronger in determination and resourcefulness than the king.

בֵּרַךְ: Bless God and . . . Be Stoned to Death?!

There are few connections between Job and the Elijah narrative, but the use of בֵּרַךְ is one. When Job's wife says to him בָּרֵךְ אֱלֹהִים וָמֻת (איוב ב:ט), it has long been proposed that ברך here (and also איוב א:ה, יא; ב:ה; תהלים י:ג) is a euphemism for the verbs ארר or קלל, both of which denote cursing. Thus Job's wife encourages him to *curse* God, not *bless* him. With that in the background, it allows us to make better sense of Jezebel's otherwise strange indictment of Naboth: בֵּרַכְתָּ אֱלֹהִים וָמֶלֶךְ (v. י). If Naboth had indeed blessed his God and his king, it certainly would not be grounds for stoning! But if he had cursed both, it makes Jezebel's call to stone him a reasonable (if duplicitous) response.

Review

Is חָפֵץ an adjective or a verb? How do you decide?

What is the difference between the *Ketiv* הַסְפָרִים and *Qere* סְפָרִים? Explain. (Hint: Where's the דָּגֵשׁ?)

מלכים א
כא, יא-טז
יא וַיַּעֲשׂוּ אַנְשֵׁי עִירוֹ הַזְּקֵנִים וְהַחֹרִים אֲשֶׁר הַיֹּשְׁבִים בְּעִירוֹ
כַּאֲשֶׁר שָׁלְחָה אֲלֵיהֶם אִיזָבֶל כַּאֲשֶׁר כָּתוּב בַּסְּפָרִים אֲשֶׁר
שָׁלְחָה אֲלֵיהֶם׃ יב קָרְאוּ צוֹם וְהֹשִׁיבוּ אֶת־נָבוֹת בְּרֹאשׁ הָעָם׃
יג וַיָּבֹאוּ שְׁנֵי הָאֲנָשִׁים בְּנֵי־בְלִיַּעַל וַיֵּשְׁבוּ נֶגְדּוֹ
וַיְעִדֻהוּ אַנְשֵׁי הַבְּלִיַּעַל אֶת־נָבוֹת נֶגֶד הָעָם לֵאמֹר
בֵּרַךְ נָבוֹת
אֱלֹהִים וָמֶלֶךְ
וַיֹּצִאֻהוּ מִחוּץ לָעִיר וַיִּסְקְלֻהוּ
בָאֲבָנִים וַיָּמֹת׃
יד וַיִּשְׁלְחוּ אֶל־אִיזֶבֶל לֵאמֹר
סֻקַּל נָבוֹת
וַיָּמֹת׃
טו וַיְהִי כִּשְׁמֹעַ אִיזֶבֶל
כִּי־סֻקַּל נָבוֹת וַיָּמֹת
וַתֹּאמֶר אִיזֶבֶל אֶל־
אַחְאָב
קוּם רֵשׁ אֶת־כֶּרֶם
נָבוֹת הַיִּזְרְעֵאלִי אֲשֶׁר
מֵאֵן לָתֶת־לְךָ בְכֶסֶף
כִּי אֵין נָבוֹת חַי כִּי־
מֵת׃
טז וַיְהִי כִשְׁמֹעַ אַחְאָב כִּי
מֵת נָבוֹת וַיָּקָם אַחְאָב
לָרֶדֶת אֶל־כֶּרֶם נָבוֹת
הַיִּזְרְעֵאלִי לְרִשְׁתּוֹ׃ ס

Reading 16

מלכים א כא:יא–טז

Words to Learn

חוּץ	NOUN M	______________
(____) מֵאֵן	VB PI	______________
(____) סֻקַּל	VB PU	______________

Going Deeper with Grammar

The Past Narrative and Perfect Verbs

The meanings of the Past Narrative and the Perfect verbs overlap in that they both regularly express past events (past tense) with a "closed" structure (perfective situation aspect), as מָלַךְ and וַיִּמְלֹךְ do in מלכים א טז:כט:

וְאַחְאָב בֶּן־עָמְרִי מָלַךְ עַל־יִשְׂרָאֵל בִּשְׁנַת שְׁלֹשִׁים וּשְׁמֹנֶה שָׁנָה לְאָסָא מֶלֶךְ
יְהוּדָה וַיִּמְלֹךְ אַחְאָב בֶּן־עָמְרִי עַל־יִשְׂרָאֵל בְּשֹׁמְרוֹן עֶשְׂרִים וּשְׁתַּיִם שָׁנָה׃

This overlap has led some scholars to claim that the two forms are distinct only in syntax (i.e., the Past Narrative occurs clause-initially whereas the Perfect is not so restricted). This is not only incorrect (e.g., בראשית ד:ג; כב:ד), but it misses notable semantic and pragmatic differences between the forms.

The Perfect is a perfective aspect conjugation (*BBH* §16), whereas the Past Narrative is a special past-tense conjugation employed for the narrative foreground (*BBH* §35). The overlap between the conjugations is due to the close semantic relationship between past tense and perfective aspect: reporting of past-time events tend to be narratival, thus portrayed as successive "closed" or "whole" events (i.e., perfective); in turn (and perhaps as a result of), perfective events default to past temporal reference.

There are, of course, syntactic differences between the two conjugations: the Past Narrative has a prefixed ו, is frequently clause-initial, and is rarely used in subordinate clauses. However, the differences are not limited to syntax but are also semantic and pragmatic. Semantically, the Past Narrative is always past tense, real mood, whereas the Perfect is not so restricted: it expresses present-performative (e.g., שמואל ב יט:ל); varieties of perfect or anterior, including future-perfect (e.g., בראשית כח:טו); and it also has irreal mood expressions (e.g., conditional, final, and so on).

Pragmatically, in narrative discourse the Past Narrative verb always expresses foregrounded events in narrative (see chap. 5 above; *BBH* §43). By contrast, the Perfect verb is not restricted to narrative discourse to the same extent, and in narrative it may express foregrounded or backgrounded events. The Perfect often expresses foregrounded events conjoined with a Past Narrative to express two coordinated (rather than narrative sequential) actions (e.g., בראשית ד:ג–ד). Background events expressed by the Perfect include scene-setting situations (e.g., בראשית לז:ב), out-of-sequence events (e.g., בראשית כב:יג), and subordinate events inside, for instance, relative clauses (e.g., בראשית כב:ט).

Identify the Perfect verbs, and explain their function in the passage.

Valency and בִּנְיָנִים (Again)

In chapter 15 we discussed that a degree of predictability among בִּנְיָנִים can be helpful for analyzing the syntax. At the same time, a lack of predictability can lead to some incorrect assumptions about the relatedness of verbs of the same root in different בִּנְיָנִים. For example, the פֻּעַל is consistently a passive valency-reduced בִּנְיָן related to the פִּעֵל of the same root. By contrast, some roots that form verbs in both the קַל and the פִּעֵל show the same syntax and have closely related or indistinguishable meanings.

וַיְשַׁלַּח יְהוֹשֻׁעַ אֶת־הָעָם אִישׁ לְנַחֲלָתוֹ
Joshua sent [פִּעֵל] the people, each to his inheritance. (יהושע כד:כח)

וְהָאֲנָשִׁים שֻׁלְּחוּ
The men were sent away [פֻּעַל]. (בראשית מד:ג)

הִנֵּה שָׁלַחְתִּי אֵלֶיךָ אֶת־נַעֲמָן עַבְדִּי
Look, I have sent [קַל] to you Na'aman my servant. (מלכים ב ה:ו)

Find and parse all the verbs of the same root in different בִּנְיָנִים in the passage.

Challenge

Valency Alternation (Again)

We discussed in chapter 11 how languages allow some unsystematic variation in how some complements are encoded with motion verbs. Similar alternations occur with other verbs, such as how the recipient is indicated by the English word *give*: *Bobby gave flowers to Sue* versus *Bobby gave Sue flowers*. Confusion can arise if variations like this are available in Hebrew but not available for the corresponding verb in one's native language. For example, in Biblical Hebrew one can oppress someone (הֱצִיקַתְהוּ, she oppressed him [שפטים יד:יז]), but more often one oppresses *to* someone (וַהֲצִיקוֹתִי לַאֲרִיאֵל, I will oppress *to* Ariel [ישעיהו כט:ב]).

Find all the VP complements in the passage, and analyze the syntax and semantics of each complement.

Reading Insights

Statives in Context

Stative verbs differ from dynamic ones morphologically and semantically (see *BBH* §38). The semantic interpretation of statives is heavily context dependent. For one, statives have a default present-time interpretation but are interpreted as past in the context of past narrative discourse:

וִיהוֹשֻׁעַ זָקֵן בָּא בַּיָּמִים וַיֹּאמֶר יְהוָה אֵלָיו אַתָּה זָקַנְתָּה בָּאתָ בַיָּמִים
Joshua was old; he had advanced in years. YHWH said to him, "You are old; you have advanced in years." (יהושע יג:א)

For another, statives may express a state or the entrance into a state (inchoative). Importantly, in narrative discourse the narrative time is "advanced" by an inchoative stative, whereas it is not advanced by a (noninchoative) stative. The latter events, like the progressive participle (chap. 12), overlap with surrounding events in the narrative. For example, the stative in the first example sets the scene for the following clause. By contrast, in the second example below the inchoative stative leads to the following ensuing event.

וְהַמִּלְחָמָה כָּבֵדָה וְהֵם לֹא יָדְעוּ כִּי־נֹגַעַת עֲלֵיהֶם הָרָעָה׃
The battle was heavy, and they did not know that disaster was about to strike them. (שפטים כ:לד)

וַתִּכְבַּד הַמִּלְחָמָה אֶל־שָׁאוּל וַיִּמְצָאֻהוּ הַמּוֹרִים אֲנָשִׁים בַּקָּשֶׁת
The battle became heavy against Saul, and the men shooting with a bow found him. (שמואל א לא:ג)

Find the statives in the passage, and decide whether they are present or past time and whether they are stative or inchoative.

Review

Find and parse all the II-ו/י verbs in the passage (see appendix B.6).

מלכים א
כא, יז-כט
יז וַיְהִי דְּבַר־יְהוָה אֶל־אֵלִיָּהוּ הַתִּשְׁבִּי לֵאמֹר׃
יח קוּם רֵד לִקְרַאת אַחְאָב מֶלֶךְ־יִשְׂרָאֵל אֲשֶׁר בְּשֹׁמְרוֹן הִנֵּה בְּכֶרֶם נָבוֹת אֲשֶׁר־יָרַד שָׁם לְרִשְׁתּוֹ׃ יט וְדִבַּרְתָּ אֵלָיו לֵאמֹר כֹּה אָמַר יְהוָה הֲרָצַחְתָּ וְגַם־יָרָשְׁתָּ וְדִבַּרְתָּ אֵלָיו לֵאמֹר כֹּה אָמַר יְהוָה בִּמְקוֹם אֲשֶׁר לָקְקוּ הַכְּלָבִים אֶת־דַּם נָבוֹת יָלֹקּוּ הַכְּלָבִים אֶת־דָּמְךָ גַּם־אָתָּה׃
כ וַיֹּאמֶר אַחְאָב אֶל־אֵלִיָּהוּ
הַמְצָאתַנִי אֹיְבִי
וַיֹּאמֶר
מָצָאתִי יַעַן הִתְמַכֶּרְךָ לַעֲשׂוֹת הָרַע בְּעֵינֵי יְהוָה׃
כא הִנְנִי מֵבִיא* אֵלֶיךָ רָעָה וּבִעַרְתִּי אַחֲרֶיךָ וְהִכְרַתִּי לְאַחְאָב מַשְׁתִּין בְּקִיר וְעָצוּר וְעָזוּב בְּיִשְׂרָאֵל׃
*Ketiv: מבי
Qere: מֵבִיא
כב וְנָתַתִּי אֶת־בֵּיתְךָ כְּבֵית יָרָבְעָם בֶּן־נְבָט וּכְבֵית בַּעְשָׁא בֶן־אֲחִיָּה אֶל־הַכַּעַס אֲשֶׁר הִכְעַסְתָּ וַתַּחֲטִא אֶת־יִשְׂרָאֵל׃
כג וְגַם־לְאִיזֶבֶל דִּבֶּר יְהוָה לֵאמֹר הַכְּלָבִים יֹאכְלוּ אֶת־אִיזֶבֶל בְּחֵל יִזְרְעֶאל׃ כד הַמֵּת לְאַחְאָב בָּעִיר יֹאכְלוּ הַכְּלָבִים וְהַמֵּת בַּשָּׂדֶה יֹאכְלוּ עוֹף הַשָּׁמָיִם׃ כה רַק לֹא־הָיָה כְאַחְאָב אֲשֶׁר הִתְמַכֵּר לַעֲשׂוֹת הָרַע בְּעֵינֵי יְהוָה אֲשֶׁר־הֵסַתָּה אֹתוֹ אִיזֶבֶל אִשְׁתּוֹ׃ כו וַיַּתְעֵב מְאֹד לָלֶכֶת אַחֲרֵי הַגִּלֻּלִים כְּכֹל אֲשֶׁר עָשׂוּ הָאֱמֹרִי אֲשֶׁר הוֹרִישׁ יְהוָה מִפְּנֵי בְּנֵי יִשְׂרָאֵל׃ ס
כז וַיְהִי כִשְׁמֹעַ אַחְאָב אֶת־הַדְּבָרִים הָאֵלֶּה וַיִּקְרַע בְּגָדָיו וַיָּשֶׂם־שַׂק עַל־בְּשָׂרוֹ וַיָּצוֹם וַיִּשְׁכַּב בַּשָּׂק וַיְהַלֵּךְ אַט׃ ס
כח וַיְהִי דְּבַר־יְהוָה אֶל־אֵלִיָּהוּ הַתִּשְׁבִּי לֵאמֹר׃
כט הֲרָאִיתָ כִּי־נִכְנַע אַחְאָב מִלְּפָנָי יַעַן כִּי־נִכְנַע מִפָּנַי לֹא־אָבִיא* הָרָעָה בְּיָמָיו בִּימֵי בְנוֹ אָבִיא הָרָעָה עַל־בֵּיתוֹ׃
*Ketiv: אבי
Qere: אָבִיא

Reading 17

מלכים א כא:יז–כט

Words to Learn

אַט NOUN M ____________________

בִּעֵר (___ ___ ___) VB PI ____________________

גִּלּוּלִים NOUN M ____________________

הֵסִית (___ ___ ___) VB HI ____________________

הִשְׁתִּין (___ ___ ___) VB HI ____________________

הִתְמַכֵּר (___ ___ ___) VB HIT ____________________

הִתְעִיב (___ ___ ___) VB HI ____________________

חֵל NOUN M ____________________

יַ֫עַן CONJ ____________________

כֶּ֫לֶב NOUN M ____________________

כַּ֫עַס NOUN M ____________________

לָקַק VB Q ____________________

נִכְנַע (___ ___ ___) VB NI ____________________

עוֹף NOUN M ____________________

צוּם VB Q _______________

קִיר NOUN M ____________________

קָרַע VB Q ____________________

רָצַח VB Q ____________________

רַק ADV ____________________

Going Deeper with Grammar

קַל Passive Participle

The קַל בִּנְיָן has both an active participle and a passive participle (see *BBH* §42). In chapter 8 we discussed participles as a special type of adjective that can encode event predicates. They can be used as other adjectives to modify a head noun or substitute for a noun (i.e., a null head relative), or as a predicate supported by a copula. The passive participle shares this range of functions.

וְאֵת הַפָּר הַשֵּׁנִי הֹעֲלָה עַל־הַמִּזְבֵּחַ הַבָּנוּי

And the second bull was offered up upon the altar that had been built. (שפטים ו:כח)

וְהֶחָלוּץ הֹלֵךְ לִפְנֵי הַכֹּהֲנִים

And the armed (ones) [i.e., those who were armed] (were) walking before the priests. (יהושע ו:ט)

וְעַתָּה אֲרוּרִים אַתֶּם

And now cursed (are) you. (יהושע ט:כג)

Unlike the active participle, the "eventive" character of the passive participle is not frequently evident because of the valency-reducing character of the passive voice. That is, when it functions as a complement of a copula, often there are no other VP complements or modifiers. Compare the third example above with the example below, which has a PP adjunct modifier of the passive participle.

וְחַרְבּוֹ שְׁלוּפָה בְּיָדוֹ

And his sword (was) drawn in his hand. (יהושע ה:יג)

Find the passive participle in the passage, and explain how it is functioning.

Verbs in Prophetic Speech

In prophetic speech prophets often convey YHWH's intention toward the addressee of the speech. There are a number of ways these statements may be constructed. One way is a conditional statement with the irreal Imperfect and/or the irreal Perfect.

וְאַתָּה אִם־תֵּלֵךְ לְפָנַי . . . וַהֲקִמֹתִי אֶת־כִּסֵּא מַמְלַכְתְּךָ עַל־יִשְׂרָאֵל לְעֹלָם

As for you, if you walk before me . . . I will establish the throne of your kingdom over Israel forever. (מלכים א ט:ד–ה)

Another way is to introduce the statement with the discourse וְהָיָה (chap. 2) followed by an irreal Imperfect or Perfect. This construction often accompanies a temporal statement about what YHWH intends to do some "day" in the future. The Perfect in this construction conveys YHWH's intention (volitional or promissory) with regard to that day.

וְהָיָה בַּיּוֹם הַהוּא וְשָׁבַרְתִּי אֶת־קֶשֶׁת יִשְׂרָאֵל בְּעֵמֶק יִזְרְעֶאל

[Irreal] On that day I will break the bow of Israel in the valley of Jezreel. (הושע א:ה)

Finally, prophetic statements may employ the participle with a prospective aspect meaning—that is, an event is portrayed as already underway in the present, but it really belongs to the future (e.g., *Joe is flying to Chicago next week*)—or irreal Perfect or some combination of these. In this construction, the irreal Perfect expresses the purpose or result of YHWH's intended action.

כֹּה אָמַר יְהוָה הִנְנִי מֵקִים עָלֶיךָ רָעָה מִבֵּיתֶךָ וְלָקַחְתִּי אֶת־נָשֶׁיךָ לְעֵינֶיךָ
וְנָתַתִּי לְרֵעֶיךָ וְשָׁכַב עִם־נָשֶׁיךָ לְעֵינֵי הַשֶּׁמֶשׁ הַזֹּאת׃

Thus says YHWH, "Hey! I am raising up against you an evil from your house so that I take your wives before your eyes and give [them] to your friend so that he might lie with your wives in the sight of this sun." (שמואל ב יב:יא)

> Explain the verb forms used in the prophetic speech in the passage.

Challenge

NPs Used Adverbially

Though PPs are the most frequent strategy for modifying how a verb's event unfolds (manner, time, location, instrument), Hebrew also allows bare NPs to serve this function (see chap. 14). That is, we find numerous cases of NPs without a preposition for which there is no obvious syntactic role other than modifying the verb. Consider the contrastive pair of examples below, both using the same noun (בֶּטַח) but one with a preposition and one without.

וַיֵּשֶׁב יְהוּדָה וְיִשְׂרָאֵל לָבֶטַח

And Judah and Israel lived securely [lit., for security]. (מלכים א ה:ה)

וַתֵּשְׁבוּ בֶּטַח

And you lived [with] security. (שמואל א יב:יא)

> Find an example of the adverbial use of a NP in the text, and explain how it modifies the verbal action.

Reading Insights

Vulgarity in the Bible?

When Ahab greets Elijah, it is not with warmth: הַמְצָאתַנִי אֹיְבִי (כא:כ). Elijah clearly holds Ahab in similar esteem, and his response in turn is both blunt and expansive. God's speech to Elijah gives him only a rhetorical question to pass on to Ahab and focuses instead on Jezebel's fate, but Elijah's speech to Ahab contains a great deal more, including a particularly vulgar reference to males as those who מַשְׁתִּין בְּקִיר (כא:כא). Yes, this is precisely what it seems—a reference to men relieving themselves against a building wall.

We will never know whether this colorful expression represents part of the divine message that was included only once for the sake of economy or whether this is Elijah's personal flourish. But it begs us to consider why he would use such vulgarity. Superficially, we might conclude that it reflects Elijah's disgust with his royal adversary, but it may be a more rhetorically useful reference. The message against Ahab may be that his entire line will be cut off (עָצוּר וְעָזוּב [כא:כא]) precisely when they are unaware, when they are preoccupied with the requirements of normal human living. In other words, none of them will see it coming.

Review

Find and parse all the II-III verbs in the passage (see appendix B.7).

Find all the occurrences of the interrogative ה in the passage (*BBH* appendix A.5).

Aleppo Codex

To review the passages of chapters 15–17, turn to the eighth page of the Aleppo Codex, and read from the eighth line of the first column (i.e., the new "paragraph," beginning with וַיְהִ֗י אַחַ֣ר הַדְּבָרִ֣ים הָאֵ֔לֶּה) through the fifteenth line of the second column of the ninth page (i.e., through the phrase עַל־בֵּיתֽוֹ).

כט וַיַּעַל מֶלֶךְ־יִשְׂרָאֵל וִיהוֹשָׁפָט מֶלֶךְ־יְהוּדָה רָמֹת גִּלְעָד׃
ל וַיֹּאמֶר מֶלֶךְ יִשְׂרָאֵל אֶל־יְהוֹשָׁפָט
הִתְחַפֵּשׂ וָבֹא בַמִּלְחָמָה
וְאַתָּה לְבַשׁ בְּגָדֶיךָ
וַיִּתְחַפֵּשׂ מֶלֶךְ יִשְׂרָאֵל וַיָּבוֹא בַּמִּלְחָמָה׃
מלכים א
כב, כט-לג
לא וּמֶלֶךְ אֲרָם צִוָּה אֶת־שָׂרֵי הָרֶכֶב
אֲשֶׁר־לוֹ שְׁלֹשִׁים וּשְׁנַיִם לֵאמֹר
לֹא תִּלָּחֲמוּ אֶת־קָטֹן
וְאֶת־גָּדוֹל כִּי אִם־אֶת־
מֶלֶךְ יִשְׂרָאֵל לְבַדּוֹ׃
לב וַיְהִי כִּרְאוֹת שָׂרֵי הָרֶכֶב אֶת־
יְהוֹשָׁפָט וְהֵמָּה אָמְרוּ
אַךְ מֶלֶךְ־יִשְׂרָאֵל הוּא
וַיָּסֻרוּ עָלָיו לְהִלָּחֵם וַיִּזְעַק יְהוֹשָׁפָט׃ לג וַיְהִי
כִּרְאוֹת שָׂרֵי הָרֶכֶב כִּי־לֹא־מֶלֶךְ יִשְׂרָאֵל הוּא
וַיָּשׁוּבוּ מֵאַחֲרָיו׃

Reading 18

מלכים א כב:כט–לג

Words to Learn

הִתְחַפֵּשׂ (__ __ __) VB HIT _______________

זָעַק VB Q _______________

לָבַשׁ, לָבֵשׁ VB Q _______________;
HI _______________

נִלְחַם (__ __ __) VB NI _______________

קָטָן, קָטֹן ADJ _______________

רֶ֫כֶב NOUN M (COLL) _______________

Going Deeper with Grammar

Adverbial Infinitive

An adverbial infinitive is frequently used with a finite verb of the same שֹׁרֶשׁ and בִּנְיָן for focus. The significance of the focusing must be discerned from the context. One common focus nuance is modal certainty or doubt, as illustrated in the two examples below, respectively (see *BBH* §25).

בְּיוֹם אֲכָלְךָ מִמֶּנּוּ מוֹת תָּמוּת
On the day you eat from it you certainly will die. (בראשית ב:יז)

הֲמָלֹךְ תִּמְלֹךְ עָלֵינוּ
Will you really reign over us? (בראשית לז:ח)

It may also function in some less common ways. One of these is as a more general (i.e., nonmodal) adverbial modifier of a finite verb.

וַיֵּלֶךְ הָלוֹךְ וְאָכֹל
He went going and eating. (שפטים יד:ט)

וָאֶכֹּת אֹתוֹ טָחוֹן הֵיטֵב
I crushed it, grinding really well. (דברים ט:כא)

Another use is as the predicate of an adjunct clause. The tense-aspect-mood (TAM) are inherited from whatever inflected finite verb exists in the main clause. The person-gender-number features are typically inherited from the main verb as well, though the second example below provides a rare example of an overt subject for the infinitive.

זָכוֹר אֶת־יוֹם הַשַּׁבָּת לְקַדְּשׁוֹ שֵׁשֶׁת יָמִים תַּעֲבֹד

Remembering the day of the Sabbath by sanctifying it, you shall toil six days. (שמות כ:ח–ט)

בְּשֵׁם הַמֶּלֶךְ אֲחַשְׁוֵרֹשׁ נִכְתָּב וְנֶחְתָּם בְּטַבַּעַת הַמֶּלֶךְ׃ וְנִשְׁלוֹחַ סְפָרִים בְּיַד הָרָצִים אֶל־כָּל־מְדִינוֹת הַמֶּלֶךְ

In the name of King Ahashverosh it was written and it was sealed with the signet ring of the king, letters being sent out by the hand of runners to all the provinces of the king. (אסתר ג:יב–יג)

Find any adverbial infinitives in the passage, and explain how they are functioning.

ו as a Phrase Edge Marker

The ו conjunction is a clitic that attaches to the front of the first word in a phrase and often serves to coordinate two phrases of the same category, in a pattern XP_1 and-XP_2:

תֹהוּ וָבֹהוּ

formless and chaotic (בראשית א:ב)

But there are cases of the asymmetric use of ו, cases in which the ו does not coordinate two phrases of the same category, XP and-YP:

אֲשֶׁר יִמָּצֵא אִתּוֹ מֵעֲבָדֶיךָ וָמֵת

[the man] who it [Joseph's silver cup] is found with him among your servants and shall die (בראשית מד:ט)

It makes no sense in this example that the ו functions as a coordinator to join the subject (the null headed relative clause) to the verb מֵת. Similarly, the ו is sometimes cliticized to an appositive (chap. 6):

אִם־לֹא אֶל־בֵּית־אָבִי תֵּלֵךְ וְאֶל־מִשְׁפַּחְתִּי

Surely to the house of my father you shall go, that is, to the house of my family. (בראשית כד:לח)

This suggests that the ו is not only a simple coordinator, but when it is present, it functions syntactically to signal the outer edge of a phrase. In contrast, when the ו is absent, phrasal edges must be determined contextually. The presence of the ו is dictated by three concerns: (1) it may be required for morphosyntactic reasons (e.g., the fused form וַיִּקְטֹל), (2) it is an information processing aid (e.g., its presence may aid in the correct identification of the sequence of NPs as a list), or (3) it may be used in a discourse-pragmatic role (e.g., to signal that an example of direct speech is the dispreferred or unexpected response in a dialogue).

Identify and explain any asymmetric uses of ו in the passage.

Challenge

Lack of Full Subject-Verb Agreement

Hebrew verbs normally match the full agreement features of their subjects, even when the subject is a compound phrase.

וַיִּקְבְּרוּ אֹתוֹ יִצְחָק וְיִשְׁמָעֵאל בָּנָיו אֶל־מְעָרַת הַמַּכְפֵּלָה

And Isaac and Ishmael, his sons, buried him at the cave of Machpelah. (בראשית כה:ט)

In such cases, the two singular nouns are combined and their agreement features are resolved as plural, thus triggering plural features in the verb.

However, there are many cases—particularly with the Past Narrative—where the verb and compound subject do not match number features.

וַיִּקַּח שֵׁם וָיֶפֶת אֶת־הַשִּׂמְלָה וַיָּשִׂימוּ עַל־שְׁכֶם שְׁנֵיהֶם

And Shem and Japheth took the garment and placed (it) upon the shoulder[s] of both of them. (בראשית ט:כג)

In this example (which illustrates a common type), the initial singular verb is followed in the next clause by a plural verb. What this seems to represent is a narrative strategy by which the first of the two subject NPs is identified by the agreement features of the verb as the more active or responsible of the two.

Identify and explain the clause in the passage that exhibits a lack of full agreement between the verb and the subject.

Word Order Notes: Null Copula Clauses

In chapter 4 we outlined the basic elements of word order variation in Hebrew. The normal order of constituents in a null copula clause is subject–null copula–complement. This parallels the order in verbal clauses: subject-verb-complement.

Concerning null copula clauses, we noted that the movement of constituents is not effected by syntactic or semantic triggers, but only by pragmatic operators like topic and focus.

Identify every null copula clause in the passage, and explain the word order.

Reading Insights

Ellipsis in Narrative

Ellipsis is the omission of a constituent in one clause whose identity is provided by its overt counterpart in a coordinate phrase or clause (chap. 7). One type of ellipsis is verb-gapping, in which the finite verb (but no argument or negative) is the elided constituent (e.g., *Rachel plays tennis, Kathy [plays] soccer*).

Another common type is VP ellipsis, in which the verb and its complement or an adjunct are elided (e.g., *Benjamin doesn't drive slowly, Colin doesn't [drive slowly] either*). VP ellipsis is less common than gapping (whether of a verb or a nonverbal constituent); below is an example from Isaiah:

צֶדֶק יָלִין בָּהּ וְעַתָּה מְרַצְּחִים
Righteousness lodged in her, but now murderers (lodge in her). (ישעיהו א:כא)

Understanding how different types of ellipsis constructions work helps us to analyze the statement made by the king of Aram to his soldiers:

לֹא תִּלָּחֲמוּ אֶת־קָטֹן וְאֶת־גָּדוֹל כִּי אִם־אֶת־מֶלֶךְ יִשְׂרָאֵל לְבַדּוֹ
(מלכים א כב:לא)

Explain the ellipsis in the king of Aram's instruction.

Review

Find and parse all the III-ה verbs in the passage (see appendix B.5).

מלכים א
כב, לד-מ
לדוְאִישׁ מָשַׁךְ בַּקֶּשֶׁת לְתֻמּוֹ
וַיַּכֶּה אֶת־מֶלֶךְ יִשְׂרָאֵל
בֵּין הַדְּבָקִים וּבֵין הַשִּׁרְיָן
וַיֹּאמֶר לְרַכָּבוֹ
הֲפֹךְ יָדְךָ וְהוֹצִיאֵנִי
מִן־הַמַּחֲנֶה כִּי
הָחֳלֵיתִי׃
להוַתַּעֲלֶה הַמִּלְחָמָה בַּיּוֹם הַהוּא וְהַמֶּלֶךְ
הָיָה מָעֳמָד בַּמֶּרְכָּבָה נֹכַח אֲרָם וַיָּמָת
בָּעֶרֶב וַיִּצֶק דַּם־הַמַּכָּה אֶל־חֵיק הָרָכֶב׃
לווַיַּעֲבֹר הָרִנָּה בַּמַּחֲנֶה כְּבֹא הַשֶּׁמֶשׁ לֵאמֹר
אִישׁ אֶל־עִירוֹ
וְאִישׁ אֶל־אַרְצוֹ׃
לזוַיָּמָת הַמֶּלֶךְ וַיָּבוֹא שֹׁמְרוֹן
וַיִּקְבְּרוּ אֶת־הַמֶּלֶךְ בְּשֹׁמְרוֹן׃
לחוַיִּשְׁטֹף אֶת־הָרֶכֶב עַל ׀ בְּרֵכַת שֹׁמְרוֹן
וַיָּלֹקּוּ הַכְּלָבִים אֶת־דָּמוֹ וְהַזֹּנוֹת רָחָצוּ
כִּדְבַר יְהוָה אֲשֶׁר דִּבֵּר׃
לטוְיֶתֶר דִּבְרֵי אַחְאָב וְכָל־אֲשֶׁר עָשָׂה וּבֵית
הַשֵּׁן אֲשֶׁר בָּנָה וְכָל־הֶעָרִים אֲשֶׁר בָּנָה
הֲלוֹא־הֵם כְּתוּבִים עַל־סֵפֶר דִּבְרֵי הַיָּמִים
לְמַלְכֵי יִשְׂרָאֵל׃ מוַיִּשְׁכַּב אַחְאָב עִם־
אֲבֹתָיו וַיִּמְלֹךְ אֲחַזְיָהוּ בְנוֹ תַּחְתָּיו׃ פ

Reading 19

מלכים א כב:לד–מ

Words to Learn

בְּרֵכָה NOUN F ______________

דֶּ֫בֶק NOUN M ______________

(__ __ __) הָחֳלָה VB HO ______________

הָפַךְ VB Q ______________

זָנָה VB Q ______________

יֶ֫תֶר NOUN M ______________

מַכָּה NOUN F ______________

מֶרְכָּבָה NOUN F ______________

מָשַׁךְ VB Q ______________

נֹ֫כַח PREP ______________

קָבַר VB Q ______________

קֶ֫שֶׁת NOUN F ______________

רַכָּב NOUN M ______________

רִנָּה NOUN F ______________

שָׁטַף VB Q ______________

שֶׁ֫מֶשׁ NOUN M/F ______________

שֵׁן NOUN F ______________

שִׁרְיוֹן NOUN M ______________

תֹּם NOUN M ______________

Going Deeper with Grammar

Organizing Narrative Time

The default temporal interpretation in narrative is iconic of the events. That is, the events are described in the order in which they occur. Departures from that default order are expressed in many languages by departures from the typical narrative verb. For example, the switch from English Simple Past to Past Perfect in the following example conveys that the forgetting preceded the walking to school: *Joe woke up, ate breakfast, and walked to school; he had forgotten to pack a lunch*. In Biblical

Hebrew the switch from Past Narrative to the Perfect form has a similar effect, as illustrated by the following example.

וַיָּשָׁב יִצְחָק וַיַּחְפֹּר אֶת־בְּאֵרֹת הַמַּיִם אֲשֶׁר חָפְרוּ בִּימֵי אַבְרָהָם אָבִיו

Isaac dug again the wells of water that they had dug in the days of Abraham his father. (בראשית כו:יח)

In more complex narrative structures, resumptive repetition may serve to reorient the reader to the main story line, much as one might backtrack an event or two in a story after being interrupted: *Now as I was saying, I came to work early today.* Recognizing the nontemporally successive material between repeated events is key to recognizing that the events are not temporally successive but that the second is a resumption of the first.

In the following account of Jonathan's attack of the Philistine garrison, the whereabouts of his father and his military force and the topography of the area Jonathan and his armor bearer cross over interrupt the beginning of the story line—Jonathan's proposal of action—which is resumed through the repetition of the proposal again. This repetition cannot be interpreted as Jonathan repeating his proposal, but rather it picks up the story by repeating it after the background information has been given.

וַיְהִי הַיּוֹם וַיֹּאמֶר יוֹנָתָן בֶּן־שָׁאוּל אֶל־הַנַּעַר נֹשֵׂא כֵלָיו לְכָה וְנַעְבְּרָה אֶל־מַצַּב פְּלִשְׁתִּים אֲשֶׁר מֵעֵבֶר הַלָּז . . . וְשָׁאוּל יוֹשֵׁב בִּקְצֵה הַגִּבְעָה תַּחַת הָרִמּוֹן אֲשֶׁר בְּמִגְרוֹן . . . וּבֵין הַמַּעְבְּרוֹת אֲשֶׁר בִּקֵּשׁ יוֹנָתָן לַעֲבֹר עַל־מַצַּב פְּלִשְׁתִּים שֵׁן־הַסֶּלַע מֵהָעֵבֶר מִזֶּה וְשֵׁן־הַסֶּלַע מֵהָעֵבֶר מִזֶּה . . . וַיֹּאמֶר יְהוֹנָתָן אֶל־הַנַּעַר נֹשֵׂא כֵלָיו לְכָה וְנַעְבְּרָה אֶל־מַצַּב הָעֲרֵלִים הָאֵלֶּה

One day Jonathan son of Saul said to the young man who carried his armor, "Come, let's cross over to the garrison of Philistines who are across there." . . . Now Saul was sitting at the outskirts of Gibeah under the pomegranate tree that is at Migron. . . . Within the pass that Jonathan sought to cross to the garrison of Philistines was a crag of rock on this side and a crag of rock on the other side. And Jonathan said to the young man who carried his armor, "Come, let's cross over to the garrison of these uncircumcised." (שמואל א יד:א–ו)

Find the resumptive repetition in the passage, and explain how it structures the narrative time.

The Quantifier כֹּל

As with numerals that precede a count noun (i.e., any noun that can be modified by a number or by adjectives such as "each," "every," and "several" and has both singular and plural forms), Hebrew כֹּל precedes and is bound to the noun that is quantified, suggesting that כֹּל is actually the head of the phrase, not the quantified noun.

וַיִּהְיוּ כָּל־יְמֵי אֱנוֹשׁ חָמֵשׁ שָׁנִים וּתְשַׁע מֵאוֹת שָׁנָה

And all of the days of Enosh were five and nine-hundred years. (בראשית ה:יא)

That כֹּל is not simply a determiner or modifier is supported by two further types of use:

אֶת־הַכֹּל נָתַן יְהוָה אֱלֹהֵינוּ לְפָנֵינוּ
the-all YHWH, our God, has set before us (דברים ב:לו)

יוֹדוּךָ עַמִּים כֻּלָּם
Let the peoples, all of them, praise you. (תהלים סז:ד)

In the first example, כֹּל appears as a free-standing constituent and even has the article ה, which indicates that כֹּל cannot itself be a determiner (two determiners may not coexist). In the second example, כֹּל has a clitic pronoun that matches the noun it follows, indicating two features: again, כֹּל itself is not a determiner, and the quantification phrase as a whole is in apposition to a NP, suggesting that כֹּל is a quantifying NP.

Identify and explain the uses of כֹּל in the passage.

Challenge

Seeing Double?

Hebrew grammars often assert that Hebrew overwhelmingly repeats the preposition on each item of a compound phrase, as in

הִנֵּה יַד־יְהוָה הוֹיָה בְּמִקְנְךָ אֲשֶׁר בַּשָּׂדֶה בַּסּוּסִים בַּחֲמֹרִים בַּגְּמַלִּים בַּבָּקָר וּבַצֹּאן
Hey! The hand of YHWH is against your livestock that is in the field, against the horses, against the asses, against the camels, against the cattle, and against the sheep. (שמות ט:ג)

But this is inaccurate. Very many of these supposed repetitions of the prepositions are actually cases of PP apposition. In the above example, בְּמִקְנְךָ is the anchor and all the other ב PPs are specifying what is covered by מִקְנֶה. Certainly there are legitimate cases of preposition repetition, especially with בֵּין:

הַמָּקוֹם אֲשֶׁר־הָיָה שָׁם אָהֳלֹה בַּתְּחִלָּה בֵּין בֵּית־אֵל וּבֵין הָעָי
the place that his tent had been there at the first, between Bethel and between Ai (בראשית יג:ג)

These uses are fairly straightforward in that there is a clear reference to a space or time that exists between two points. Most prepositions do not function this way.

The real patterns of repetition or nonrepetition with prepositions are fascinating. For instance, in the clause below, there is only one preposition used for the recipient of YHWH's speech. This indicates that Moses and Aaron are understood as a single, compound unit.

וַיֹּאמֶר יְהוָה אֶל־מֹשֶׁה וְאַהֲרֹן
and YHWH said <u>to</u> Moses and Aaron (שמות יב:מג)

So why is the preposition used twice below while there are five elements in the compound complement NP?

עָשׂוּ מִלְחָמָה אֶת־בֶּרַע מֶלֶךְ סְדֹם וְאֶת־בִּרְשַׁע מֶלֶךְ עֲמֹרָה שִׁנְאָב מֶלֶךְ אַדְמָה וְשֶׁמְאֵבֶר מֶלֶךְ צְבֹיִים וּמֶלֶךְ בֶּלַע
They made war <u>with</u> Bera, king of Sodom, and <u>with</u> Birsha, king of Gomorrah, Shinab, king of Admah, Shemeber, king of Zeboim, and the king of Bela. (בראשית יד:ב)

The likeliest answer is that the preposition is used above to distinguish groups within the compound. That is, the war was fought against two groups, one consisting only of Bera, king of Sodom, and the other consisting of a group of kings.

Identify and explain any repetition of prepositions in the passage.

Valency of Reflexive and Reciprocal Verbs

Narrative economy motivates (among other things) null complements (chap. 3) and implicit complements (chap. 10). The primary difference between these two is whether there is an antecedent in the text: null complements are equivalent to pronouns, which must refer back to something in the context; implicit complements tend to be nonspecific and therefore not identifiable with anything in the text.

הִנֵּה הַנִּשְׁאָר שִׂים־לְפָנֶיךָ אֱכֹל
Hey, set the leftover before you; eat (it). (שמואל א ט:כד)

אֱכֹל וּשְׁתֵה יֹאמַר לָךְ
"Eat (something) and drink (something)," they say to you. (משלי כג:ז)

Verbs classified as reflexive or reciprocal present a different sort of case in that the argument structure can be quite different depending on whether the complement is overt or not. Consider the following contrasting examples.

רַחֲצוּ הִזַּכּוּ
Wash (yourselves), clean (yourselves). (ישעיהו א:טז)

וְרַחֲצוּ רַגְלֵיכֶם
Wash your feet. (בראשית יח:ד)

צֶדֶק וְשָׁלוֹם נָשָׁקוּ
Righteousness and peace have kissed (each other). (תהלים פה:יא)

עֲגָלִים יִשָּׁקוּן
They will kiss calves. (הושע יג:ב)

Find all the null and implicit complements in the passage. Which ones are reflexive or reciprocal?

Reading Insights

Where to Break the Clause?

Because the ו is not always a hard-and-fast sign for determining the edge of a clause (chap. 18), it is not always clear how to interpret a sequence of constituents. For example, in מלכים א כב:לד, some translations take לְתֻמּוֹ with the second clause (e.g,. "and unknowingly struck the king of Israel," NRSV), while others take it with the first clause (e.g., "someone drew his bow at random," NIV).

וְאִישׁ מָשַׁךְ בַּקֶּשֶׁת לְתֻמּוֹ וַיַּכֶּה אֶת־מֶלֶךְ יִשְׂרָאֵל

Given that Hebrew does allow (contrary to what most grammars will tell you) a constituent to be fronted before a *wayyiqtol*, both translations given above are fine grammatical options. Two features suggest (but do not determine) placing the לְתֻמּוֹ with the first clause. First, the Masoretes read it that way. The word has a זָקֵף קָטֹן accent, indicating that they read it as the last word of the first clause. Second, תֹּם means "completeness" or "perfection" and more likely refers to the way the bow was drawn rather than any sort of intention on the part of the soldier. Hebrew narrative rarely gives access to characters' inner states, especially of one-dimensional stock characters.

Taken this way, it seems better to take לְתֻמּוֹ as a comment about either the soldier giving his "complete" strength to drawing the bow, or a comment about the bow itself being completely bent. This latter option requires taking קֶשֶׁת as masculine, which occurs in only one other text: שמואל ב א:כב.

Review

Find and parse the doubly weak verbs in the passage (see appendix B.8).

Aleppo Codex

To review the passages of chapters 18–19, turn to the tenth page of the Aleppo Codex, and read from the third word of the fifteenth line in the third column (i.e., וַיַּעַל) through the first line of the second column on the eleventh page (i.e., through the word תַּחְתָּיו).

מלכים ב
א, ב-ח
בוַיִּפֹּל אֲחַזְיָה בְּעַד הַשְּׂבָכָה בַּעֲלִיָּתוֹ אֲשֶׁר
בְּשֹׁמְרוֹן וַיָּחַל וַיִּשְׁלַח מַלְאָכִים וַיֹּאמֶר אֲלֵהֶם
לְכוּ דִרְשׁוּ בְּבַעַל זְבוּב אֱלֹהֵי
עֶקְרוֹן אִם־אֶחְיֶה מֵחֳלִי זֶה: ס
גוּמַלְאַךְ יְהוָה דִּבֶּר
אֶל־אֵלִיָּה הַתִּשְׁבִּי
קוּם עֲלֵה לִקְרַאת מַלְאֲכֵי מֶלֶךְ־
שֹׁמְרוֹן וְדַבֵּר אֲלֵהֶם הַמִבְּלִי אֵין־
אֱלֹהִים בְּיִשְׂרָאֵל אַתֶּם הֹלְכִים
לִדְרֹשׁ בְּבַעַל זְבוּב אֱלֹהֵי עֶקְרוֹן: דוְלָכֵן
כֹּה־אָמַר יְהוָה הַמִּטָּה אֲשֶׁר־עָלִיתָ
שָּׁם לֹא־תֵרֵד מִמֶּנָּה כִּי מוֹת תָּמוּת
וַיֵּלֶךְ אֵלִיָּה:
הוַיָּשׁוּבוּ הַמַּלְאָכִים אֵלָיו וַיֹּאמֶר אֲלֵיהֶם
מַה־זֶּה שַׁבְתֶּם:
ווַיֹּאמְרוּ אֵלָיו
אִישׁ ׀ עָלָה לִקְרָאתֵנוּ וַיֹּאמֶר אֵלֵינוּ לְכוּ
שׁוּבוּ אֶל־הַמֶּלֶךְ אֲשֶׁר־שָׁלַח אֶתְכֶם
וְדִבַּרְתֶּם אֵלָיו כֹּה אָמַר יְהוָה הֲמִבְּלִי אֵין־
אֱלֹהִים בְּיִשְׂרָאֵל אַתָּה שֹׁלֵחַ לִדְרֹשׁ בְּבַעַל
זְבוּב אֱלֹהֵי עֶקְרוֹן לָכֵן הַמִּטָּה אֲשֶׁר־
עָלִיתָ שָּׁם לֹא־תֵרֵד מִמֶּנָּה כִּי־מוֹת תָּמוּת:
זוַיְדַבֵּר אֲלֵהֶם
מֶה מִשְׁפַּט הָאִישׁ אֲשֶׁר עָלָה לִקְרַאתְכֶם
וַיְדַבֵּר אֲלֵיכֶם אֶת־הַדְּבָרִים הָאֵלֶּה:
חוַיֹּאמְרוּ אֵלָיו
אִישׁ
בַּעַל שֵׂעָר וְאֵזוֹר
עוֹר אָזוּר בְּמָתְנָיו
וַיֹּאמַר
אֵלִיָּה הַתִּשְׁבִּי הוּא:

Reading 20

מלכים ב א:ב–ח

Words to Learn

אֵזוֹר NOUN M ____________

בְּלִי NOUN M ____________;
CONJ (WITH מִן) ____________

בַּ֫עַד PREP ____________

בַּ֫עַל NOUN M ____________;
PN ____________

דָּרַשׁ VB Q ____________

עוֹר NOUN M ____________

שְׂבָכָה NOUN F ____________

שֵׂעָר NOUN M ____________

Going Deeper with Grammar

What's the כִּי *(Redux)?*

Though the various uses of כִּי may not be distilled down to a core function (chap. 6), they do fall into two distinct categories: (1) כִּי that introduces subordinate clauses (causal, temporal, conditional, complement, etc.) and (2) כִּי that is a positive exclamative, "indeed!" or "certainly!"

The former use of כִּי serves a clear syntactic role—it categorizes the clause that follows the כִּי as a non-main clause that depends on (or is within the phrasal structure of) the verb of a hierarchically higher clause. This is, in a nutshell, the description of subordination. The latter use of כִּי does not affect a clause's categorization but reflects the speaker's interest in affirming the veracity or applicability of the following proposition.

There are, unfortunately, many occasions when deciding between כִּי's two categories of usage is difficult. The clause כִּי מוֹת תָּמוּת in מלכים ב א:ד is a good case in point.

Is the כִּי in this verse a subordinator or a positive exclamative? Explain your interpretation.

Parataxis and Hypotaxis

Parataxis (Gk. παράταξις, placing side by side) and *hypotaxis* (Gk. ὑπόταξις, subjection, submission; lit., under + arrangement) refer to whether or not a constituent's syntactic role is overtly marked by, for example, a morphological or lexical marker. Hebrew is a heavily hypotactic language, though the precise semantics of many constituent relationships is left ambiguous due to the extreme use of ו to conjoin constituents.

Hypotactic coordination exhibits an overt coordinator, such as ו between two NP conjuncts or between a string of narrative clauses (on the ו, see chap. 18).

אֶת הַשָּׁמַיִם וְאֵת הָאָרֶץ
the heavens and the earth (בראשית א:א)

וַיֹּאמֶר אֱלֹהִים יְהִי אוֹר וַיְהִי־אוֹר׃ וַיַּרְא אֱלֹהִים אֶת־הָאוֹר כִּי־טוֹב
And God said, "Let light exist." And light existed. And God saw the light, that it was good. (בראשית א:ג–ד)

Paratactic coordination lacks an overt coordinator even though the larger syntactic context suggests that the two constituents are in a coordinate relationship.

בִּימֵי עֻזִּיָּה יוֹתָם אָחָז יְחִזְקִיָּה מַלְכֵי יְהוּדָה
in the days of Uzziah, Jotham, Ahaz, Hezekiah, kings of Judah (הושע א:א)

The same is true for subordination: paratactic subordination lacks an overt subordinator, while hypotactic subordination exhibits one.

Parataxis

וַיֹּאמֶר אֱלֹהִים יְהִי אוֹר
And God said, "Let light exist!" (בראשית א:ג)

אֶת־הַדֶּרֶךְ יֵלְכוּ בָהּ
the way (that) they should walk in it (שמות יח:כ)

Hypotaxis

וַתֹּאמֶר לָהֶם לֵאמֹר רְאוּ
And she said to them, [quote marker] "See!" (בראשית לט:יד)

אֶת־הַדֶּרֶךְ אֲשֶׁר תֵּלְכוּ־בָהּ
the way that you should walk in it (יהושע ג:ד)

In the passage, find and describe one example each of the following: hypotactic coordination, hypotactic subordination, paratactic coordination, and paratactic subordination.

Challenge

Hebrew Doesn't Have No Problem with Double Negatives

In English, the use of two negatives in the same clause, such as *I have never owed nothing to no one*, is generally considered ungrammatical or at least grammatically marginal. The rule in formal English is that two negatives create a positive, as in *It has not gone unnoticed*, with the logical equivalence of *it has been noticed*. Thus the combination of negatives without intending a positive can be confusing.

Hebrew, in contrast, apparently permits the use of two negatives in order to reinforce the negation in the statement. This occurs particularly with בְּלִי:

הַמִבְּלִי אֵין־קְבָרִים בְּמִצְרַיִם
Is it because graves do *not* exist in Egypt? (שמות יד:יא)

The use of the double negative in such questions may be a strategy to highlight their rhetorical nature.

Find and explain the double negative in the passage.

Story Lines within Story Lines

You are already familiar with the fact that the Past Narrative expresses foregrounded story line events in narrative (chap. 5; *BBH* §43). These are events that carry the story line forward and are typically but not always in natural sequence; that is, the events are told in the order in which they occur in the narrative world. By contrast, backgrounded events are those that serve to set scenes, report events out of narrative sequence, or appear in subordinate clauses (see chap. 16).

Despite this neat division, narrative allows for multiple layers of story line, so that subsidiary foregrounded narrative sequences may appear *within* scene-setting passages or subordinate expressions. Consider the example below: the narrative reports Joash's death and then indicates the out-of-sequence event of Elisha's earlier illness by avoiding the Past Narrative and instead employing the Perfect verb; the subsidiary story line of Joash coming to Elisha during his illness continues with the Past Narrative, and goes on for some verses, after being "set back" in time by the initial Perfect verb.

וַיִּקָּבֵר יוֹאָשׁ בְּשֹׁמְרוֹן עִם מַלְכֵי יִשְׂרָאֵל׃ וֶאֱלִישָׁע חָלָה אֶת־חָלְיוֹ אֲשֶׁר
יָמוּת בּוֹ וַיֵּרֶד אֵלָיו יוֹאָשׁ מֶלֶךְ־יִשְׂרָאֵל וַיֵּבְךְּ עַל־פָּנָיו

Joash was buried in Samaria with the kings of Israel. Now Elisha had become ill with his illness of which he would die, and Joash the king of Israel went down to him and wept upon his face. (מלכים ב יג:יג–יד)

Find the subsidiary story line in the passage.

Reading Insights

Seeking Contexts

Context is an important indicator of the particular meaning of a lexical item. While it would be an overstatement to say that meaning is entirely contextual, language economizes by relying on context to distinguish sometimes very different meanings for a lexical item. For example, the English word *cleave* can mean to split something (e.g., *He cleaved wood for the fire*) or to stick to someone or something (e.g., *Her tongue cleaved to the roof of her mouth*).

Rather than appealing to "context" generally, it is preferable to identify *what* specifically about the context indicates the most felicitous meaning for a term. In the case of the verb דָּרַשׁ, the syntax and semantics of the immediate context serve to distinguish a fairly wide range of meanings. Consider the following examples.

- Monovalent of carrying out a legal investigation

  וְדָרַשְׁתָּ הֵיטֵב
  You should investigate carefully. (דברים יז:ד)

- Bivalent with NP of what or who is sought for vengeance or care

  וְאַךְ אֶת־דִּמְכֶם לְנַפְשֹׁתֵיכֶם אֶדְרֹשׁ
  Only your blood for your lives I will seek vengeance. (בראשית ט:ה)

  הִנְנִי־אָנִי וְדָרַשְׁתִּי אֶת־צֹאנִי
  Hey, I myself will look after my sheep. (יחזקאל לד:יא)

- Bivalent with deity or intermediary sought after for worship or an oracle

  וַתֵּלֶךְ לִדְרֹשׁ אֶת־יְהוָה
  And she went to inquire of YHWH. (בראשית כה:כב)

Seeking after a deity is a common use of the verb דָּרַשׁ, though the complement sought is syntactically expressed in various ways. It can appear as a NP (above), or a ל preposition, or a ב preposition. Interestingly, the ב preposition construction appears only twice with reference to YHWH (דברי הימים א י:יד and דברי הימים ב לד:כו,

below). The other instances appear to denote illicit seeking of oracles or guidance from spirit mediums.

וּפֶן־תִּדְרֹשׁ לֵאלֹהֵיהֶם
and lest you inquire after/worship their gods (דברים יב:ל)

הַשֹּׁלֵחַ אֶתְכֶם לִדְרוֹשׁ בַּיהוָה
who sent you to inquire of YHWH (דברי הימים ב לד:כו)

> Explain the particular meaning of דָּרַשׁ in the passage based on the syntactic and semantic context.

מַה זֶה

The interrogative phrases מַה זֶה and לָמָּה זֶה can be followed by a verbal clause whose syntactic relationship to the interrogative is not transparently easy to determine.

לָמָּה זֶּה תִּשְׁאַל לִשְׁמִי
Why is this, you ask my name? (בראשית לב:ל)

The insertion of "that" in many English translations (e.g., "Why is this *that* you ask my name") is not wrong, but it can be misunderstood. English "that" in such cases may be mistaken as a type of relative clause. Though there is some overlap between what we see here and relative clauses, it is not quite accurate to call these relatives, since זֶה rarely hosts its own relative and, unlike relative clauses, in these examples the זֶה has no role within the following clause (see chap. 2). In these cases, "that" nominalizes the following clause so that it may act syntactically like a NP. Newly categorized, the clause may stand in apposition (chap. 6) to the demonstrative.

> Find and explain the appositive מַה זֶה example in the text.

Review

> Find the case of dislocation in the passage.
>
> Parse דִּרְשׁוּ. Review the characteristics of II-guttural verbs.
>
> Find and parse every II-ו/י and III-ה verb in the passage.

ט וַיִּשְׁלַח אֵלָיו שַׂר־חֲמִשִּׁים וַחֲמִשָּׁיו וַיַּעַל אֵלָיו
וְהִנֵּה יֹשֵׁב עַל־רֹאשׁ הָהָר וַיְדַבֵּר אֵלָיו
אִישׁ הָאֱלֹהִים הַמֶּלֶךְ דִּבֶּר רֵדָה׃
י וַיַּעֲנֶה אֵלִיָּהוּ וַיְדַבֵּר אֶל־שַׂר הַחֲמִשִּׁים
וְאִם־אִישׁ אֱלֹהִים אָנִי תֵּרֶד אֵשׁ מִן־הַשָּׁמַיִם וְתֹאכַל אֹתְךָ וְאֶת־חֲמִשֶּׁיךָ
וַתֵּרֶד אֵשׁ מִן־הַשָּׁמַיִם וַתֹּאכַל אֹתוֹ וְאֶת־חֲמִשָּׁיו׃
מלכים ב
א, ט-י

מלכים ב
א, יא-יב
יא וַיָּשָׁב וַיִּשְׁלַח אֵלָיו שַׂר־חֲמִשִּׁים אַחֵר וַחֲמִשָּׁיו וַיַּעַן וַיְדַבֵּר אֵלָיו
אִישׁ הָאֱלֹהִים כֹּה־אָמַר הַמֶּלֶךְ מְהֵרָה רֵדָה׃
יב וַיַּעַן אֵלִיָּה וַיְדַבֵּר אֲלֵיהֶם
אִם־אִישׁ הָאֱלֹהִים אָנִי תֵּרֶד אֵשׁ מִן־הַשָּׁמַיִם וְתֹאכַל אֹתְךָ וְאֶת־חֲמִשֶּׁיךָ
וַתֵּרֶד אֵשׁ־אֱלֹהִים מִן־הַשָּׁמַיִם וַתֹּאכַל אֹתוֹ וְאֶת־חֲמִשָּׁיו׃

Reading 21

מלכים ב א:ט–יב

Words to Learn

אַחֵר ADJ ______________

מְהֵרָה NOUN F ______________;
ADV ______________

רֹאשׁ NOUN M ______________

Going Deeper with Grammar

Verbal Hendiadys

In chapter 12 we discussed how Hebrew can combine the verbs שׁוב or יסף with another verb to express the idea of doing something "again." This strategy is part of a larger phenomenon of verbal hendiadys, whereby two verbs are coordinated to express a single event, usually with one verb adverbially modifying the event expressed by the other.

וַתְּמַהֵר וַתֵּרֶד מֵעַל הַחֲמוֹר

She <u>hurried</u> and she <u>got down</u> from upon the donkey.
or She <u>quickly got down</u> from the donkey. (שמואל א כה:כג)

One place where verbal hendiadys often occurs is in the narrative framing of speech using multiple verbs.

וַיְדַבֵּר אֱלֹהִים אֶל־מֹשֶׁה וַיֹּאמֶר אֵלָיו אֲנִי יְהוָה

God <u>spoke</u> to Moses <u>and said</u> to him, "I am YHWH."
or <u>Speaking</u> to Moses, God <u>said</u> to him, "I am YHWH." (שמות ו:ב)

וַיִּשָּׂא קוֹלוֹ וַיִּקְרָא

He <u>lifted up</u> his voice <u>and he called</u>.
or <u>Lifting up</u> his voice, <u>he called</u>. (שפטים ט:ז)

וַיֶּעְתַּר מָנוֹחַ אֶל־יְהוָה וַיֹּאמַר

Manoah <u>entreated</u> YHWH <u>and said</u>
or <u>Entreating</u> YHWH, Manoah <u>said</u> (שפטים יג:ח)

Identify a case of verbal hendiadys in the passage.

Challenge

Where's the Subject?

Null subjects (chaps. 1, 4, and 14) are quite common with finite verbs, whose inflectional features provide information about the null subject's person-gender-number.

וַיֵּדְעוּ כִּי עֵירֻמִּם הֵם
ø (They) knew that they were naked. (בראשית ג:ז)

And null subjects are common in null copula and participial clauses, particularly in contexts such as complement and relative clauses, and in infinitival phrases:

וַיַּרְא אֱלֹהִים אֶת־הָאוֹר כִּי־טוֹב
And God saw the light, that ø (it) (was) good. (בראשית א:ד)

כֵּאלֹהִים יֹדְעֵי טוֹב וָרָע
like gods (who) ø (they) know good and bad (בראשית ג:ה)

וַיִּתֵּן אֹתָם אֱלֹהִים בִּרְקִיעַ הַשָּׁמָיִם לְהָאִיר עַל־הָאָרֶץ
And God put them in the firmament of the heavens to ø (they) make light over the earth. (בראשית א:יז)

In the third example, the null subject for the infinitive is difficult to gloss; the next example provides an infinitive with an overt subject for comparison.

מִקֵּץ עֶשֶׂר שָׁנִים לְשֶׁבֶת אַבְרָם בְּאֶרֶץ כְּנָעַן
at the end of ten years of Abram's dwelling in the land of Canaan (בראשית טז:ג)

In nonsubordinate contexts, it is much rarer to find a null subject clause when the predication is a null copula.

טוֹב
ø (It) ø (is) good. (רות ג:יג)

The obvious reason that such examples are rare is that they are more difficult to process mentally.

Find and explain an example of a null subject, null copula clause in the passage.

Reading Insights

What the ה?

Occasionally a Hebrew MS imperative will include an extra ָה־ suffix that is not part of the inflectional paradigm.

תְּנָה־לִּי אֶת־כַּרְמְךָ
Give me your vineyard. (מלכים א כא:ב)

This "paragogic" ה is added to the imperative when the action is directed toward the speaker or is for the benefit of the speaker. Thus in the example above, Ahab's command to Naboth is for Ahab's benefit.

Identify and explain the two cases of the extra ה in the passage.

Review

Identify every I-י/ו verb in the passage. Review the paradigm for those verbs.

Identify every III-ה verb in the passage. Review the paradigm for those verbs, and then explain the form of the verbs in the passage—that is, whether the ה appears and why it does or does not. (Notice the unshortened form of וַיַּעֲנֶה, a phenomenon that mostly occurs in מלכים א–ב and ירמיהו.)

מלכים ב
א, יג-יח
יג וַיָּשָׁב וַיִּשְׁלַח שַׂר־חֲמִשִּׁים
שְׁלִשִׁים וַחֲמִשָּׁיו
וַיַּעַל וַיָּבֹא שַׂר־הַחֲמִשִּׁים הַשְּׁלִישִׁי
וַיִּכְרַע עַל־בִּרְכָּיו ׀ לְנֶגֶד אֵלִיָּהוּ
וַיִּתְחַנֵּן אֵלָיו וַיְדַבֵּר אֵלָיו
אִישׁ הָאֱלֹהִים תִּיקַר־נָא נַפְשִׁי וְנֶפֶשׁ עֲבָדֶיךָ
אֵלֶּה חֲמִשִּׁים בְּעֵינֶיךָ׃ יד הִנֵּה יָרְדָה אֵשׁ מִן־
הַשָּׁמַיִם וַתֹּאכַל אֶת־שְׁנֵי שָׂרֵי הַחֲמִשִּׁים הָרִאשֹׁנִים
וְאֶת־חֲמִשֵּׁיהֶם וְעַתָּה תִּיקַר נַפְשִׁי בְּעֵינֶיךָ׃ ס
טו וַיְדַבֵּר מַלְאַךְ יְהוָה אֶל־אֵלִיָּהוּ
רֵד אוֹתוֹ אַל־תִּירָא מִפָּנָיו
וַיָּקָם וַיֵּרֶד אוֹתוֹ
אֶל־הַמֶּלֶךְ׃ טז וַיְדַבֵּר
אֵלָיו
כֹּה־אָמַר יְהוָה יַעַן אֲשֶׁר־שָׁלַחְתָּ מַלְאָכִים לִדְרֹשׁ
בְּבַעַל זְבוּב אֱלֹהֵי עֶקְרוֹן הַמִבְּלִי אֵין־אֱלֹהִים
בְּיִשְׂרָאֵל לִדְרֹשׁ בִּדְבָרוֹ לָכֵן הַמִּטָּה אֲשֶׁר־עָלִיתָ
שָּׁם לֹא־תֵרֵד מִמֶּנָּה כִּי־מוֹת תָּמוּת׃
יז וַיָּמָת כִּדְבַר יְהוָה ׀ אֲשֶׁר־דִּבֶּר אֵלִיָּהוּ וַיִּמְלֹךְ
יְהוֹרָם תַּחְתָּיו פ בִּשְׁנַת שְׁתַּיִם לִיהוֹרָם בֶּן־
יְהוֹשָׁפָט מֶלֶךְ יְהוּדָה כִּי לֹא־הָיָה לוֹ בֵּן׃
יח וְיֶתֶר דִּבְרֵי אֲחַזְיָהוּ אֲשֶׁר עָשָׂה הֲלוֹא־
הֵמָּה כְתוּבִים עַל־סֵפֶר דִּבְרֵי הַיָּמִים
לְמַלְכֵי יִשְׂרָאֵל׃ פ

Reading 22

מלכים ב א:יג–יח

Words to Learn

(__ __ __) הִתְחַנֵּן VB HIT ______________

יָקַר VB Q ______________

Going Deeper with Grammar

O Vocative!

Vocatives are referential NPs that address the listener directly. Vocative constituents have a deictic connection to the agreement features of the verb but are not fully integrated into the clause as arguments of the verb.

שֹׁבְנָה בְנֹתַי
Return ø (you), O my daughters. (רות א:יב)

וַתַּעַל מִשַּׁחַת חַיַּי יְהוָה אֱלֹהָי
And ø (you) brought my life up from the pit, O YHWH, my God. (יונה ב:ז)

In each case, the vocative constituent is contained within the domain of the clause but does not function as a subject, complement, or even adjunct. Rather, most vocatives are in apposition to a subject or complement constituent. In the first example, the vocative בְּנֹתַי is in apposition to the null subject pronoun of the imperative; in the second example, the vocative יְהוָה אֱלֹהָי is extraposed though still appositional to the null subject pronoun, which is presumably in its normal position following the *wayyiqtol*.

The other position for vocatives is not in apposition to a subject, whether overt or null, but standing at or near the front of the clause.

וַתֹּאמֶר לָהּ נָעֳמִי חֲמוֹתָהּ בִּתִּי הֲלֹא אֲבַקֶּשׁ־לָךְ מָנוֹחַ אֲשֶׁר יִיטַב־לָךְ
Naomi, her mother-in-law, said to her, "My daughter, should I not seek for you a resting-place where it will be better for you?" (רות ג:א)

Identify and explain the syntax of the vocative in the passage.

Complements and Adjuncts with Direction Verbs

Direction verbs often have implicit or null directional complements (chap. 10). Only a set number of directional complements (usually one) are licensed by direction verbs. In cases where multiple PPs appear, therefore, the directional PP that fits most closely with the direction verb's semantics is the complement, while additional PPs are adjuncts that elaborate on the core directional construction. For example, the verb יָצָא most frequently has a complement expressing the location from which one departs. When it appears with both a directional "from" PP and "to" PP, the former will be a complement and the latter an adjunct phrase.

כֹּל אֲשֶׁר־יֵצֵא מִדַּלְתֵי בֵיתֵךְ הַחוּצָה דָּמוֹ בְרֹאשׁוֹ

Anyone who goes out <u>from</u> the doors of your house <u>into</u> the street, his blood (is) on his head. (יהושע ב:יט)

Find the direction verbs in the passage, and identify their complements and adjuncts.

Challenge

Ambiguous Morphology

In the majority of cases, Hebrew morphology provides enough information about person, gender, and/or number that syntactic relationships are clear, such as whether or not a given adjective modifies a nearby noun or whether or not a given noun is the subject of a nearby verb. However, sometimes the verb does not agree with what appears to be the full subject (see chap. 18). And some verbal forms are homophonous, such as the 3FS and 2MS Imperfect.

Identify the case of morphological ambiguity in the text, and provide a solution. (Hint: it is a precious example.)

Reading Insights

Spelling Variations

The differential object marker (DOM) identifying the NP complement of a verb and the preposition אֵת (with) are spelled identically (אֵת/אֶת־) except when they have attached pronouns: אוֹתִי (me) versus אִתִּי (with me).

Sometimes these spellings with attached pronouns are confused or switched in the text, so that what looks like the DOM is actually the preposition meaning "with." In such cases, the inappropriateness of a complement (e.g., a complement is not licensed by the verb) and the appropriateness of a PP are the only indication of the spelling variation.

אוּלַי יְהוָה אוֹתִי

Perhaps YHWH (is) <u>with me</u>. (יהושע יד:יב)

Identify and distinguish the object marker את and the preposition את in the text.

Review

Find the dislocated structure in the passage, and identify the resumptive element.

Aleppo Codex

To review the passages of chapters 20–22, turn to the eleventh page of the Aleppo Codex, and read from the third word of the twenty-first line in the third column (i.e., וַיִּפֹּל) through the twelfth page.

א וַיְהִי בְּהַעֲלוֹת יְהוָה אֶת־אֵלִיָּהוּ בַּסְעָרָה הַשָּׁמָיִם וַיֵּלֶךְ אֵלִיָּהוּ וֶאֱלִישָׁע מִן־הַגִּלְגָּל׃
ב וַיֹּאמֶר אֵלִיָּהוּ אֶל־אֱלִישָׁע
שֵׁב־נָא פֹה כִּי יְהוָה שְׁלָחַנִי עַד־בֵּית־אֵל
וַיֹּאמֶר אֱלִישָׁע
חַי־יְהוָה וְחֵי־נַפְשְׁךָ אִם־אֶעֶזְבֶךָּ
מלכים ב
ב, א-ה
וַיֵּרְדוּ בֵּית־אֵל׃
ג וַיֵּצְאוּ בְנֵי־הַנְּבִיאִים אֲשֶׁר־בֵּית־אֵל אֶל־אֱלִישָׁע וַיֹּאמְרוּ אֵלָיו
הֲיָדַעְתָּ כִּי הַיּוֹם יְהוָה לֹקֵחַ אֶת־אֲדֹנֶיךָ מֵעַל רֹאשֶׁךָ
וַיֹּאמֶר
גַּם־אֲנִי יָדַעְתִּי הֶחֱשׁוּ׃
ד וַיֹּאמֶר לוֹ אֵלִיָּהוּ
אֱלִישָׁע | שֵׁב־נָא פֹה כִּי יְהוָה שְׁלָחַנִי יְרִיחוֹ
וַיֹּאמֶר
חַי־יְהוָה וְחֵי־נַפְשְׁךָ אִם־אֶעֶזְבֶךָּ
וַיָּבֹאוּ יְרִיחוֹ׃
ה וַיִּגְּשׁוּ בְנֵי־הַנְּבִיאִים אֲשֶׁר־בִּירִיחוֹ אֶל־אֱלִישָׁע וַיֹּאמְרוּ אֵלָיו
הֲיָדַעְתָּ כִּי הַיּוֹם יְהוָה לֹקֵחַ אֶת־אֲדֹנֶיךָ מֵעַל רֹאשֶׁךָ
וַיֹּאמֶר
גַּם־אֲנִי יָדַעְתִּי הֶחֱשׁוּ׃

Reading 23

מלכים ב ב:א–ה

Words to Learn

הֶחֱשָׁה (__ __ __) VB HI ______________

סְעָרָה NOUN F ______________

Going Deeper with Grammar

Prospective Aspect Participle

The participle can predicatively portray events when used as the complement of a copula (*BBH* §42). Typically it describes an event as ongoing or progressive, with the temporal location (i.e., past, present, future) determined by the copula (if overt) or context (chap. 12).

וַיֵּרָא אֵלָיו יְהוָה בְּאֵלֹנֵי מַמְרֵא וְהוּא יֹשֵׁב פֶּתַח־הָאֹהֶל כְּחֹם הַיּוֹם

YHWH appeared to him at the oaks of Mamre, and he (was) sitting at the opening of the tent during the heat of the day. (בראשית יח:א)

We mentioned briefly that prophetic pronouncements may feature the participle with a prospective aspect sense (chap. 17). This function of the participle is not limited to prophetic speech but occurs fairly frequently in all sorts of discourse. The participle in these cases portrays an event that, though in the future, has already begun in some sense; it's a done deal, so to speak. The English progressive is similar: *I am flying to New York* versus *I will fly to New York* sometimes implies that the ticket is already purchased.

Distinguishing between progressive and prospective meanings for the participle, like its temporal location generally, often relies on the context: if the event portrayed by the participle is not yet ongoing, then prospective aspect is the most appropriate sense. At other times, adverbial temporal expressions will point to a prospective interpretation. Both cases are illustrated in the following example.

בְּעוֹד שְׁלֹשֶׁת יָמִים אַתֶּם עֹבְרִים אֶת־הַיַּרְדֵּן הַזֶּה לָבוֹא לָרֶשֶׁת אֶת־הָאָרֶץ
אֲשֶׁר יְהוָה אֱלֹהֵיכֶם נֹתֵן לָכֶם לְרִשְׁתָּהּ

In yet three days you are going to cross this Jordan to enter to take possession of the land that YHWH your God is going to give to you to possess it. (יהושע א:יא)

Find the participles in the passage, and describe how they are functioning (*BBH* §42). If they are predicative, what is the temporal/aspectual meaning?

Challenge

Complement Variation with ידע

The verb יָדַע is bivalent, but the syntax of the complement varies. Very frequently it is a clausal complement introduced by כִּי.

וַיֵּדַע דָּוִד כִּי־הֱכִינוֹ יְהוָה לְמֶלֶךְ עַל־יִשְׂרָאֵל
And David knew <u>that</u> YHWH had established him for a king over Israel. (שמואל ב ה:יב)

At other times, the complement is an attached pronoun or a NP.

וְאַתָּה יָדַעְתָּ אֶת־עַבְדְּךָ אֲדֹנָי יְהוִה
And you know <u>your servant</u>, Lord YHWH. (שמואל ב ז:כ)

These two structures are combined in other instances, with an appositive כִּי clause modifying a NP.

יָדַעְתָּ אֶת־אַבְנֵר בֶּן־נֵר כִּי לְפַתֹּתְךָ בָּא
You know <u>Abner, son of Ner</u>, <u>that</u> he came to deceive you. (שמואל ב ג:כה)

Finally, less often the complement is a null anaphora referring to something in the earlier context, which avoids unnecessary repetition in the narrative or dialogue.

וַיֵּצֵא יוֹאָב מֵעִם דָּוִד וַיִּשְׁלַח מַלְאָכִים אַחֲרֵי אַבְנֵר וַיָּשִׁבוּ אֹתוֹ מִבּוֹר
הַסִּרָה וְדָוִד לֹא יָדָע
And Joab went out from David and sent messengers after Abner, and they brought him back from the Cistern of Sirah, but David did not know <u>ø (it)</u>. (שמואל ב ג:כו)

Find all the occurrences of ידע in the passage, and describe the complement syntax.

Reading Insights

Grammar and Interpersonal Dynamics

Like many languages, Hebrew has a variety of strategies to encode the relative social status of speakers and their addressees. Besides the use of a separate morpheme for politeness (נָא), the choice between imperative, second-person jussive, and even third-person jussive directed at the addressee sends a complicated signal concerning the objective social status of the speaker and addressee (e.g., a king and his subjects) as well as the stance (deferential or not) of the speaker.

Identify and explain the grammatical clues concerning the relationships of the participants in the dialogues in the passage.

Review

Explain the lack of a דָּגֵשׁ after the preposition-article in the word בַּסְּעָרָה (v. א).

Identify and parse every weak verb in the passage.

Find the oath formula in the passage, and describe its syntax and semantics.

Find the lack of subject-verb agreement in the passage, and provide an explanation for it.

מלכים ב
ב, ו-י
וַיֹּאמֶר לוֹ אֵלִיָּהוּ
שֵׁב־נָא פֹה כִּי יְהוָה שְׁלָחַנִי הַיַּרְדֵּנָה
וַיֹּאמֶר
חַי־יְהוָה וְחֵי־נַפְשְׁךָ אִם־אֶעֶזְבֶךָּ
וַיֵּלְכוּ שְׁנֵיהֶם:
ז וַחֲמִשִּׁים אִישׁ מִבְּנֵי הַנְּבִיאִים הָלְכוּ וַיַּעַמְדוּ מִנֶּגֶד מֵרָחוֹק וּשְׁנֵיהֶם עָמְדוּ עַל־הַיַּרְדֵּן:
ח וַיִּקַּח אֵלִיָּהוּ אֶת־אַדַּרְתּוֹ וַיִּגְלֹם וַיַּכֶּה אֶת־הַמַּיִם וַיֵּחָצוּ הֵנָּה וָהֵנָּה
וַיַּעַבְרוּ שְׁנֵיהֶם בֶּחָרָבָה: ט וַיְהִי כְעָבְרָם וְאֵלִיָּהוּ אָמַר אֶל־אֱלִישָׁע
שְׁאַל מָה אֶעֱשֶׂה־לָּךְ בְּטֶרֶם אֶלָּקַח מֵעִמָּךְ
וַיֹּאמֶר אֱלִישָׁע
וִיהִי־נָא פִּי־שְׁנַיִם בְּרוּחֲךָ אֵלָי:
י וַיֹּאמֶר
הִקְשִׁיתָ לִשְׁאוֹל אִם־תִּרְאֶה אֹתִי לֻקָּח מֵאִתָּךְ יְהִי־לְךָ כֵן וְאִם־אַיִן לֹא יִהְיֶה:

מלכים ב
ב, יא-יב
יאוַיְהִ֗י הֵ֚מָּה הֹלְכִ֤ים הָלוֹךְ֙ וְדַבֵּ֔ר וְהִנֵּ֤ה רֶֽכֶב־אֵשׁ֙ וְס֣וּסֵי
אֵ֔שׁ וַיַּפְרִ֖דוּ בֵּ֣ין שְׁנֵיהֶ֑ם וַיַּ֙עַל֙ אֵֽלִיָּ֔הוּ בַּסְּעָרָ֖ה הַשָּׁמָֽיִם׃
יבוֶאֱלִישָׁ֣ע רֹאֶ֗ה וְה֣וּא מְצַעֵק֙
אָבִ֣י ׀ אָבִ֗י רֶ֤כֶב
יִשְׂרָאֵל֙ וּפָ֣רָשָׁ֔יו

יב וְלֹא רָאָהוּ עוֹד
וַֽיַּחֲזֵק בִּבְגָדָיו וַֽיִּקְרָעֵם לִשְׁנַיִם קְרָעִים׃ יג וַיָּרֶם אֶת־אַדֶּרֶת
אֵלִיָּהוּ אֲשֶׁר נָפְלָה מֵעָלָיו
מלכים ב
ב, יב-יד
וַיָּשָׁב וַיַּעֲמֹד עַל־שְׂפַת הַיַּרְדֵּן׃
יד וַיִּקַּח אֶת־אַדֶּרֶת אֵלִיָּהוּ אֲשֶׁר־נָפְלָה מֵעָלָיו וַיַּכֶּה אֶת־הַמַּיִם
וַיֹּאמַר
אַיֵּה יְהוָה אֱלֹהֵי אֵלִיָּהוּ
אַף־הוּא ׀
וַיַּכֶּה אֶת־הַמַּיִם וַיֵּחָצוּ הֵנָּה וָהֵנָּה וַיַּעֲבֹר אֱלִישָׁע׃
BIBLE

Reading 24

מלכים ב ב:ו–יד

Words to Learn

אַיֵּה	INTER ______________
אַף	ADV ______________
גָּלַם	VB Q ______________
הֵ֫נָּה	ADV ______________
הִפְרִיד (___ ___ ___)	VB HI ______________
הִקְשָׁה (___ ___ ___)	VB HI ______________
הֵרִים (___ ___ ___)	VB HI ______________
חָצָה	VB Q ______________
חָרָבָה	NOUN F ______________
טֶ֫רֶם	ADV ______________
פָּרָשׁ	NOUN M ______________
צִעֵק (___ ___ ___)	VB PI ______________
קְרָעִים	NOUN MP ______________
רָחוֹק	ADJ ______________; NOUN M ______________
שָׂפָה	NOUN F ______________

Going Deeper with Grammar

Play It Again or Not

In chapter 12 we discussed the use of the verbs שׁוּב and יָסַף with another verb to express the idea of "again." Usually this verbal hendiadys is recognizable from the close coordination of the two verbs. At other times, these verbs might be coordinate with another but express *not* the idea of again but two separate events. The context will guide you as to which interpretation is best. For example, the narrative account of the attack of Ai tells how Joshua set an ambush for the city while he drew the military out. When Joshua and the men with him see the success of the ambush party, they do not strike the men of Ai *again*, but turn around (from their feigned flight) and strike them.

וִיהוֹשֻׁעַ וְכָל־יִשְׂרָאֵל רָאוּ כִּי־לָכַד הָאֹרֵב אֶת־הָעִיר וְכִי עָלָה עֲשַׁן הָעִיר
וַיָּשֻׁבוּ וַיַּכּוּ אֶת־אַנְשֵׁי הָעָי׃

And Joshua and all Israel saw that the ambush party had captured the city [of Ai] and that the smoke of the city had risen. And they turned around and struck the men of Ai. (יהושע ח:כא)

> Find potential examples of verbal hendiadys expressing "again" in the passage, and explain whether it expresses one "again" event or two separate events.

Reading Insights

A Mouthful of Two?

Elisha's request of Elijah in verse ט (וִיהִי־נָא פִּי־שְׁנַיִם בְּרוּחֲךָ אֵלָי) uses the noun פֶּה in an idiomatic way. The denotation of פֶּה is clear and univocal: it refers to the eating and speaking orifice, the "mouth." Like the English usage (e.g., "mouth of the river"), Hebrew פֶּה is used in numerous figurative ways. Besides the expected "mouth of a cave," it is used to represent the product of the mouth in speaking—that is, an edict or declaration. It is also used to refer to the edge of a sword, perhaps because the edge is what "bites." The connotation of פֶּה in this passage is much less common: it refers to a mouthful and by extension a portion. Thus Elisha's polite (perhaps hesitant) request is that he receive a "portion of two" with regard to (בְּ) Elijah's spirit.

Review

> Find the adverbial infinitives in the passage, and describe how they are functioning.
>
> Explain all the syntactic relationships in the following (v. יא): וַיְהִי הֵמָּה הֹלְכִים הָלוֹךְ וְדַבֵּר וְהִנֵּה רֶכֶב־אֵשׁ וְסוּסֵי אֵשׁ.

Aleppo Codex

To review the passages of chapters 23–24, turn to the thirteenth page of the Aleppo Codex, and read from the beginning through the eighth line in the third column (i.e., through the phrase וַיַּעֲבֹר אֱלִישָׁע).

Appendixes and Glossaries

Appendix A

Aleppo Codex

The Aleppo Codex (ca. 925 CE) is considered by most biblical scholars to be "the oldest and best codex of the entire OT in the masoretic tradition."[1] Moshe Goshen-Gottstein goes so far as to characterize it as "the perfect original masterpiece which authenticates itself by internal criteria."[2] Of all the manuscripts from the Masoretic period (ca. 600–1100 CE), the Aleppo Codex is the only one in which the Masorah accurately corresponds to what is found in the text. In other manuscripts, such as the Leningrad Codex, the Masorah does not correspond exactly to the text, indicating that the two have been copied from different sources.

A product of the medieval Jewish scribal tradition, the Masorah ("tradition") consists of marginal notations intended to ensure the accurate copying of the text. The notes in the side margins of the text constitute the מְסוֹרָה קְטַנָּה ("small Masorah"; also called the Masorah parva), which includes textual notes such as the *Qere* forms of *Qere-Ketiv* variations and the number of occurrences of rare words or spellings. The notes at the top and bottom of the text constitute theמְסוֹרָה גְּדוֹלָה ("large Masorah"; also called the Masorah magna). It typically expands on details offered in the מְסוֹרָה קְטַנָּה, such as listing the verse references where a rare word or spelling occurs. Some ancient manuscripts also include textual notes, often in the form of lists, at the beginning or end of the biblical book.

According to most accounts, the Aleppo Codex was damaged in a fire from an anti-Jewish riot in reaction to the creation of the State of Israel in 1947. However, the accuracy of this account has recently been questioned in light of evidence that the codex was mostly complete when it left Aleppo.[3] Regardless of when and how the damage came about, most of the beginning and ending of the codex is now lost, including the Pentateuch; small portions of 2 Kings, Jeremiah, the Minor Prophets, Chronicles, and Psalms; and most of Song of Songs, Lamentations, Esther, Daniel, Ezra, and Nehemiah.[4]

1. Ellis R. Brotzman and Eric J. Tully, *Old Testament Textual Criticism: A Practical Introduction*, 2nd ed. (Grand Rapids: Baker Academic, 2016), 57.
2. Moshe H. Goshen-Gottstein, "The Aleppo Codex and the Rise of the Masoretic Bible Text," *Biblical Archaeologist* 42, no. 3 (1979): 150.
3. Matti Friedman, *The Aleppo Codex: A True Story of Obsession, Faith, and the Pursuit of an Ancient Bible* (Chapel Hill, NC: Algonquin Books, 2012).
4. Goshen-Gottstein, "Aleppo Codex," 149.

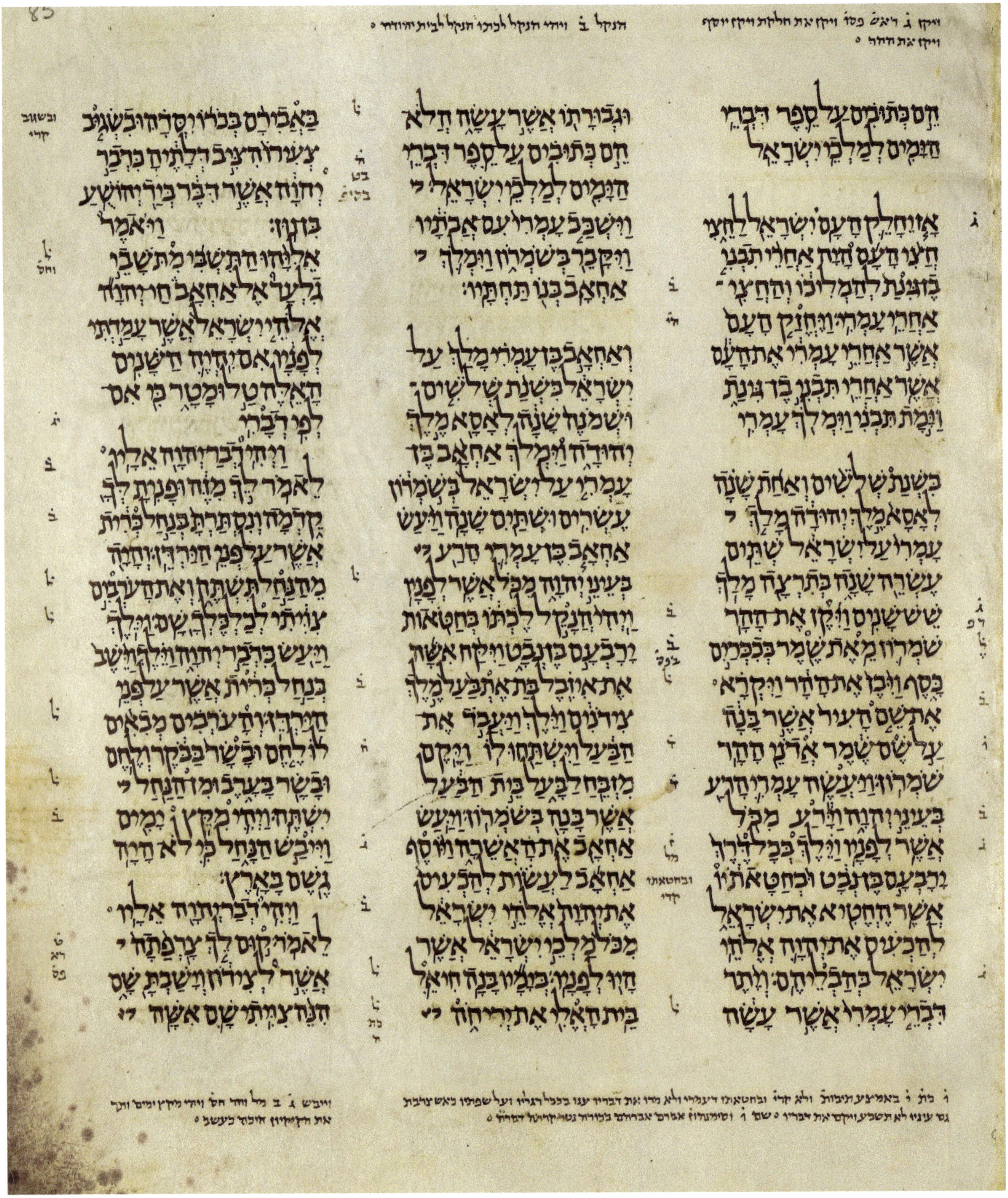

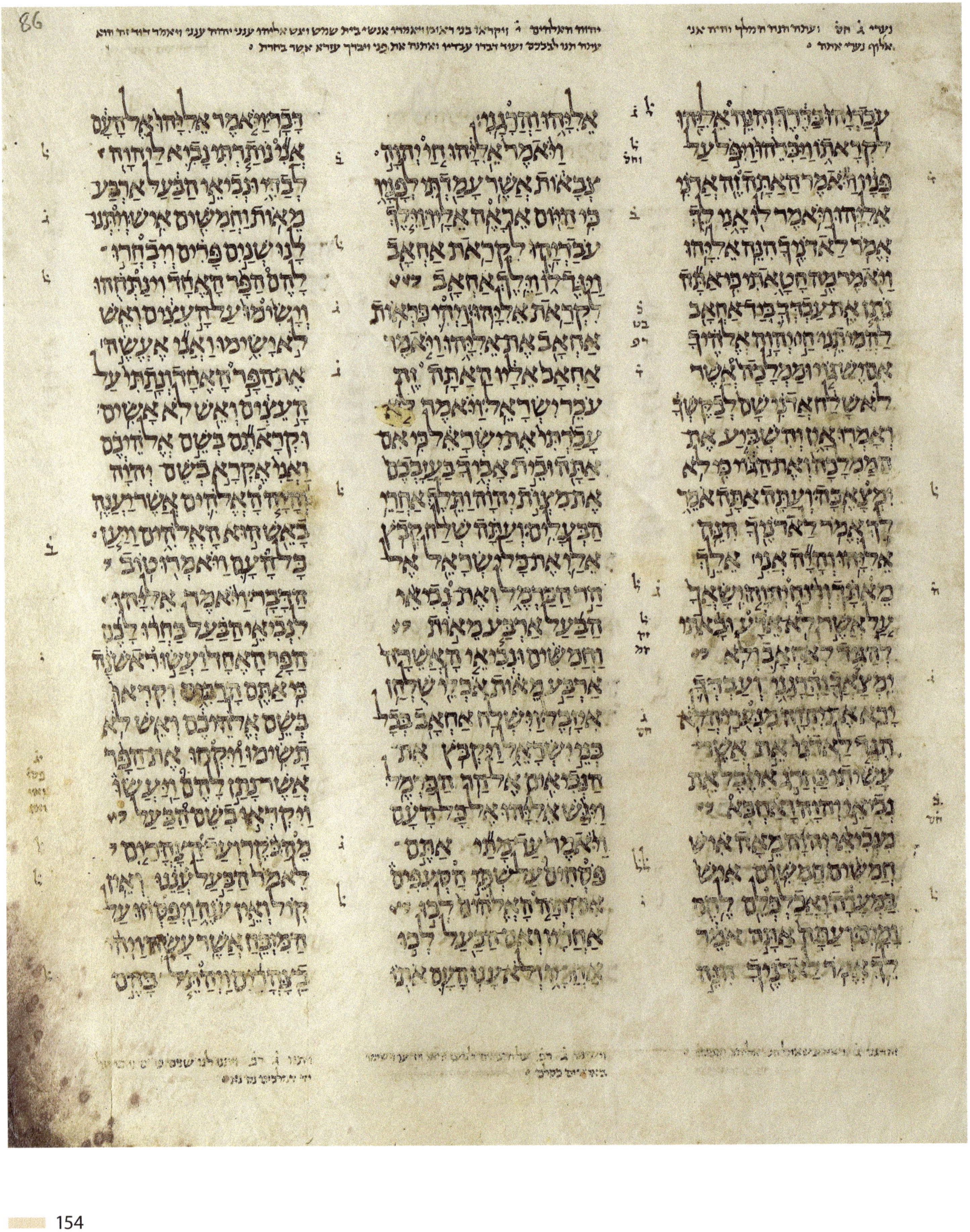

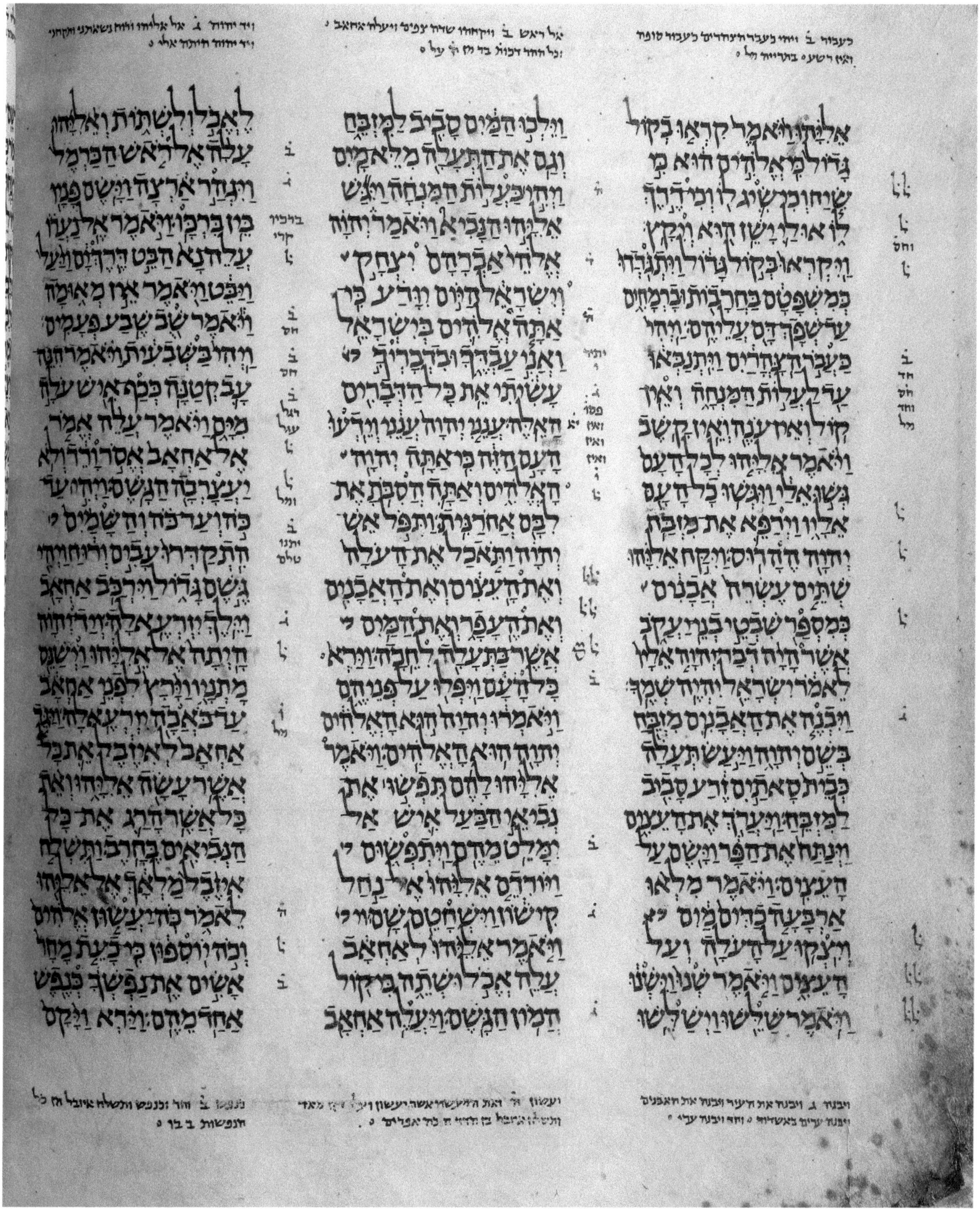

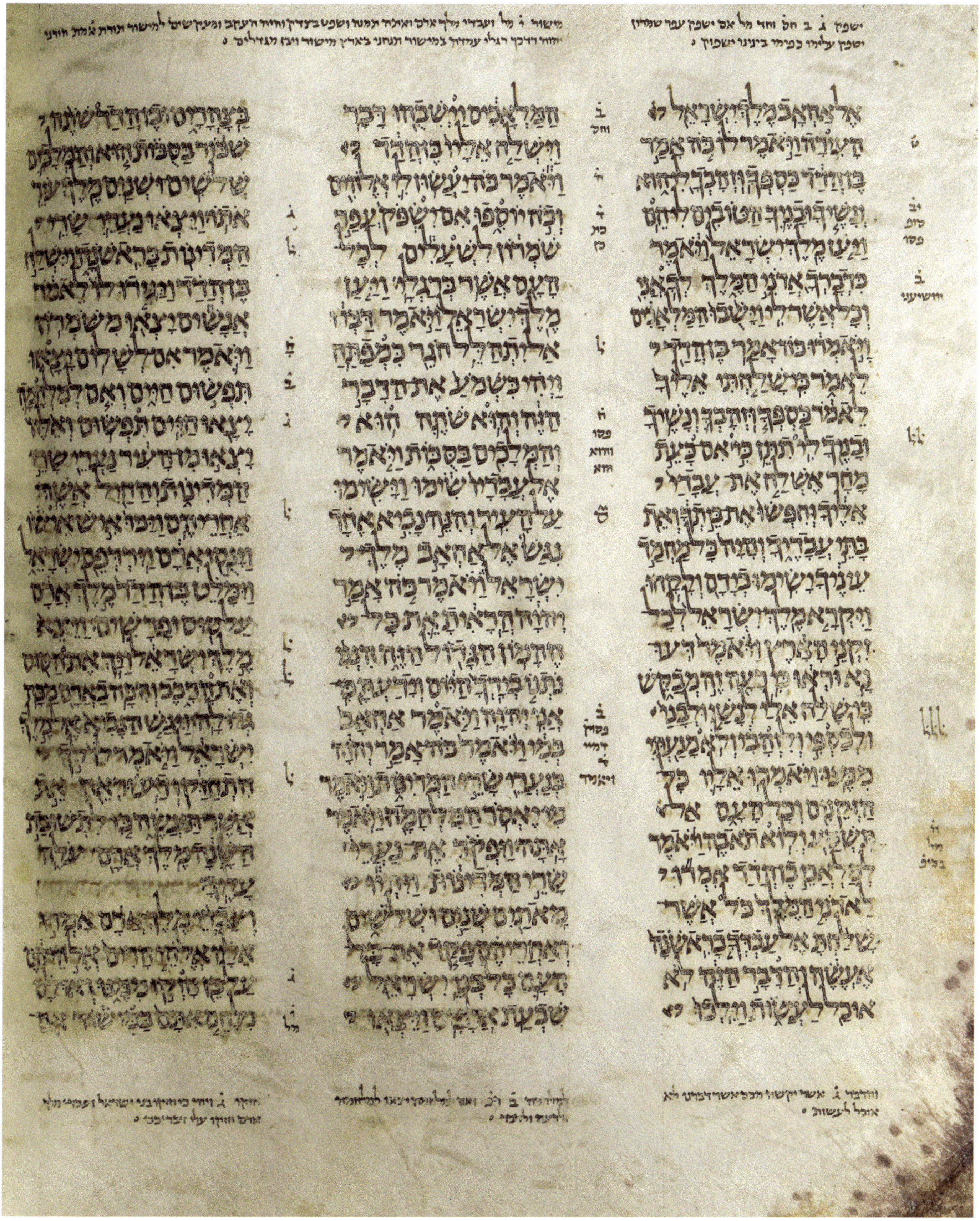

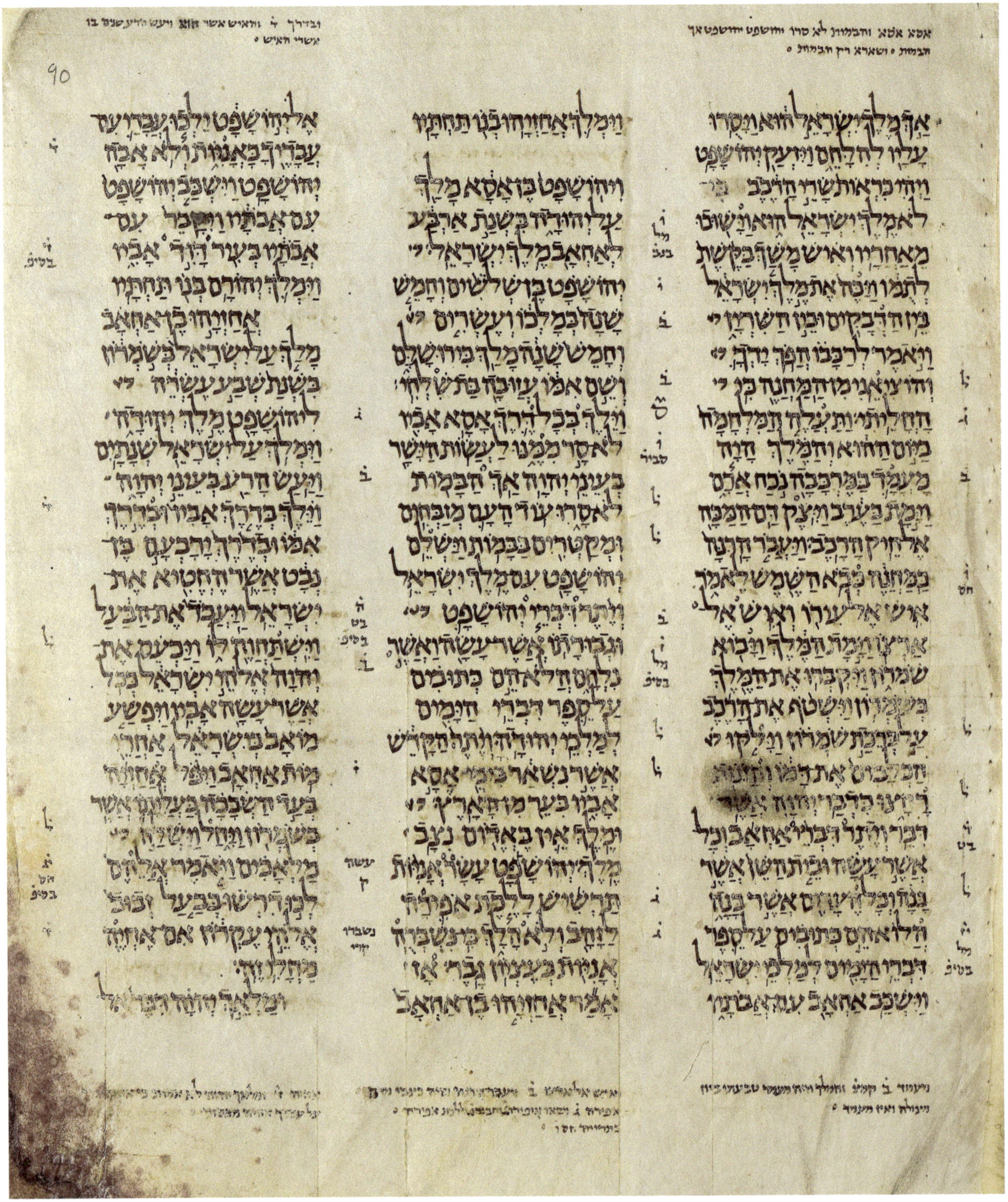

Appendix B

Weak Verb Paradigms

Introduction to Weak Verbs

The paradigms in the lessons of this book use שָׁרָשִׁים that have three regular consonants (i.e., no gutturals or glides). These are referred to as *strong verbs*. Hebrew, however, contains many more weak verbs than strong. *Weak verbs* have one or more "weak" (e.g., glide) consonants in the שֹׁרֶשׁ that may affect the form's vowel pattern.

Weak verbs fall into one of *four* main classes (Roman numerals are used to refer to the position of the weak letter in the שֹׁרֶשׁ):

- A שֹׁרֶשׁ that begins or ends with א: I-א, III-א
- A שֹׁרֶשׁ that begins with נ: I-נ
- A שֹׁרֶשׁ with ו or י (i.e., glides): I-ו/י, II-ו/י, III-ה (originally III-ו/י)
- A שֹׁרֶשׁ with an identical consonant in second and third positions: II-III

This chart lists all the classes of weak verbs:

Class	Traditional Name	Example
I-א	*Pe ʾAlef*	אָמַר
III-א	*Lamed ʾAlef*	מָצָא
I-נ	*Pe Nun*	נָפַל
I-ו/י	*Pe Vav/Yod*	יָשַׁב, יָרַשׁ
III-ה	*Lamed Heʾ*	גָּלָה
II-ו/י	*ʿAyin Vav/Yod*	קוּם, שִׂים
II-III	*ʿAyin ʿAyin*	סָבַב

Weak Verbs Quick Reference Chart: Representative Forms

	Strong	I-א	III-א	I-נ	I-ו/י	III-ה	II-ו/י	II-III
PERF 3MS	שָׁמַר	אָמַר	מָצָא	נָגַשׁ	יָשַׁב	גָּלָה	קָם	סָב
IMPF 3MS	יִשְׁמֹר	יֹאמַר	יִמְצָא	יִגַּשׁ	יֵשֵׁב	יִגְלֶה	יָקוּם	יָסֹב
PAST 3MS	וַיִּשְׁמֹר	וַיֹּאמֶר	וַיִּמְצָא	וַיִּגַּשׁ	וַיֵּשֶׁב	וַיִּגֶל	וַיָּקָם	וַיָּסָב
IMPV MS	שְׁמֹר	אֱמֹר	מְצָא	גַּשׁ	שֵׁב	גְּלֵה	קוּם	סֹב
INF	שְׁמֹר	אֱמֹר	מְצֹא	גֶּשֶׁת	שֶׁבֶת	גְּלוֹת	קוּם	סֹב
ADV INF	שָׁמוֹר	אָמוֹר	מָצוֹא	נָגוֹשׁ	יָשׁוֹב	גָּלֹה	קוֹם	סָבוֹב
PTCP MS	שֹׁמֵר	אֹמֵר	מֹצֵא	נֹגֵשׁ	יֹשֵׁב	גֹּלֶה	קָם	סֹבֵב

1. I-א Verbs

The majority of verbs that begin with א are classified as I-Guttural verbs and follow that pattern:

Qal 3MS Imperfect (dynamic) of אָזַר is יֶאֱזֹר.
Qal 3MS Imperfect (stative) of אָהֵב is יֶאֱהַב.

However, five verbs are classified as I-א weak verbs because they have a unique vocalization in the Qal Imperfect and Past Narrative conjugations. In all the other conjugations and בִּנְיָנִים, these roots behave exactly as I-Gutturals.

The five שָׁרָשִׁים that are I-א can be learned by a traditional mnemonic device:

He *said*: "I am *willing* to *eat* what I *bake* even if I *perish*!"

אָמַר	he said
אָבָה	he was willing
אָכַל	he ate
אָפָה	he baked
אָבַד	he perished

In the Qal Imperfect and Past Narrative conjugations, the initial א in these five שָׁרָשִׁים becomes quiescent; that is, it loses its consonantal status. The following changes take place:

- An R_2 בְּגַד כְּפַת lacks a דָּגֵשׁ קַל:

  יֹאכַל (cf. יִכְתֹּב)

- The prefix vowel becomes a ֹ (חוֹלָם):

  יֹאכַל (cf. יֶאֱהַב)

- The theme vowel (the vowel between R_2 and R_3) becomes ַ (פַּתַח):

  יֹאכַל (cf. יֶאֱזֹר)

The theme vowel also appears as ֵ (צֵרֵי) in pausal forms, as in יֹאכֵל, and as ֶ (סֶגוֹל) in the Past Narrative of אמר as וַיֹּאמֶר:

- Often the R_1 א is not written in the 1cs form.

  אֹכַל instead of *אאֹכַל

Paradigm: אָמַר "Say" (also אָבַד "perish"; אָבָה "be willing"; אָכַל "eat"; and אָפָה "bake")

	Impf 3ms	Impf 1cs	Past
Qal	יֹאמַר	אֹמַר	וַיֹּאמֶר

These five שָׁרָשִׁים behave differently only in the Qal Imperfect and Past Narrative; they conform to I-Guttural in other conjugations and בִּנְיָנִים.

2. III-א Verbs

A phenomenon similar to I-א verbs takes place in III-א verbs. The א becomes quiescent and cannot close a syllable:

מָצָאת instead of *מָצַאְתְּ

- The א *cannot* be vocalized with a שְׁוָא.
- A בְּגַד כְּפַת letter following the א *never* has a דָּגֵשׁ קַל.
- The vowel preceding the א *lengthens*.

Here are the other characteristics to note about the III-א verbs:

- ֶ (סֶגוֹל) appears before א in the 3fp/2fp Imperfect in all בִּנְיָנִים:

Qal	תִּמְצֶאנָה	Nifal	תִּמָּצֶאנָה
Piel	תְּמַצֶּאנָה	Pual	תְּמֻצֶּאנָה
Hitpael	תִּתְמַצֶּאנָה		
Hifil	תַּמְצֶאנָה	Hofal	תֻּמְצֶאנָה

- Only Qal Perfect shows a distinction in vowel pattern between dynamic and stative:

Perfect **מָצָא** (dynamic) *versus* **מָלֵא** (stative)
Imperfect **יִמְצָא** (dynamic) *like* **יִמְלָא** (stative)

- Nifal, Piel, and Hifil Perfect have a ֵ (צֵ֫רֵי) theme vowel instead of a ַ (פַּ֫תַח) before consonantal inflectional suffixes:

	Nifal	Piel	Hifil
2MS	נִמְצֵ֫אתָ	מִצֵּ֫אתָ	הִמְצֵ֫אתָ
2FS	נִמְצֵאת	מִצֵּאת	הִמְצֵאת
1CS	נִמְצֵ֫אתִי	מִצֵּ֫אתִי	הִמְצֵ֫אתִי
2MP	נִמְצֵאתֶם	מִצֵּאתֶם	הִמְצֵאתֶם
2FP	נִמְצֵאתֶן	מִצֵּאתֶן	הִמְצֵאתֶן
1CP	נִמְצֵ֫אנוּ	מִצֵּ֫אנוּ	הִמְצֵ֫אנוּ

- Hofal has a ֻ (קִבּוּץ) instead of ָ (קָמֵץ חָטוּף) under the prefix:

הֻמְצָא instead of *הָמְצָא
יֻמְצָא instead of *יָמְצָא

Paradigm: מָצָא "Find"

	Qal	Nifal	Piel	Pual	Hitpael	Hifil	Hofal
PERF 3MS	מָצָא	נִמְצָא	מִצֵּא	מֻצָּא	הִתְמַצֵּא	הִמְצִיא	הֻמְצָא
3FS	מָצְאָה	נִמְצְאָה	מִצְּאָה	מֻצְּאָה	הִתְמַצְּאָה	הִמְצִ֫יאָה	הֻמְצְאָה
2MS	מָצָ֫אתָ	נִמְצֵ֫אתָ	מִצֵּ֫אתָ	מֻצֵּ֫אתָ	הִתְמַצֵּ֫אתָ	הִמְצֵ֫אתָ	הֻמְצֵ֫אתָ
2FS	מָצָאת	נִמְצֵאת	מִצֵּאת	מֻצֵּאת	הִתְמַצֵּאת	הִמְצֵאת	הֻמְצֵאת
1CS	מָצָ֫אתִי	נִמְצֵ֫אתִי	מִצֵּ֫אתִי	מֻצֵּ֫אתִי	הִתְמַצֵּ֫אתִי	הִמְצֵ֫אתִי	הֻמְצֵ֫אתִי
3CP	מָצְאוּ	נִמְצְאוּ	מִצְּאוּ	מֻצְּאוּ	הִתְמַצְּאוּ	הִמְצִ֫יאוּ	הֻמְצְאוּ
2MP	מְצָאתֶם	נִמְצֵאתֶם	מִצֵּאתֶם	מֻצֵּאתֶם	הִתְמַצֵּאתֶם	הִמְצֵאתֶם	הֻמְצֵאתֶם
2FP	מְצָאתֶן	נִמְצֵאתֶן	מִצֵּאתֶן	מֻצֵּאתֶן	הִתְמַצֵּאתֶן	הִמְצֵאתֶן	הֻמְצֵאתֶן
1CP	מָצָ֫אנוּ	נִמְצֵ֫אנוּ	מִצֵּ֫אנוּ	מֻצֵּ֫אנוּ	הִתְמַצֵּ֫אנוּ	הִמְצֵ֫אנוּ	הֻמְצֵ֫אנוּ
IMPF 3MS	יִמְצָא	יִמָּצֵא	יְמַצֵּא	יְמֻצָּא	יִתְמַצֵּא	יַמְצִיא	יֻמְצָא
3FS/2MS	תִּמְצָא	תִּמָּצֵא	תְּמַצֵּא	תְּמֻצָּא	תִּתְמַצֵּא	תַּמְצִיא	תֻּמְצָא

	Qal	Nifal	Piel	Pual	Hitpael	Hifil	Hofal
2FS	תִּמְצְאִי	תִּמָּצְאִי	תְּמַצְּאִי	תְּמֻצְּאִי	תִּתְמַצְּאִי	תַּמְצִיאִי	תֻּמְצְאִי
1CS	אֶמְצָא	אֶמָּצֵא	אֲמַצֵּא	אֲמֻצָּא	אֶתְמַצֵּא	אַמְצִיא	אֻמְצָא
3MP	יִמְצְאוּ	יִמָּצְאוּ	יְמַצְּאוּ	יְמֻצְּאוּ	יִתְמַצְּאוּ	יַמְצִיאוּ	יֻמְצְאוּ
3FP/2FP	תִּמְצֶאנָה	תִּמָּצֶאנָה	תְּמַצֶּאנָה	תְּמֻצֶּאנָה	תִּתְמַצֶּאנָה	תַּמְצֶאנָה	תֻּמְצֶאנָה
2MP	תִּמְצְאוּ	תִּמָּצְאוּ	תְּמַצְּאוּ	תְּמֻצְּאוּ	תִּתְמַצְּאוּ	תַּמְצִיאוּ	תֻּמְצְאוּ
1CP	נִמְצָא	נִמָּצֵא	נְמַצֵּא	נְמֻצָּא	נִתְמַצֵּא	נַמְצִיא	נֻמְצָא

III-א: Representative Forms

	Qal	Nifal	Piel	Pual	Hitpael	Hifil	Hofal
PAST 3MS	וַיִּמְצָא	וַיִּמָּצֵא	וַיְמַצֵּא	וַיְמֻצָּא	וַיִּתְמַצֵּא	וַיַּמְצֵא	וַיֻּמְצָא
JUSS 3MS	יִמְצָא	יִמָּצֵא	יְמַצֵּא	יְמֻצָּא	יִתְמַצֵּא	יַמְצֵא	יֻמְצָא
1CS	אֶמְצְאָה	אִמָּצְאָה	אֲמַצְּאָה		אֶתְמַצְּאָה	אַמְצִיאָה	
IMPV MS	מְצָא	הִמָּצֵא	מַצֵּא		הִתְמַצֵּא	הַמְצֵא	
FS	מִצְאִי	הִמָּצְאִי	מַצְּאִי		הִתְמַצְּאִי	הַמְצִיאִי	
MP	מִצְאוּ	הִמָּצְאוּ	מַצְּאוּ		הִתְמַצְּאוּ	הַמְצִיאוּ	
FP	מְצֶאנָה	הִמָּצֶאנָה	מַצֶּאנָה		הִתְמַצֶּאנָה	הַמְצֶאנָה	
INF	מְצֹא	הִמָּצֵא	מַצֵּא	מֻצָּא	הִתְמַצֵּא	הַמְצִיא	הֻמְצָא
ADV INF	מָצוֹא	נִמְצֹא	מַצֹּא		הִתְמַצֵּא	הַמְצֵא	
PTCP MS	מֹצֵא	נִמְצָא	מְמַצֵּא	מְמֻצָּא	מִתְמַצֵּא	מַמְצִיא	מֻמְצָא
FS	מֹצְאָה	נִמְצָאָה	מְמַצְּאָה	מְמֻצָּאָה	מִתְמַצְּאָה	מַמְצִיאָה	מֻמְצָאָה
	מֹצֵאת	נִמְצֵאת	מְמַצֵּאת	מְמֻצֵּאת	מִתְמַצֵּאת	מַמְצֵאת	מֻמְצֵאת
MP	מֹצְאִים	נִמְצָאִים	מְמַצְּאִים	מְמֻצָּאִים	מִתְמַצְּאִים	מַמְצִיאִים	מֻמְצָאִים
FP	מֹצְאוֹת	נִמְצָאוֹת	מְמַצְּאוֹת	מְמֻצָּאוֹת	מִתְמַצְּאוֹת	מַמְצִיאוֹת	מֻמְצָאוֹת

3. I-נ Verbs

I-נ weak verbs undergo *two* changes that make them weak:

- When the נ closes a syllable (i.e., it does not have a vowel and is preceded by a verbal prefix), it *assimilates* to the following consonant, lengthening it (i.e., the following consonant will have a דָּגֵשׁ חָזָק):

Qal 3MS Imperfect יִפֹּל (instead of *יִנְפֹּל)
Nifal 3MS Perfect נִגַּשׁ (instead of *נִנְגַּשׁ)
Hifil MS Participle מַגִּישׁ (instead of *מַנְגִּישׁ)

But נ does *not* assimilate to gutturals, as in יִנְהַג.

- When the נ occurs at the beginning of a form and it does not have a vowel, it may undergo *aphaeresis*; that is, the initial נ drops out. This occurs only in the Qal Imperative and Infinitive:

  Qal 2MS Imperative גַּשׁ (instead of *נְגַשׁ)
  Qal Infinitive גֶּשֶׁת from *גַּשְׁתְּ (instead of *נְגַשׁ)

The דָּגֵשׁ in the ג is a דָּגֵשׁ קַל, because the ג now stands at the beginning of the word. The Infinitive forms that drop the נ also add a ת to the end of the form.
But the נ remains with a few שָׁרָשִׁים:

Qal Infinitive/2MS Imperative נְפֹל

נָתַן and לָקַח

The verb לָקַח follows the I-נ pattern:

- The ל assimilates (just like a נ would) to the ק:

  Qal 3MS Imperfect יִקַּח
  Qal 3FS Imperfect תִּקַּח

  However, the ל does not assimilate in the Nifal:

  Nifal 3MS Perfect נִלְקַח

- The ל undergoes aphaeresis in the Imperative and Infinitive forms:

  Qal 2MS Imperative קַח
  Qal Infinitive קַ֫חַת

The verb נָתַן is not only a I-נ verb; it also has a נ as the final consonant of the שֹׁרֶשׁ. When inflectional endings are added and the final נ in נָתַן does not have a full vowel, it assimilates to the following consonant (just like the initial נ in the same environment). This does not happen in other שָׁרָשִׁים that end in נ:

Qal 2MS Perfect נָתַ֫תָּ (from *נָתַנְתָּ)
Qal 2FS Perfect נָתַתְּ (from *נָתַנְתְּ)
Qal 1CS Perfect נָתַ֫תִּי (from *נָתַנְתִּי)
Qal Infinitive תֵּת (with suffixes, -תִּת, from *תִּנְתְּ)

Paradigm: נָפַל "Fall"; נָגַשׁ "Draw Near"

	Qal	Qal	Nifal	Pi/Pu/Hit	Hifil	Hofal
PERF 3MS	נָפַל	נָגַשׁ	נִגַּשׁ		הִגִּישׁ	הֻגַּשׁ
3FS	נָפְלָה	נָגְשָׁה	נִגְּשָׁה		הִגִּ֫ישָׁה	הֻגְּשָׁה
2MS	נָפַ֫לְתָּ	נָגַ֫שְׁתָּ	נִגַּ֫שְׁתָּ		הִגַּ֫שְׁתָּ	הֻגַּ֫שְׁתָּ
2FS	נָפַ֫לְתְּ	נָגַ֫שְׁתְּ	נִגַּ֫שְׁתְּ		הִגַּ֫שְׁתְּ	הֻגַּ֫שְׁתְּ
1CS	נָפַ֫לְתִּי	נָגַ֫שְׁתִּי	נִגַּ֫שְׁתִּי		הִגַּ֫שְׁתִּי	הֻגַּ֫שְׁתִּי
3CP	נָפְלוּ	נָגְשׁוּ	נִגְּשׁוּ		הִגִּ֫ישׁוּ	הֻגְּשׁוּ
2MP	נְפַלְתֶּם	נְגַשְׁתֶּם	נִגַּשְׁתֶּם	R	הִגַּשְׁתֶּם	הֻגַּשְׁתֶּם
2FP	נְפַלְתֶּן	נְגַשְׁתֶּן	נִגַּשְׁתֶּן	E	הִגַּשְׁתֶּן	הֻגַּשְׁתֶּן
1CP	נָפַ֫לְנוּ	נָגַ֫שְׁנוּ	נִגַּ֫שְׁנוּ	G	הִגַּ֫שְׁנוּ	הֻגַּ֫שְׁנוּ
				U		
IMPF 3MS	יִפֹּל	יִגַּשׁ	יִנָּגֵשׁ	L	יַגִּישׁ	יֻגַּשׁ
3FS/2MS	תִּפֹּל	תִּגַּשׁ	תִּנָּגֵשׁ	A	תַּגִּישׁ	תֻּגַּשׁ
2FS	תִּפְּלִי	תִּגְּשִׁי	תִּנָּגְשִׁי	R	תַּגִּ֫ישִׁי	תֻּגְּשִׁי
1CS	אֶפֹּל	אֶגַּשׁ	אֶנָּגֵשׁ		אַגִּישׁ	אֻגַּשׁ
3MP	יִפְּלוּ	יִגְּשׁוּ	יִנָּגְשׁוּ		יַגִּ֫ישׁוּ	יֻגְּשׁוּ
3FP	תִּפֹּ֫לְנָה	תִּגַּ֫שְׁנָה	תִּנָּגַ֫שְׁנָה		תַּגֵּ֫שְׁנָה	תֻּגַּ֫שְׁנָה
2MP	תִּפְּלוּ	תִּגְּשׁוּ	תִּנָּגְשׁוּ		תַּגִּ֫ישׁוּ	תֻּגְּשׁוּ
2FP	תִּפֹּ֫לְנָה	תִּגַּ֫שְׁנָה	תִּנָּגַ֫שְׁנָה		תַּגֵּ֫שְׁנָה	תֻּגַּ֫שְׁנָה
1CP	נִפֹּל	נִגַּשׁ	נִנָּגֵשׁ		נַגִּישׁ	נֻגַּשׁ

I-נ: Representative Forms

	Qal	Qal	Nifal	Pi/Pu/Hit	Hifil	Hofal
PAST 3MS	וַיִּפֹּל	וַיִּגַּשׁ	וַיִּנָּגֵשׁ	R	וַיַּגֵּשׁ	וַיֻּגַּשׁ
JUSS 3MS	יִפֹּל	יִגַּשׁ	יִנָּגֵשׁ	E G	יַגֵּשׁ	יֻגַּשׁ
1CS	אֶפְּלָה	אֶגְּשָׁה	אֶנָּגְשָׁה	U	אַגִּ֫ישָׁה	
IMPV MS	נְפֹל	גַּשׁ	הִנָּגֵשׁ	L A	הַגֵּשׁ	
FS	נִפְלִי	גְּשִׁי	הִנָּגְשִׁי	R	הַגִּ֫ישִׁי	

	Qal	Qal	Nifal	Pi/Pu/Hit	Hifil	Hofal
MP	נִפְלוּ	גְּשׁוּ	הִנָּגְשׁוּ		הַגִּישׁוּ	
FP	נְפֹּלְנָה	גַּשְׁנָה	הִנָּגַשְׁנָה	R	הַגֵּשְׁנָה	
INF	נְפֹל	גֶּשֶׁת	הִנָּגֵשׁ	E	הַגִּישׁ	הֻגַּשׁ
ADV INF	נָפוֹל	נָגוֹשׁ	הִנָּגֵשׁ	G	הַגֵּשׁ	הֻגֵּשׁ
PTCP MS	נֹפֵל	נֹגֵשׁ	נִגָּשׁ	U	מַגִּישׁ	מֻגָּשׁ
FS	נֹפְלָה	נֹגְשָׁה	נִגָּשָׁה	L	מַגִּישָׁה	מֻגָּשָׁה
	נֹפֶלֶת	נֹגֶשֶׁת	נִגָּשֶׁת	A	מַגֶּשֶׁת	מֻגֶּשֶׁת
MP	נֹפְלִים	נֹגְשִׁים	נִגָּשִׁים	R	מַגִּישִׁים	מֻגָּשִׁים
FP	נֹפְלוֹת	נֹגְשׁוֹת	נִגָּשׁוֹת		מַגִּישׁוֹת	מֻגָּשׁוֹת

4. I-ו/י Verbs

I-ו/י weak verbs undergo *two* changes:

- The ו or י contracts with the preceding vowel:

  Qal 3MS Imperfect יֵשֵׁב (from *יִיְשֵׁב)
  Qal 3MS Imperfect יִירַשׁ (from *יִיְרַשׁ)
  Hifil 3MS Perfect הוֹשִׁיב (from *הַוְשִׁיב)
  Hofal 3MS Perfect הוּשַׁב (from *הֻוְשַׁב)

- The ו or י undergoes aphaeresis when it lacks a full vowel at the beginning of the word (only in Qal Imperative and Infinitive of *some* שָׁרָשִׁים that are I-ו). This is similar to the form of I-נ weak verbs:

  2MS Imperative שֵׁב, instead of *יְשֵׁב
  Infinitive שֶׁבֶת (from [1]*שֵׁבְתְּ), instead of *יְשֵׁב

But ירא is an example of a שֹׁרֶשׁ that retains the initial י in the Imperative (יְרָא) and Infinitive (יְרֹא).

There are *three* different types of I-ו/י weak verbs:

- Original I-ו verbs—these verbs originally began with ו:

The ו is replaced with a י in Qal, Piel, Pual, and Hitpael:

Qal 3MS Perfect יָשַׁב and Imperfect יֵשֵׁב

1. Morphologically, the ת is a feminine ending—with no semantic value—that was added after the י underwent aphaeresis.

The original ו appears (as consonant or vowel marker) in Nifal, Hifil, and Hofal:

Nifal 3MS Perfect נוֹשַׁב and Imperfect יִוָּשֵׁב
Hifil 3MS Perfect הוֹשִׁיב and Imperfect יוֹשִׁיב

Qal Prefix verbs of dynamic I-ו/י roots have an *a-i* pattern:

Dynamic (*a-i*) יֵשֵׁב from *יַיְשִׁב

Qal Prefix verbs of stative I-ו/י roots have an *i-a* pattern:

Stative (*i-a*) יִירַשׁ from *יִיְרַשׁ

• Original I-י verbs—these verbs originally began with י. The י appears in all forms (as a consonant or a vowel marker):

Qal 3MS Imperfect יִיבַשׁ and Infinitive יְבֹשׁ
Hifil 3MS Perfect הֵיטִיב and 3MS Imperfect יֵיטִיב

There are only *seven* I-י type שָׁרָשִׁים (all have stative *i-a* Prefix pattern):

יָבֵשׁ	Q it was dry
יָטַב	Q he was good
ילל	HI he howled
יָשַׁר	Q it was straight, upright
ימן	HI he chose/used the right arm
יָנַק	Q he suckled
*יָקַץ	Q he awoke

• I-י-צ verbs—these roots begin with -יצ and undergo changes like I-נ weak verbs. The י assimilates into the צ when it closes a syllable (this is similar to the assimilation of the נ in I-נ verbs):

Hifil 3MS Perfect הִצִּיב (from *הִיְצִיב)

There are only *six* I-י-צ roots (all with stative *i-a* in the Prefix pattern):

יצב	HIT he stationed himself
יצג	HI he set, placed
יצע	HI he spread, lay
יָצַק	Q he poured
יָצַר	Q he formed, fashioned
יָצַת	Q it kindled, burned

The Verb הָלַךְ

The verb הָלַךְ follows the original I-ו pattern:

Qal 3MS Perfect הָלַךְ
Qal 3MS Imperfect יֵלֵךְ
Qal 3MS Past Narrative וַיֵּלֶךְ
Qal 2MS Imperative לֵךְ
Qal Infinitive לֶכֶת
Hifil 3MS Perfect הוֹלִיךְ
Hifil 3MS Imperfect יוֹלִיךְ

Paradigm: יָרַשׁ "Possess"; יָשַׁב "Sit"; יָטַב "Be Good"

	Qal	Qal	Nifal	Pi/Pu/Hit	Hifil	Hofal	Qal	Hifil
PERF 3MS	יָרַשׁ	יָשַׁב	נוֹשַׁב		הוֹשִׁיב	הוּשַׁב	יָטַב	הֵיטִיב
3FS	יָרְשָׁה	יָשְׁבָה	נוֹשְׁבָה		הוֹשִׁיבָה	הוּשְׁבָה	יָטְבָה	הֵיטִיבָה
2MS	יָרַשְׁתָּ	יָשַׁבְתָּ	נוֹשַׁבְתָּ		הוֹשַׁבְתָּ	הוּשַׁבְתָּ	יָטַבְתָּ	הֵיטַבְתָּ
2FS	יָרַשְׁתְּ	יָשַׁבְתְּ	נוֹשַׁבְתְּ		הוֹשַׁבְתְּ	הוּשַׁבְתְּ	יָטַבְתְּ	הֵיטַבְתְּ
1CS	יָרַשְׁתִּי	יָשַׁבְתִּי	נוֹשַׁבְתִּי		הוֹשַׁבְתִּי	הוּשַׁבְתִּי	יָטַבְתִּי	הֵיטַבְתִּי
3CP	יָרְשׁוּ	יָשְׁבוּ	נוֹשְׁבוּ	R	הוֹשִׁיבוּ	הוּשְׁבוּ	יָטְבוּ	הֵיטִיבוּ
2MP	יְרַשְׁתֶּם	יְשַׁבְתֶּם	נוֹשַׁבְתֶּם	E	הוֹשַׁבְתֶּם	הוּשַׁבְתֶּם	יְטַבְתֶּם	הֵיטַבְתֶּם
2FP	יְרַשְׁתֶּן	יְשַׁבְתֶּן	נוֹשַׁבְתֶּן	G	הוֹשַׁבְתֶּן	הוּשַׁבְתֶּן	יְטַבְתֶּן	הֵיטַבְתֶּן
1CP	יָרַשְׁנוּ	יָשַׁבְנוּ	נוֹשַׁבְנוּ	U	הוֹשַׁבְנוּ	הוּשַׁבְנוּ	יָטַבְנוּ	הֵיטַבְנוּ
				L				
IMPF 3MS	יִירַשׁ	יֵשֵׁב	יִוָּשֵׁב	A	יוֹשִׁיב	יוּשַׁב	יִיטַב	יֵיטִיב
3FS/2MS	תִּירַשׁ	תֵּשֵׁב	תִּוָּשֵׁב	R	תּוֹשִׁיב	תּוּשַׁב	תִּיטַב	תֵּיטִיב
2FS	תִּירְשִׁי	תֵּשְׁבִי	תִּוָּשְׁבִי		תּוֹשִׁיבִי	תּוּשְׁבִי	תִּיטְבִי	תֵּיטִיבִי
1CS	אִירַשׁ	אֵשֵׁב	אֶוָּשֵׁב		אוֹשִׁיב	אוּשַׁב	אִיטַב	אֵיטִיב
3MP	יִירְשׁוּ	יֵשְׁבוּ	יִוָּשְׁבוּ		יוֹשִׁיבוּ	יוּשְׁבוּ	יִיטְבוּ	יֵיטִיבוּ
3FP	תִּירַשְׁנָה	תֵּשַׁבְנָה	תִּוָּשַׁבְנָה		תּוֹשֵׁבְנָה	תּוּשַׁבְנָה	תִּיטַבְנָה	תֵּיטַבְנָה
2MP	תִּירְשׁוּ	תֵּשְׁבוּ	תִּוָּשְׁבוּ		תּוֹשִׁיבוּ	תּוּשְׁבוּ	תִּיטְבוּ	תֵּיטִיבוּ
2FP	תִּירַשְׁנָה	תֵּשַׁבְנָה	תִּוָּשַׁבְנָה		תּוֹשֵׁבְנָה	תּוּשַׁבְנָה	תִּיטַבְנָה	תֵּיטַבְנָה
1CP	נִירַשׁ	נֵשֵׁב	נִוָּשֵׁב		נוֹשִׁיב	נוּשַׁב	נִיטַב	נֵיטִיב

I-ו/י: Representative Forms

	Qal	Qal	Nifal	Pi/Pu/Hit	Hifil	Hofal	Qal	Hifil
PAST 3MS	וַיִּרַשׁ	וַיֵּשֶׁב	וַיִּוָּשֵׁב		וַיֹּשֶׁב	וַיּוּשַׁב	וַיִּיטַב	וַיֵּיטֵב
JUSS 3MS	יִירַשׁ	יֵשֵׁב	יִוָּשֵׁב		יוֹשֵׁב		יִיטַב	יֵיטֵב
1CS	אִירְשָׁה	אֵשְׁבָה	אֶוָּשְׁבָה		אוֹשִׁיבָה		אִיטְבָה	אֵיטִיבָה
IMPV MS	רֵשׁ	שֵׁב	הִוָּשֵׁב	R	הוֹשֵׁב		יְטַב	הֵיטֵב
FS	רְשִׁי	שְׁבִי	הִוָּשְׁבִי	E	הוֹשִׁיבִי		יִטְבִי	הֵיטִיבִי
MP	רְשׁוּ	שְׁבוּ	הִוָּשְׁבוּ	G	הוֹשִׁיבוּ		יִטְבוּ	הֵיטִיבוּ
FP	רַשְׁנָה	שֵׁבְנָה	הִוָּשַׁבְנָה		הוֹשֵׁבְנָה		יְטַבְנָה	הֵיטֵבְנָה
INF	רֶשֶׁת	שֶׁבֶת	הִוָּשֵׁב	U	הוֹשִׁיב	הוּשַׁב	יְטֹב	הֵיטִיב
ADV INF	יָרוֹשׁ	יָשׁוֹב	הִוָּשֵׁב	L	הוֹשֵׁב	הוּשֵׁב	יָטוֹב	הֵיטֵב
PTCP MS	יֹרֵשׁ	יֹשֵׁב	נוֹשָׁב	A	מוֹשִׁיב	מוּשָׁב	יֹטֵב	מֵיטִיב
FS	יֹרְשָׁה יֹרֶשֶׁת	יֹשְׁבָה יֹשֶׁבֶת	נוֹשָׁבָה נוֹשֶׁבֶת	R	מוֹשִׁיבָה מוֹשֶׁבֶת	מוּשָׁבָה מוּשֶׁבֶת	יֹטְבָה יֹטֶבֶת	מֵיטִיבָה מֵיטֶבֶת
MP	יֹרְשִׁים	יֹשְׁבִים	נוֹשָׁבִים		מוֹשְׁבִים	מוּשָׁבִים	יֹטְבִים	מֵיטִיבִים
FP	יֹרְשׁוֹת	יֹשְׁבוֹת	נוֹשָׁבוֹת		מוֹשְׁבוֹת	מוּשָׁבוֹת	יֹטְבוֹת	מֵיטִיבוֹת

5. III-ה Verbs

Most III-ה weak verbs originally ended with י (or ו). The ה in the 3MS Perfect form is only a vowel letter marking the long final vowel. This vowel letter was added after the final י or ו was lost. The original R_3 י or ו shows up only rarely.

Qal Passive Participle (שָׁמוּר) exhibits the original י:

גָּלוּי uncovered

Qal 3MS Perfect of some verbs shows the original ו:

שָׁלֵו he was at ease

The few שָׁרָשִׁים that actually have a ה as their original R_3 have a מַפִּיק in the ה (i.e., הּ). This signifies that the הּ is a consonant rather than a vowel letter:

גָּבַהּ it was high/lofty/tall

- All forms *without* an inflectional suffix end in ה (except the Infinitive, which has וֹת-):

  Perfect—3MS גָּלָה
  Imperfect—3MS יִגְלֶה
  Imperative—2MS גְּלֵה
  Infinitive—גְּלוֹת
  Adverbial Infinitive—גָּלֹה
  Participle—MS גֹּלֶה; MS נִסְמָךְ FORM גֹּלֵה

- Forms with a vocalic inflectional suffix or an attached pronoun with a linking vowel drop the R_3 ה:

  Qal Perfect 3CP גָּלוּ
  Qal Perfect 3MS + 1CS suffix גָּלַנִי

- In all forms with a consonantal suffix, the R_3 contracts:
  1. Into ִי in the active בִּנְיָנִים (Qal, Piel, Hitpael, and Hifil):

     Qal Perfect 2MS גָּלִיתָ

  2. Into ֵי in the passive בִּנְיָנִים (Nifal, Pual, and Hofal):

     Nifal Perfect 2MS נִגְלֵיתָ

  3. Into ֶי in Prefix verb 3FP/2FP in all בִּנְיָנִים:

     Qal Imperfect 3FP/2FP תִּגְלֶינָה

- In Past and Jussive forms *without* an inflectional suffix, the R_3 ה drops:

  יִגֶל let him uncover; וַיִּגֶל he uncovered

Paradigm: גָּלָה "Reveal"

	Qal	Nifal	Piel	Pual	Hitpael	Hifil	Hofal
PERF 3MS	גָּלָה	נִגְלָה	גִּלָּה	גֻּלָּה	הִתְגַּלָּה	הִגְלָה	הָגְלָה
3FS	גָּלְתָה	נִגְלְתָה	גִּלְּתָה	גֻּלְּתָה	הִתְגַּלְּתָה	הִגְלְתָה	הָגְלְתָה
2MS	גָּלִיתָ	נִגְלֵיתָ	גִּלִּיתָ	גֻּלֵּיתָ	הִתְגַּלִּיתָ	הִגְלִיתָ	הָגְלֵיתָ
2FS	גָּלִית	נִגְלֵית	גִּלִּית	גֻּלֵּית	הִתְגַּלִּית	הִגְלִית	הָגְלֵית
1CS	גָּלִיתִי	נִגְלֵיתִי	גִּלִּיתִי	גֻּלֵּיתִי	הִתְגַּלִּיתִי	הִגְלִיתִי	הָגְלֵיתִי
3CP	גָּלוּ	נִגְלוּ	גִּלּוּ	גֻּלּוּ	הִתְגַּלּוּ	הִגְלוּ	הָגְלוּ
2MP	גְּלִיתֶם	נִגְלֵיתֶם	גִּלִּיתֶם	גֻּלֵּיתֶם	הִתְגַּלִּיתֶם	הִגְלִיתֶם	הָגְלֵיתֶם
2FP	גְּלִיתֶן	נִגְלֵיתֶן	גִּלִּיתֶן	גֻּלֵּיתֶן	הִתְגַּלִּיתֶן	הִגְלִיתֶן	הָגְלֵיתֶן
1CP	גָּלִינוּ	נִגְלֵינוּ	גִּלִּינוּ	גֻּלֵּינוּ	הִתְגַּלִּינוּ	הִגְלִינוּ	הָגְלֵינוּ

	Qal	Nifal	Piel	Pual	Hitpael	Hifil	Hofal
IMPF 3MS	יִגְלֶה	יִגָלֶה	יְגַלֶה	יְגֻלֶה	יִתְגַלֶה	יַגְלֶה	יָגְלֶה
3FS/2MS	תִגְלֶה	תִגָלֶה	תְגַלֶה	תְגֻלֶה	תִתְגַלֶה	תַגְלֶה	תָגְלֶה
2FS	תִגְלִי	תִגָלִי	תְגַלִי	תְגֻלִי	תִתְגַלִי	תַגְלִי	תָגְלִי
1CS	אֶגְלֶה	אֶגָלֶה	אֲגַלֶה	אֲגֻלֶה	אֶתְגַלֶה	אַגְלֶה	אָגְלֶה
3MP	יִגְלוּ	יִגָלוּ	יְגַלוּ	יְגֻלוּ	יִתְגַלוּ	יַגְלוּ	יָגְלוּ
3FP	תִגְלֶינָה	תִגָלֶינָה	תְגַלֶינָה	תְגֻלֶינָה	תִתְגַלֶינָה	תַגְלֶינָה	תָגְלֶינָה
2MP	תִגְלוּ	תִגָלוּ	תְגַלוּ	תְגֻלוּ	תִתְגַלוּ	תַגְלוּ	תָגְלוּ
2FP	תִגְלֶינָה	תִגָלֶינָה	תְגַלֶינָה	תְגֻלֶינָה	תִתְגַלֶינָה	תַגְלֶינָה	תָגְלֶינָה
1CP	נִגְלֶה	נִגָלֶה	נְגַלֶה	נְגֻלֶה	נִתְגַלֶה	נַגְלֶה	נָגְלֶה

III-ה: Representative Forms

	Qal	Nifal	Piel	Pual	Hitpael	Hifil	Hofal
PAST 3MS	וַיִגֶל	וַיִגָל	וַיְגַל		וַיִתְגַל	וַיֶגֶל	
JUSS 3MS	יִגֶל	יִגָל	יְגַל		יִתְגַל	יֶגֶל	
1CS	No distinct 1CS Jussive form; identical to 1CS Imperfect						
IMPV MS	גְלֵה	הִגָלֵה	גַלֵה		הִתְגַלֵה	הַגְלֵה	
FS	גְלִי	הִגָלִי	גַלִי		הִתְגַלִי	הַגְלִי	
MP	גְלוּ	הִגָלוּ	גַלוּ		הִתְגַלוּ	הַגְלוּ	
FP	גְלֶינָה	הִגָלֶינָה	גַלֶינָה		הִתְגַלֶינָה	הַגְלֶינָה	
INF	גְלוֹת	הִגָלוֹת	גַלוֹת	גֻלוֹת	הִתְגַלוֹת	הַגְלוֹת	הַגְלוֹת
ADV INF	גָלֹה	נִגְלֹה	גַלֹה	גֻלֹה	הִתְגַלֹה	הַגְלֵה	הָגְלֵה
PTCP MS	גֹלֶה	נִגְלֶה	מְגַלֶה	מְגֻלֶה	מִתְגַלֶה	מַגְלֶה	מָגְלֶה
FS	גֹלָה	נִגְלָה	מְגַלָה	מְגֻלָה	מִתְגַלָה	מַגְלָה	מָגְלָה
MP	גֹלִים	נִגְלִים	מְגַלִים	מְגֻלִים	מִתְגַלִים	מַגְלִים	מָגְלִים
FP	גֹלוֹת	נִגְלוֹת	מְגַלוֹת	מְגֻלוֹת	מִתְגַלוֹת	מַגְלוֹת	מָגְלוֹת

6. II-ו/י Verbs

II-ו/י weak verbs have a ו or י as R_2. They are classified as weak verbs because the ו or י undergoes one of *two* changes:

- It *elides* (i.e., drops out):

    Qal 3MS Perfect/MS Participle קָם, בָּא, שָׂם

- It *contracts* with a preceding or following vowel—the ו or י in these forms is merely a vowel letter, not a remnant of the original ו or י consonant:

    Qal 3MS Imperfect יָקוּם, יָבוֹא, יָשִׂים

Several common שָׁרָשִׁים retain their R_2 ו or י as a consonant (and thus the ו or י does not disappear or contract):

הָיָה he is; חָיָה he is alive; קִוָּה he waited

Lexicon Tip 1: The II-ו/י weak verbs are listed in your lexicon by their Infinitive form because this form (unlike the 3MS Perfect, used for other verbs) better reflects the three consonants of these weak שָׁרָשִׁים.

Lexicon Tip 2: A few שָׁרָשִׁים are listed as both II-ו and II-י because they exhibit two Infinitive forms: an R_2 ו and an R_2 י:

שׂוּם and שִׂים

לוּן and לִין

Though these שָׁרָשִׁים should be classified as II-י forms, some older lexica list them as II-ו:

- Some שָׁרָשִׁים exhibit a distinction between *dynamic* and *stative* patterns in the Qal:

    קָם (dynamic) versus מֵת (stative)

- Instead of Piel, Pual, and Hitpael, *most* שָׁרָשִׁים that are II-ו/י roots have Polel, Polal, and Hitpolel בִּנְיָנִים:

    קוֹמֵם, קוֹמַם, הִתְקוֹמֵם; but Piel צִוָּה and Pual צֻוָּה

- Linking vowels often connect the שֹׁרֶשׁ to the consonantal inflectional suffixes: וֹ in Nifal and Hifil Perfect, יֶ in Qal and Hifil Imperfect:

    Nifal 2MS Perfect נְקוּמוֹתָ
    Hifil 2MS Perfect הֲקִימוֹתָ
    Qal 3FP/2FP Imperfect תְּקוּמֶינָה
    Hifil 3FP/2FP Imperfect תְּקִימֶינָה (sometimes תָּקֵמְנָה)

Paradigm: מוּת "Die"; שִׂים "Set"; קוּם "Arise"

	Qal Stative	Qal II-י	Qal II-ו	Nifal	Polel	Hifil	Hofal
PERF 3MS	מֵת	שָׂם	קָם	נָקוֹם	קוֹמֵם	הֵקִים	הוּקַם
3FS	מֵ֫תָה	שָׂ֫מָה	קָ֫מָה	נָ֫קוֹמָה	קוֹמְמָה	הֵקִ֫ימָה	הוּקְמָה
2MS	מַ֫תָּה	שַׂ֫מְתָּ	קַ֫מְתָּ	נְקוּמ֫וֹתָ	קוֹמַ֫מְתָּ	הֲקִימ֫וֹתָ	הוּקַ֫מְתָּ
2FS	מַ֫תְּ	שַׂ֫מְתְּ	קַ֫מְתְּ	נְקוּמוֹת	קוֹמַ֫מְתְּ	הֲקִימוֹת	הוּקַ֫מְתְּ
1CS	מַ֫תִּי	שַׂ֫מְתִּי	קַ֫מְתִּי	נְקוּמ֫וֹתִי	קוֹמַ֫מְתִּי	הֲקִימ֫וֹתִי	הוּקַ֫מְתִּי
3CP	מֵ֫תוּ	שָׂ֫מוּ	קָ֫מוּ	נָ֫קוֹמוּ	קוֹמְמוּ	הֵקִ֫ימוּ	הוּקְמוּ
2MP	מַתֶּם	שַׂמְתֶּם	קַמְתֶּם	נְקוּמוֹתֶם	קוֹמַמְתֶּם	הֲקִימוֹתֶם	הוּקַמְתֶּם
2FP	מַתֶּן	שַׂמְתֶּן	קַמְתֶּן	נְקוּמוֹתֶן	קוֹמַמְתֶּן	הֲקִימוֹתֶן	הוּקַמְתֶּן
1CP	מַ֫תְנוּ	שַׂ֫מְנוּ	קַ֫מְנוּ	נְקוּמ֫וֹנוּ	קוֹמַ֫מְנוּ	הֲקִימ֫וֹנוּ	הוּקַ֫מְנוּ
IMPF 3MS	יָמוּת	יָשִׂים	יָקוּם	יִקּוֹם	יְקוֹמֵם	יָקִים	יוּקַם
3FS/2MS	תָּמוּת	תָּשִׂים	תָּקוּם	תִּקּוֹם	תְּקוֹמֵם	תָּקִים	תּוּקַם
2FS	תָּמ֫וּתִי	תָּשִׂ֫ימִי	תָּק֫וּמִי	תִּקּ֫וֹמִי	תְּקוֹמֲמִי	תָּקִ֫ימִי	תּוּקְמִי
1CS	אָמוּת	אָשִׂים	אָקוּם	אֶקּוֹם	אֲקוֹמֵם	אָקִים	אוּקַם
3MP	יָמ֫וּתוּ	יָשִׂ֫ימוּ	יָק֫וּמוּ	יִקּ֫וֹמוּ	יְקוֹמֲמוּ	יָקִ֫ימוּ	יוּקְמוּ
3FP	תְּמוּתֶ֫ינָה	תְּשִׂימֶ֫ינָה	תְּקוּמֶ֫ינָה	תִּקּ֫וֹמְנָה	תְּקוֹמֵ֫מְנָה	תָּקֵ֫מְנָה תְּקִימֶ֫ינָה	תּוּקַ֫מְנָה
2MP	תָּמ֫וּתוּ	תָּשִׂ֫ימוּ	תָּק֫וּמוּ	תִּקּ֫וֹמוּ	תְּקוֹמֲמוּ	תָּקִ֫ימוּ	תּוּקְמוּ
2FP	תְּמוּתֶ֫ינָה	תְּשִׂימֶ֫ינָה	תְּקוּמֶ֫ינָה	תִּקּ֫וֹמְנָה	תְּקוֹמֵ֫מְנָה	תָּקֵ֫מְנָה תְּקִימֶ֫ינָה	תּוּקַ֫מְנָה
1CP	נָמוּת	נָשִׂים	נָקוּם	נִקּוֹם	נְקוֹמֵם	נָקִים	נוּקַם

II-ו/י: Representative Forms

	Qal Stative	Qal II-י	Qal II-ו	Nifal	Polel	Hifil	Hofal
PAST 3MS	וַיָּ֫מָת	וַיָּ֫שֶׂם	וַיָּ֫קָם	וַיִּקּוֹם	וַיְקוֹמֵם	וַיָּ֫קֶם	וַיּוּקַם
JUSS 3MS	יָמֹת	יָשֵׂם	יָקֹם	יִקּוֹם	יְקוֹמֵם	יָקֵם	

	Qal Stative	Qal II-י	Qal II-ו	Nifal	Polel	Hifil	Hofal
1CS	אָמ֫וּתָה	אָשִׂ֫ימָה	אָק֫וּמָה	אֶקֹ֫ומָה	אֲקוֹמֲמָה	אָקִ֫ימָה	
IMPV MS	מוּת	שִׂים	קוּם	הִקּוֹם	קוֹמֵם	הָקֵם	
FS	מ֫וּתִי	שִׂ֫ימִי	ק֫וּמִי	הִקּ֫וֹמִי	קוֹמֲמִי	הָקִ֫ימִי	
MP	מ֫וּתוּ	שִׂ֫ימוּ	ק֫וּמוּ	הִקּ֫וֹמוּ	קוֹמֲמוּ	הָקִ֫ימוּ	
FP	מֹ֫תְנָה	שֵׂ֫מְנָה	קֹ֫מְנָה	הִקּ֫וֹמְנָה	קוֹמֵ֫מְנָה	הָקֵ֫מְנָה	
INF	מוּת	שִׂים	קוּם	הִקּוֹם	קוֹמֵם	הָקִים	הוּקַם
ADV INF	מוֹת	שׂוֹם	קוֹם	הִקּוֹם	קוֹמֵם	הָקֵם	הוּקֵם
PTCP MS	מֵת	שָׂם	קָם	נָקוֹם	מְקוֹמֵם	מֵקִים	מוּקָם
FS	מֵתָה	שָׂמָה	קָמָה	נְקוֹמָה	מְקוֹמְמָה	מְקִימָה	מוּקָמָה
MP	מֵתִים	שָׂמִים	קָמִים	נְקוֹמִים	מְקוֹמְמִים	מְקִימִים	מוּקָמִים
FP	מֵתוֹת	שָׂמוֹת	קָמוֹת	נְקוֹמוֹת	מְקוֹמְמוֹת	מְקִימוֹת	מוּקָמוֹת

7. II-III Verbs

The II-III weak verbs are roots with identical second (R_2) and third (R_3) root letters. They have the following characteristics:

- The identical root letters may *assimilate*:

  Qal 3CP Perfect סַ֫בּוּ or סָבְבוּ

When the lengthened (from assimilation) consonant is at the end of the word, the דָּגֵשׁ חָזָק drops out:

Qal 3MS Perfect סַב (from *סַבּ)

Sometimes instead of R_2 assimilating forward into R_3, it assimilates backward into R_1:

Qal 3MP Imperfect יָסֹ֫בּוּ but also יִסֹּ֫בוּ

- Instead of Piel, Pual, and Hitpael, most II-III weak verbs have Poel, Poal, and Hitpoel:

  Poel סוֹבֵב *but* Piel קִלֵּל

- Linking vowels often appear before consonantal inflectional suffixes in some forms: Qal, Nifal, Hifil, and Hofal Perfect forms have וֹ, and Qal, Nifal, Hifil, and Hofal Imperfect, Imperative, and Past Narrative forms have ֵי:

2MS PERF:	Q	סַבּוֹתָ	NI	נְסַבּוֹתָ	HI	הֲסִבּוֹתָ
2/3FP IMPF:	Q	תְּסֻבֶּינָה	NI	תִּסַּבֶּינָה	HI	תְּסִבֶּינָה
FP IMPV:	Q	סֻבֶּינָה	NI	הִסַּבֶּינָה	HI	הֲסִבֶּינָה

Paradigm: קַל "Be Slight"; סָבַב "Surround"

	Qal Stative	Qal Dynamic	Nifal	Poel	Hifil	Hofal
PERF 3MS	קַל	סָבַב/סָב	נָסַב	סוֹבֵב	הֵסֵב	הוּסַב
3FS	קַלָּה	סַבָּה/סָבְבָה	נָסַבָּה	סוֹבְבָה	הֵסַבָּה	הוּסַבָּה
2MS	קַלּוֹתָ	סַבּוֹתָ	נְסַבּוֹתָ	סוֹבַבְתָּ	הֲסִבּוֹתָ	הוּסַבּוֹתָ
2FS	קַלּוֹת	סַבּוֹת	נְסַבּוֹת	סוֹבַבְתְּ	הֲסִבּוֹת	הוּסַבּוֹת
1CS	קַלּוֹתִי	סַבּוֹתִי	נְסַבּוֹתִי	סוֹבַבְתִּי	הֲסִבּוֹתִי	הוּסַבּוֹתִי
3CP	קַלּוּ	סַבּוּ/סָבְבוּ	נָסַבּוּ	סוֹבְבוּ	הֵסַבּוּ	הוּסַבּוּ
2MP	קַלּוֹתֶם	סַבּוֹתֶם	נְסַבּוֹתֶם	סוֹבַבְתֶּם	הֲסִבּוֹתֶם	הוּסַבּוֹתֶם
2FP	קַלּוֹתֶן	סַבּוֹתֶן	נְסַבּוֹתֶן	סוֹבַבְתֶּן	הֲסִבּוֹתֶן	הוּסַבּוֹתֶן
1CP	קַלּוֹנוּ	סַבּוֹנוּ	נְסַבּוֹנוּ	סוֹבַבְנוּ	הֲסִבּוֹנוּ	הוּסַבּוֹנוּ
IMPF 3MS	יֵקַל	יִסֹּב/יָסֹב	יִסַּב	יְסוֹבֵב	יָסֵב	יוּסַב/יֻסַּב
3FS/2MS	תֵּקַל	תִּסֹּב/תָּסֹב	תִּסַּב	תְּסוֹבֵב	תָּסֵב	תּוּסַב
2FS	תֵּקַלִּי	תִּסְבִי/תָּסֹבִּי	תִּסַּבִּי	תְּסוֹבְבִי	תָּסֵבִּי	תּוּסַבִּי
1CS	אֵקַל	אֶסֹּב/אָסֹב	אֶסַּב	אֲסוֹבֵב	אָסֵב	אוּסַב
3MP	יֵקַלּוּ	יִסְבוּ/יָסֹבּוּ	יִסַּבּוּ	יְסוֹבְבוּ	יָסֵבּוּ	יוּסַבּוּ
3FP	תְּקַלֶּינָה	תִּסֹּבְנָה/ תְּסֻבֶּינָה	תִּסַּבֶּינָה	תְּסוֹבֵבְנָה	תְּסִבֶּינָה	תּוּסַבֶּינָה
2MP	תֵּקַלּוּ	תִּסְבוּ/תָּסֹבּוּ	תִּסַּבּוּ	תְּסוֹבְבוּ	תָּסֵבּוּ	תּוּסַבּוּ
2FP	תְּקַלֶּינָה	תִּסֹּבְנָה/ תְּסֻבֶּינָה	תִּסַּבֶּינָה	תְּסוֹבֵבְנָה	תְּסִבֶּינָה	תּוּסַבֶּינָה
1CP	נֵקַל	נִסֹּב/נָסֹב	נִסַּב	נְסוֹבֵב	נָסֵב	נוּסַב

II-III: Representative Forms

	Qal Stative	Qal Dynamic	Nifal	Poel	Hifil	Hofal
PAST 3MS	וַיֵּקַל	וַיָּ֫סָב	וַיִּסַּב	וַיְסוֹבֵב	וַיָּ֫סֶב	וַיּוּסַב
JUSS 3MS	יֵקַל	יָסֹב	יִסַּב	יְסוֹבֵב	יָסֵב	יוּסַב
1CS	אֵקַ֫לָּה	אָסֹ֫בָּה	אֶסַּ֫בָּה	אֲסוֹבְבָה	אָסֵ֫בָּה	
IMPV MS		סֹב	הִסַּב	סוֹבֵב	הָסֵב	
FS		סֹ֫בִּי	הִסַּ֫בִּי	סוֹבֲבִי	הָסֵ֫בִּי	
MP		סֹ֫בּוּ	הִסַּ֫בּוּ	סוֹבֲבוּ	הָסֵ֫בּוּ	
FP		סֳבֶּ֫ינָה	הִסַּבֶּ֫ינָה	סוֹבֵ֫בְנָה	הֲסִיבֶּ֫נָה	
INF	קֹל	סֹב	הִסַּב	סוֹבֵב	הָסֵב	הוּסַב
ADV INF	קָלוֹל	סָבוֹב	הִסּוֹב	סוֹבֵב	הָסֵב	הוּסֵב
PTCP MS	קַל	סֹבֵב	נָסָב	מְסוֹבֵב	מֵסֵב	מוּסָב
FS	קַלָּה	סֹבְבָה	נְסַבָּה	מְסוֹבְבָה	מְסִבָּה	מוּסַבָּה
MP	קַלִּים	סֹבְבִים	נְסַבִּים	מְסוֹבְבִים	מְסִבִּים	מוּסַבִּים
FP	קַלּוֹת	סֹבְבוֹת	נְסַבּוֹת	מְסוֹבְבוֹת	מְסִבּוֹת	מוּסַבּוֹת

8. Doubly Weak Verbs

By this point, you have studied all of the major categories of weak שָׁרָשִׁים in Biblical Hebrew. However, many verb שָׁרָשִׁים contain more than one weak consonant. Such שָׁרָשִׁים are referred to as doubly weak. Below are listed some common doubly weak שָׁרָשִׁים:

אָבָה	I-א, III-ה
יָרָה	I-ו/י, III-ה
יָצָא	I-ו/י, III-א
נָשָׂא	I-נ, III-א
נָטָה	I-נ, III-ה
בּוֹא	II-ו/י, III-א
הָיָה	II-ו/י, III-ה

Although most of these שָׁרָשִׁים are still relatively simple to identify, other שָׁרָשִׁים become more difficult to identify since it is possible that up to two of their three שָׁרָשִׁים consonants may not be apparent, as in the verb וַיַּךְ.

The key to correctly identifying and parsing these doubly weak verbs is to use a *three-step process of elimination.*

Step 1: Identify what parts of the verb form are inflectional affixes and what parts are remnants of the שֹׁרֶשׁ:

וַיַּךְ: the וַ and יַּ are clearly inflectional affixes for the Past Narrative conjugation; thus ךְ is the only remaining consonant from the שֹׁרֶשׁ of this verb.

Step 2: Rule out which weak consonants *cannot* be part of the verbal שֹׁרֶשׁ, or vice versa, and identify which weak consonants can account for what is left of the verbal שֹׁרֶשׁ in the verb form.

ךְ: Since we have only one consonant of the שֹׁרֶשׁ left, the other two consonants must be ones that disappear in some way:

- Of the weak consonants (the gutturals, ה, ו, י, and נ), only ה, ו, and י *elide*, and נ *assimilates*. Hence, the remaining consonants of this verb's שֹׁרֶשׁ cannot be א, ח, ע, or ר.
- נ only assimilates at the beginning of a שֹׁרֶשׁ (except in נתן), so we can rule out a שֹׁרֶשׁ that ends in נ.
- ה only drops out at the end of a שֹׁרֶשׁ, so we rule out a שֹׁרֶשׁ beginning with ה.
- ו and י often drop out in II-ו/י verbs; however, these weak verbs never have a final ה that drops out or an initial נ that assimilates. Thus we can conclude that this verb is not a II-ו/י.

For the verb וַיַּךְ we are left with two logical possibilities after the first two steps: the שֹׁרֶשׁ is either נכה or יכה.

Step 3: Use your lexicon to identify which of your logical שָׁרָשִׁים actually exists in the Hebrew Bible. If both exist, then scan through the existing forms in each שֹׁרֶשׁ to aid you in identifying which is your verb's שֹׁרֶשׁ.

In the case of וַיַּךְ the lexicon should tell you that יכה as a שֹׁרֶשׁ does not exist. *Therefore*, the שֹׁרֶשׁ for this verb is נכה HI "smite, strike":

וַיַּךְ: Hifil 3MS Past of the שֹׁרֶשׁ נכה (from *וַיַּנְכֶה)

Appendix C

Masoretic Accents

The טְעָמִים, or accents, serve to break up the text into sense units so that when the text is read or chanted, a pause (or breath) is taken in a logical place. Knowing the accents, therefore, enables the reader to know both where to place word stress and how to phrase groups of words.

The accents are categorized as disjunctive (those that make a sense break with what follows) and conjunctive (those that make a sense connection with what follows). In addition, the disjunctive accents are of different levels depending on the strength of their disjunction. Level 1 accents make the greatest disjunction and frequently affect the syllable they appear in by lengthening the vowel.

Listed below is the set of accents used in the majority of the books of the Bible. They are organized into four disjunctive levels, followed by a list of the conjunctive accents (a slightly different set is used in Psalms, Job, and Proverbs):

Disjunctive: Level 1

Silluq	◌ֽ	סִילֽוּק׃	(always with *sof pasuq* סוֹף פָּסוּק)
Atnah̩	◌֑	אַתְנָ֑ח	

Disjunctive: Level 2

Tifh̩a	◌֖	טִפְחָ֖א	
Zaqef Qatan	◌֔	זָקֵף קָטָ֔ן	
Zaqef Gadol	◌֕	זָקֵף גָּד֕וֹל	(variant of *zaqef qatan*)
Segolta	◌֒	סְגֹלְתָּא֒	(postpositive)
Shalshelet	◌֓	שַׁלְשֶׁ֓לֶת	(variant of *segolta*)

Disjunctive: Level 3

Revia	◌֗	רְבִ֗יעַ	
Zarqa	◌֮	זַרְקָא֮	(postpositive)
Pashta	◌֙	פַּשְׁטָא֙	(postpositive)
Yetiv	◌֚	יְ֚תִיב	(prepositive)
Tevir	◌֛	תְּבִ֛יר	

Disjunctive: Level 4

Geresh	◌֜	גֵּ֜רֶשׁ
Gershayim	◌֞	גֵּרְשַׁ֞יִם
Legarmeh	◌֣ ׀	לְגַרְמֵ֣ה ׀
Pazer Qatan	◌֡	פָּזֵר קָטָ֡ן
Pazer Gadol	◌֟	פָּזֵר גָּדוֹ֟ל
Telisha Gedola	◌֠	תְּלִישָׁא גְּדוֹ֠לָה

If two of the same disjunctive accents appear within one clause, most often the first of the two will mark the more disjunctive sense break.

Conjunctive

Munaḥ	◌֣	מוּנָ֣ח	
Mahpak	◌֤	מַהְפָּ֤ךְ	
Merka	◌֥	מֵרְכָ֥א	
Merka Kefula	◌֦	מֵרְכָא כְּפוּלָ֦א	
Darga	◌֧	דַּרְגָּ֧א	
Azla	◌֨	אַזְלָ֨א	
Telisha Qetana	◌֩	תְּלִישָׁא קְטַנָּה֩	(postpositive)
Galgal	◌֪	גַּלְגַּ֪ל	
Mayela	◌֖	מַיְלָ֖א	(cf. *tifḥa*; marks secondary stress)

Verse divisions by the accents can be understood as operating on a continuous dichotomy: the strongest disjunctive divides the verse in half, the next strongest divides each half in half again, and so forth.

Linguistics Glossary

Like all technical fields, linguistics thrives on specialized terminology. Unfortunately, the terminology often results in some opacity, if not confusion, for biblical and textual studies students and scholars who have not been trained in linguistics. And yet, it is often not desirable to avoid all technical terminology. Doing so would not only result in unwieldy verbosity but would remove studies like this from their explicit grounding in a linguistic theory and/or specific linguistic studies.

To facilitate the student's use of this textbook, we provide here a short list of linguistic terms used in our discussions. For convenience and to point the student to perhaps the single most useful linguistics volume for the nonlinguist, we have based several definitions on David Crystal, *A Dictionary of Linguistics and Phonetics*, 6th ed. (Oxford: Blackwell, 2008). The number in brackets after the glossary term is the page number in Crystal where the definition can be found.

adjectival. *See* adjective.

adjective [11]. A word specifying the attribute of a noun.

adjunct [12]. An "optional or secondary element in a construction." Removing an adjunct will not affect the structural identity of the rest of the construction.

adposition. A relational word that heads a noun complement and signals location, direction, means, manner, time, or possession as well as marking a noun as the complement of a multivalent verb. Adpositions are distinguished by whether they precede (preposition) or follow (postposition) their complement. Hebrew uses prepositions except for one postposition (i.e., the directional ה). *See also* postposition; prepositional phrase.

adverb(ial) [14]. A word specifying the mode of action of a verb, such as "how" (manner), "where" (place), "when" (time), or "why" (purpose).

adversative [15]. A word expressing "an antithetical circumstance. Adversative meaning can be expressed in several grammatical ways (as 'adversatives'), such as through a conjunction (*but*), adverbial (*however*, *nevertheless*, *yet*, *in spite of that*, *on the other hand*), or preposition (*despite*, *except*, *apart from*, *notwithstanding*)."

agreement [18]. The "formal relationship between elements, whereby a form of one word requires a corresponding form of another (i.e., the forms agree)."

anacoluthon [24]. "A syntactic break in the expected grammatical sequence within a sentence, as when a sentence begins with one construction and remains unfinished, e.g., *The man came and—are you listening?* 'Anacolutha' have come to be especially noticed in linguistic studies as an area of performance features which a grammar of a language would aim to exclude."

anaphora [25]. The process or result of a linguistic item (e.g., pronoun) deriving its interpretation from some previously expressed unit of meaning (the antecedent). Anaphoric reference is one way of marking the identity between what is being expressed and what has already been expressed. In such a sentence as *He did that there*, each word is anaphoric and is thus anaphorically related to a corresponding referent in the preceding context. Anaphora operates *within* clause boundaries, and the greater the distance between the anaphor and its antecedent, the greater potential there is for other constituents that also agree with the anaphor to intervene and create difficulty for interpretation.

apocopation [30]. "The deletion of the final element in a word," in contrast to aphaeresis (omission of a beginning element) and syncope (omission of an interior element).

apposition(al) [31]. Words "at the same grammatical level, and which have an identity or similarity of reference."

appositive. The second (or third, fourth, etc.) item in an appositional structure.

appositive head. The first item in an appositional structure.

appositive of attribution. An appositive that describes the head: X, being Y.

appositive of equivalence. An appositive that is equated with the head: X, that is/namely Y.

appositive of inclusion. An appositive that is one specific or exemplary instance of the head: X, for example/especially Y.

nonrestrictive appositive. An appositive that does not define or limit the head.

restrictive appositive. An appositive that defines or limits the head.

argument. A major constituent that contributes to the grammaticality of a clause; largely identical with complement. *See* complement.

aspect. *See* tense-aspect-mood.

asseverative כִּי. The use of כִּי to reinforce an affirmation.[1] Translatable by English as "certainly, indeed."

assimilation [39]. When one sound segment influences "the articulation of another, so that the sounds become more alike, or identical."

avalent. *See* valency.

bivalent. *See* valency.

bound construction [59]. A morpheme is bound if it "cannot occur on its own as a separate word." The so-called "construct state" of nouns involves a variant form of the noun that is bound to the following noun (bound construction).

casus pendens. *See* dislocation.

1. See Paul Joüon and Takamitsu Muraoka, *A Grammar of Biblical Hebrew*, 2nd ed., 3rd reprint with corrections (Rome: Gregorian and Biblical Press, 2011), §164b, although we take it to be a stronger reinforcement than described there.

clause [78]. A syntactical unit that is "smaller than the sentence but larger than phrases, words, or morphemes."

comparative clause. A clause in which two items are compared (e.g., מִכֶּסֶף וּמִזָּהָב חֵן טוֹב, favor is better than silver and than gold [משלי כב:א]).

conditional clause [99]. A clause expressing a hypothesis or condition.

nominalized clause. A subordinate clause, typically introduced by כי or אשר, which functions syntactically in the main clause as a noun phrase would. Nominalized clauses can thus function as the subject of the main clause or as a complement of the verb.

nonrestrictive relative. A relative clause that does not define or limit the modified noun phrase.

null copula clause. *See* copula.

purpose clause. A clause expressing the reason an action was taken.

reduced. *See* small clause.

relative clause. A subordinate clause that modifies a noun phrase.

relative head. The relative head, or pivot, is the word modified by the relative clause.

restrictive relative. A relative clause that defines or limits the modified noun phrase.

result clause [415]. A clause expressing consequence or effect.

small clause [440]. A "clause that contains neither a finite verb nor an infinitival *to*."

subordinate clause. A clause (of any kind) that is subordinated within a larger clause. *See* subordination.

temporal clause. A subordinate clause indicating when the events of the main clause occur.

unmarked relative. A relative clause that is not introduced by a relative pronoun.

clitic [80]. A form that resembles a word but "cannot stand on its own as a normal utterance, being phonologically dependent upon a neighboring word (its host) in a construction."

complement [92]. "A major constituent of sentence or clause structure, traditionally associated with 'completing' the action specified by the verb. In its broadest sense, complement therefore is a very general notion, subsuming all obligatory features of the predicate other than the verb, e.g., objects (e.g., *She kicked the ball*) and adverbials (e.g., *She was in the garden*)." This notion of *obligatory completion* extends to prepositional phrases and noun phrases as well, so that these phrases also can require complements (e.g., *to the bank*).

concessive [98]. "A word or construction which expresses the meaning of 'concession.' The point expressed in the main clause continues to be valid despite the point being made in the subordinate clause (the concessive clause). In English, the most widely used markers of concession are *although* and *though*."

conjunction [101]. An "item or a process whose primary function is to connect words or other constructions."

constituent [104]. "A linguistic unit which is a functional component of a larger construction."

construct. *See* bound construction.

copula (verbal, nonverbal, null) [116]. A "linking verb, i.e., a verb which has little independent meaning, and whose main function is to relate other elements of clause structure, especially subject and complement." In Hebrew, the verbal copula is היה. The verbal copula is omitted more often than not in favor of a null copula (i.e., a phonologically unexpressed copula) that defaults to the tense-aspect of the discourse context. Null copula clauses are variously referred to as "nominal clauses" or "verbless clauses." A nonverbal copula is an overt constituent (i.e., not a null item but an overt item such as a pronoun) that is used to link the two components of a copular clause.

covert. *See* null.

deixis/deictic [133]. The process of (and as an adjective, the words used in) referring directly to the personal, temporal, or locational characteristics of the situation within which an utterance takes place, whose meaning is thus relative to that situation. The first- and second-person pronouns אֲנִי, אֲנַחְנוּ, אַתָּה, אַתְּ, אַתֶּם, and אַתֶּן are deictic, as are the demonstrative זֶה, זאת, and אֵלֶּה and also nonpronominal words such as הִנֵּה and עַתָּה. Within a discourse, deixis is relativized and thus concerns the backward or forward reference in discourse (anaphora and cataphora respectively)—for example, English *that*, *the following*, *the former*.

demonstrative [135]. A class of items whose function is to point to an entity in the situation or elsewhere in a sentence. The Hebrew items זֶה, זאת, and אֵלֶּה (and when used to modify nouns, הוּא, הִיא, הֵם, and הֵן) have their reference fixed by gestures, speaker knowledge, or other means. Depending on their grammatical role, they are often called "demonstrative determiners" (בַּיּוֹם הַהוּא, on that day) or "demonstrative pronouns" (מַה־זֹּאת עָשִׂית, what is this you have done?). Demonstratives fall within the general class of deictic expressions and are sometimes contrasted with "pure indexicals."

dislocation (left and right) [273, s.v. "Left Dislocation"; 418, s.v. "Right Dislocation"]. A type of sentence in which one of the constituents appears in initial (left) or final (right) position, and its canonical position is filled by a pronoun or a full lexical noun phrase with the same reference (e.g., *John, I like him/the old chap* or *I know that woman/her, Julie*).

exceptional case marking (ECM). A term used in generative linguistic theory for a class of verbs, such as *believe* and *consider*, which may take a clausal complement and assign accusative (object) case to the subject of the embedded clause (e.g., *John considers him a genius*). Though not studied for Biblical Hebrew, an example is identified with the verb מצא (find) in קהלת ז:כו.

exclamative [177]. "Any emotional utterance, usually lacking the grammatical structure of a full sentence, and marked by strong intonation, e.g., *Gosh! Good grief!*" The most common exclamative in Hebrew is the deictic הִנֵּה, though the exclamative use of כי also occurs (this is sometimes referred to as the asseverative כי [see above]).

extraposition/extraposed [182]. Refers "to the process or result of moving (or extraposing) an element from its normal position to a position at or near the end of the sentence."

focus (fronting) [192–93]. "A term used by some linguists in a two-part analysis of sentences which distinguishes between the information assumed by speakers, and that which is at the centre (or 'focus') of their communicative interest; 'focus' in this sense is opposed to presupposition. (The contrast between given and new information makes an analogous distinction.) For example, in the sentence *It was Mary who came to tea*, Mary is the focus (as the intonation contour helps to signal). Taking such factors into account is an important aspect of intersentence relationships: it would not be possible to have the above sentence as the answer to the question *What did Mary do?*, but only to *Who came to tea?*" In Hebrew, constituents are typically fronted (*see* fronting) to indicate focus.

fronting [201]. The transposition of "a constituent from the middle or end of a string to initial position. For example, the rule of '*Wh*-fronting' places a *Wh*-phrase (e.g. *where*, *which books*) in initial position, transposing it from the underlying noninitial position (cf. *John walked there* → *John walked where* → *where did John walk*)."

gapping [166]. Gapping occurs when an unambiguously specifiable "part of the structure has been omitted, which is recoverable from a scrutiny of the context."

genitive. A term properly used to describe a particular *case*, borrowed in the study of Hebrew to describe various ways in which a noun can be modified along the lines of the English *of*.

gnomic. A clause, or a verb within a clause, that communicates a general truth or maxim.

grammaticalization [218, s.v. "Grammar"]. The process whereby a word with semantic content is used to express grammatical functions. "An example of grammaticalization (grammaticization) is the use of the English motion verb *go*, as in *She is going to London*, which has become a marker of tense in *It's going to rain*." A case of grammaticalization in Hebrew concerns the word אֲשֶׁר, which (based on Semitic evidence) seems to have been a noun "step, place" in pre-Biblical Hebrew but has grammaticalized into a function introducing nominal (relative, complement) clauses.

heavy noun phrase shift (HNPS). A cross-linguistically common phenomenon wherein "heavy" or complex constituents are moved to the right of "lighter" or less complex constituents.

interrogative [251]. A type of sentence "usually seen in contrast to declarative. It refers to verb forms or sentence/clause types typically used in the expression of questions, e.g. the inverted order of *is he coming?*, or the use of an interrogative word (or simply 'interrogative'), often subclassified as interrogative adjectives (e.g. *which*), adverbs (e.g. *why*) and pronouns (e.g. *who*)."

inversion [254]. A syntactic change "in which a specific sequence of constituents is seen as the reverse of another."

linguistic typology [499, s.v. "Typological Linguistics"]. A branch of linguistics that studies the structural similarities between languages, regardless of their history, in an attempt to establish a satisfactory classification, or typology, of languages. Typological comparison is thus distinguished from the historical comparison of languages—the province of comparative philology and historical linguistics—and its groupings may not coincide with those set up by the historical method. For example, in respect of the paucity of inflectional endings, English is closer to Chinese than it is to Latin.

mood. *See* tense-aspect-mood.

monovalent. *See* valency.

nominal clause. *See* copula.

noun phrase (NP) [367, 333]. "A single element of structure [consisting] minimally of the noun." A NP may consist of a single noun (e.g., דָּבָר, thing) or may contain additional constituents that modify the noun (e.g., הַדָּבָר הַקָּשֶׁה אֲשֶׁר אֶעֱשֶׂה מָחָר, the difficult thing that I am going to do tomorrow).

null copula. *See* copula.

null (covert) [335]. Generative grammar uses this mathematical term for "empty" or "zero" to refer to a "phonologically empty constituent" or "null element"—that is, a constituent that exists but is not phonologically overt (verbalized).

null (covert) complement. A constituent that must exist, given the argument structure of a verb or noun phrase, but that is not phonologically overt. Null complements may or may not be reconstructable from context.

null (covert) subject. A subject that must exist, given the argument structure of a verb, but that is not phonologically overt. Null subjects may or may not be reconstructable from context.

null (covert) verb. A verb that is not phonologically overt. *See* gapping.

overt. *See* null.

partitive. A preposition referring to only part of what is designated by the noun or noun equivalent (e.g., אֶחָד מִן־הַסָּרִיסִים, one of the eunuchs).[2]

pivot. *See* clause: relative clause; clause: relative head.

postposition [377]. "The closed set of items which follow noun phrases (or single nouns or pronouns) to form a single constituent of structure. The analogous construction in English involves prepositions. A rare English postposition is -ward(s) (e.g., *it floated upward*)." A similarly rare Hebrew postposition is the directional ה. *See also* adposition; prepositional phrase.

predicate [381]. A "major constituent of sentence structure . . . containing all obligatory constituents other than the subject," within a "two-part analysis" of clauses. *See* subject.

2. See Bruce K. Waltke and Michael Patrick O'Connor, *An Introduction to Biblical Hebrew Syntax* (Winona Lake, IN: Eisenbrauns, 1990), §11.2.11e.

prepositional phrase (PP) [383]. The "set of items which typically precede noun phrases (often single nouns or pronouns), to form a single constituent of structure." Prepositions "can combine with not only an NP but also a PP (e.g., *since before breakfast*) [or] a clause (e.g., *since they finished their breakfast*)." *See also* adposition; postposition.

pronoun [391–92]. A word that can substitute syntactically for a noun phrase. Pronouns are often divided into classes, such as personal, demonstrative, interrogative, reflexive, indefinite, and relative. Additionally, anaphoric and deictic differences indicate that first- and second-person pronouns must be distinguished from third-person pronouns. Such a divide is clear in Hebrew, where the third-person subject pronouns הוּא, הִיא, הֵם, and הֵן are also used as distal demonstratives and, as argued above, nonverbal copulas.

proper noun (PN) [392]. "The name of an individual person, place, etc."

relative clause. *See under* clause.

relative head. *See under* clause.

resumptive/resumption [415]. An "element or structure which repeats or in some way recapitulates the meaning of a prior element." In Hebrew, resumption occurs especially in relative clauses, where pronouns are the typical resumptive element; for example, הָאָרֶץ אֲשֶׁר עָבַרְנוּ בָהּ, the land that they explored *it* (במדבר יג:לב).

small clause. *See under* clause.

subject [461]. "A major constituent of sentence or clause structure, traditionally associated with the 'doer' of an action, as in *The cat bit the dog*. [Many] approaches make a twofold distinction in sentence analysis between subject and predicate." *See* predicate.

subordination [462]. "The process or result of linking linguistic units so that they have different syntactic status, one being dependent upon the other, and usually a constituent of the other."

substantive [463]. "Items which function as nouns, though lacking some of the formal characteristics of that class (cf. the 'substantival function' of adjectives, in *the poor*, *the rich*, etc.)."

tense. *See* tense-aspect-mood.

tense-aspect-mood (TAM). A bundle of features present in verbs.

aspect [38]. Refers "primarily to the way the grammar marks the duration or type of temporal activity denoted by the verb."

mood [312]. "Mood (modality, or mode) refers to a set of syntactic and semantic contrasts signaled by alternative paradigms of the verb, e.g. indicative (the unmarked form), subjunctive, imperative. Semantically, a wide range of meanings is involved, especially attitudes on the part of the speaker toward the factual content of the utterance, e.g. uncertainty, definiteness, vagueness, possibility."

tense [479]. Refers "primarily to the way the grammar marks the time at which the action denoted by the verb took place."

topic (fronting) [48]. "The entity (person, thing, etc.) about which something is said, whereas the further statement made about this entity is the comment." In Hebrew, constituents are fronted (*see* fronting) to indicate topic.

trivalent. *See* valency.

valency [507]. "The number and type of bonds which syntactic elements may form with each other." In this book, the term refers particularly to the number of arguments necessary to complete a verb phrase.

- **avalent.** The valency of a verb requiring no arguments (subject and complements).
- **bivalent.** The valency of a verb requiring two arguments.
- **monovalent.** The valency of a verb requiring one argument.
- **trivalent.** The valency of a verb requiring three arguments.

verb phrase (VP). The phrase of which the verb is the head, that is, the predicate of a verbal clause. *See* predicate.

verbless clause. *See* copula.

Hebrew-English Glossary

Verbs are listed alphabetically by the Perfect 3MS forms for each בִּנְיָנִים in which they occur, and by שֹׁרֶשׁ (or קַל Perfect 3MS if it occurs) in cases where they differ in alphabetization (e.g., הִפְעִיל).

NOUN M father	אָב; אָבוֹת P
VB Q be willing, consent	אָבָה
PN Abiram	אֲבִירָם
PN Abel	אָבֵל
NOUN F stone	אֶ֫בֶן; אֲבָנִים P, אַבְנֵי P NIS
PN Abraham	אַבְרָהָם
NOUN M master, lord	אָדוֹן, אֲדוֹן NIS; אֲדֹנִים P, אֲדֹנֵי P NIS
NOUN F ground, land	אֲדָמָה, אַדְמַת NIS; אֲדָמוֹת P
PN (EPITHET) the Lord	אֲדֹנָי
NOUN F robe	אַדֶּ֫רֶת; אַדַּרְתּוֹ W. ENCL PRON
CONJ or	אוֹ
ADV perhaps	אוּלַי
CONJ but	אוּלָם
NOUN M girdle, waistcloth	אֵזוֹר
NOUN F ear	אֹ֫זֶן; אָזְנַ֫יִם DU, אָזְנֵי DU NIS
VB Q gird, equip	אָזַר
NOUN M brother	אָח, אֲחִי NIS; אַחִים P, אֲחֵי P NIS
PN Ahab	אַחְאָב
ADJ one, each one	אֶחָד, אַחַת F
PN Ahaziah	אֲחַזְיָה; אֲחַזְיָהוּ
PN Ahijah	אֲחִיָּה
PREP, ADV, CONJ behind, after	אַחַר, אַחֲרֵי
ADJ another	אַחֵר, אַחֶ֫רֶת F; אֲחֵרִים MP, אֲחֵרִין FP
ADJ at the back, western, last	אַחֲרוֹן
ADV backward	אֲחֹרַנִּית
NOUN M dejected mood, gentleness	אַט; אַטִּי W. ENCL PRON

אֹיֵב/אוֹיֵב	NOUN M (= Q PTCP) enemy
אַיֵּה	INTER where?
אִיזֶבֶל	PN Jezebel
אֵין, אַיִן	EXST ADV there is/are not
אִישׁ; אֲנָשִׁים P, אַנְשֵׁי P NIS	NOUN M man
אַךְ	ADV only, surely; nevertheless
אֲכִילָה	NOUN F food
אָכַל	VB Q eat
אָכְלָה	NOUN F food, eating
אֶל	PREP to, toward
אַל	ADV not (with commands)
אֵל	NOUN M god, God, mighty one
אֵלֶּה	CP DEM these
אֱלֹהִים	NOUN M God; gods
אֵלִיָּה/אֵלִיָּהוּ	PN Elijah
אֱלִישָׁע	PN Elisha
אַלְמָנָה; אַלְמָנוֹת P	NOUN F widow
אֶלֶף; אֲלָפִים P, אַלְפֵי P NIS	NOUN M (only P) thousand, clan; cattle
אִם	COND if; *also marks alternative condition, i.e.,* or
אֵם; אִמּוֹת P	NOUN F mother
אָמַר	VB Q say (*see also* וַיֹּאמֶר and לֵאמֹר)
אֱמֶת	NOUN F truth, faithfulness
אֲנִי, אָנֹכִי	PRON 1CS
אָסָא	PN Asa
אָסַר	VB Q tie, bind, keep in confinement
אַף	ADV also, even, moreover
אֵצֶל	NOUN M proximity; PREP beside
אַרְבַּע; אַרְבָּעָה F; אַרְבָּעִים P	PN Arba; CARD four; P forty
אֲרָם	PN Aram
אֶרֶץ; אֲרָצוֹת P, אַרְצוֹת P NIS	NOUN F earth, land
אֵשׁ	NOUN M, F fire
אִשָּׁה, אֵשֶׁת NIS; נָשִׁים P, נְשֵׁי P NIS	NOUN F woman, wife
אֲשֶׁר	CONJ that, which, who; COMP that
אֲשֵׁרָה	NOUN F grove; PN Asherah
אֶת־, אֵת; אֹתִי W. ENCL PRON	*differential object marker*
אֶת־, אֵת; אִתִּי W. ENCL PRON	PREP with
אַתָּה	PRON 2MS you
אַתֶּם	PRON 2MP you

בְּ	PREP in, at, with, by
בְּאֵר שֶׁבַע	PN Beersheba
בֶּ֫גֶד; בְּגָדִים P, בִּגְדֵי P NIS	NOUN M garment
בַּד	NOUN M solitude (mostly with לְ, i.e., לְבַד)
בְּהֵמָה, בֶּהֱמַת NIS; בְּהֵמוֹת P, בַּהֲמוֹת P NIS	NOUN F cattle
בּוֹא	VB Q come, enter; HI bring, make enter
בָּחַר	VB Q choose
בֵּין	PREP (*only* NIS) between
בַּ֫יִת, בֵּית NIS; בָּתִּים P, בָּתֵּי P NIS	NOUN M house
בֵּית־אֵל	PN Bethel
בְּלִי	NOUN M ending; CONJ without (with מִן)
בְּלִיַּ֫עַל	NOUN M uselessness, wickedness; a good for nothing
בֵּן, בֶּן־ NIS; בָּנִים P, בְּנֵי P NIS	NOUN M son
בָּנָה	VB Q build
בַּ֫עַד; בְּעַד NIS	PREP behind, on behalf of, away from
בַּ֫עַל; בְּעָלִים P, בַּעֲלֵי P NIS	NOUN M owner, lord; PN Baal
בַּעֲלָה; בַּעֲלַת NIS	NOUN F female owner, mistress
בִּעֵר	VB PI sweep away, remove; devastate (בער)
בַּעְשָׁא	PN Baasha
בָּקָר, בְּקַר NIS; בְּקָרִים P	NOUN M cattle, herd, ox
בֹּ֫קֶר; בְּקָרִים P	NOUN M morning
בִּקֵּשׁ	VB PI seek (בקשׁ)
בְּרִית	NOUN F covenant
בֵּרַךְ	VB PI bless; PU, NI be blessed (ברך)
בֶּ֫רֶךְ; בִּרְכַּ֫יִם DU, בִּרְכֵּי DU NIS	NOUN F knee
בְּרֵכָה, בְּרֵכַת NIS; בְּרֵכוֹת P	NOUN F pool
בָּשָׂר, בְּשַׂר NIS; בְּשָׂרִים P	NOUN M flesh
בִּשֵּׁל	VB PI boil (בָּשַׁל)
בַּת; בָּנוֹת P	NOUN F daughter

גָּאַל	VB Q redeem, act as a kinsman
גֹּאֵל	NOUN M (= Q PTCP) kinsman-redeemer, close relative
גָּדוֹל, גְּדוֹלָה F; גְּדוֹלִים MP, גְּדוֹלוֹת FP; גְּדֹלֵי MP NIS	ADJ great
גָּהַר	VB Q bend down
גּוֹי; גּוֹיִם P, גּוֹיֵי P NIS	NOUN M nation, people
גִּלְגָּל	PN Gilgal
גִּלּוּל; גִּלּוּלִים P	NOUN M idols
גָּלַם	VB Q wrap, wrap up

גִּלְעָד	PN Gilead
גַּם	ADV also, even
גַּן; גַּנִּים P	NOUN M garden
גֶּשֶׁם; גְּשָׁמִים P, גִּשְׁמֵי P NIS	NOUN M rain

דָּאַג	VB Q be anxious, worry
דֶּבֶק; דְּבָקִים P	NOUN M scale of armor
דָּבָר, דְּבַר NIS; דְּבָרִים P, דִּבְרֵי P NIS	NOUN M word, thing
דִּבֵּר	VB PI speak (דבר)
דָּם, דַּם NIS; דָּמִים P, דְּמֵי P NIS	NOUN M blood, P bloodguilt
דְּמָמָה	NOUN F calm, silence
דַּמֶּשֶׂק	PN Damascus
דַּק; דַּקָּה F	ADJ thin, soft, small
דֶּרֶךְ; דְּרָכִים P, דַּרְכֵי P NIS	NOUN M/F way, road
דָּרַשׁ	VB Q seek

הַ•	DET the
הֲ	INTER *marker for yes/no question*
-ָה	ADV to, toward (attached to NOUN)
הֵבִיא	VB HI bring, make enter (בּוֹא)
הִבִּיט	VB HI look, gaze (נבט)
הִגִּיד	VB HI declare (נגד)
הוּא	MS PRON he; DEM that
הוֹסִיף	VB HI multiply, do again, continue (יָסַף)
הוֹצִיא	VB HI bring forth (יָצָא)
הוֹשִׁיב	VB HI settle, set, cause to sit, inhabit (יָשַׁב)
הֶחְבִּיא	VB HI hide (something) (חבא)
הָחֳלָה	VB HO be wounded (חָלָה)
הֶחֱשָׁה	VB HI be silent (חשה)
הִיא	FS PRON she; DEM that
הָיָה	VB Q become, be
הֵיכָל, הֵיכַל NIS; הֵיכָלוֹת P, הֵיכְלֵי P NIS	NOUN M palace, temple
הִכָּה	VB HI smite, strike (נכה)
הִכִּיר	VB HI recognize, regard (נכר)
הִכְעִיס	VB HI provoke to anger (כָּעַס)
הִלְוִיט	VB HI wrap (לוט)
הָלַךְ	VB Q walk, go
הֵם, הֵמָּה	MP PRON they; DEM those
הָמוֹן	NOUN M multitude, crowd; commotion, (up)roar

הֵמִית	VB HI kill (מות)
הֵ֫נָּה	ADV here
הִנֵּה	INTJ behold! see! hey!
הֵנִיחַ/הִנִּיחַ	VB HI cause to rest, make quiet; set down; let remain, leave (נוּחַ)
הֵסִיב	VB HI make go around; turn away (סבב)
הֵסִית	VB HI incite, mislead; entice away (סות)
הֵעִיד	VB HI bear witness against, admonish (עוד)
הֶעֱלָה	VB HI cause to rise up, lead up (עָלָה)
הָעֳמַד	VB HO be set up, caused to stand (עָמַד)
הָפַךְ	VB Q overturn, destroy
הִפְרִיד	VB HI divide, separate (something) (פרד)
הֵקִים	VB HI raise, erect (קום)
הִקְשָׁה	VB HI make hard/difficult, harden (קשה)
הַר; הָרִים P; הָהָר, הֶהָרִים W. DET	NOUN M mountain, hill country
הֶרְאָה	VB HI show, exhibit (רָאָה)
הָרַג	VB Q kill, slay
הֵרִים	VB HI raise up, lift up (רום)
הָרַס	VB Q tear down
הֵרַע	VB HI do evil, treat badly (רעע)
הִשְׁאִיר	VB HI leave over, behind (שָׁאַר)
הִשְׁבִּיעַ	VB HI cause to swear (an oath) (שׁבע)
הִשְׁלִיךְ	VB HI throw (שׁלך)
הִשְׁתַּחֲוָה	VB HISHTAFEL bow down, prostrate oneself (חוה)
הִשְׁתִּין	VB HI urinate (שׁתן)
הִתְגֹּדֵד	VB HITPOEL make incisions on oneself, cut oneself (גדד)
הִתְגּוֹרֵר	VB HITPOLEL to stay as a sojourner/guest (גור)
הִתְחַנֵּן	VB HIT make supplication, implore; favor (חָנַן)
הִתְחַפֵּשׂ	VB HIT hide oneself, disguise oneself (חפשׂ)
הִתֵּל	VB PI to mock (התל)
הִתְמֹדֵד	VB HITPOEL stretch oneself out (מָדַד)
הִתְמַכֵּר	VB HIT sell oneself (מָכַר)
הִתְנַבֵּא	VB HIT prophesy (נבא)
הִתְעִיב	VB HI act abominably (תעב)
הִתְקַדֵּר	VB HIT become dark (קָדַר)

וְ	CONJ and
וַיֹּ֫אמֶר	VB Q 3MS PAST he said (אָמַר)

זְבוּב	NOUN M fly (PN בַּ֫עַל זְבוּב)
זָבַח	VB Q, PI slaughter, sacrifice
זֶה	MS DEM this
זָכַר	VB Q remember
זָנָה	VB Q act as prostitute, fornicate
זָעֵף	ADJ furious
זָעַק	VB Q cry, call out
זָקֵן, זְקֵנָה F; זְקַן M NIS; זְקֵנִים MP, זְקֵנוֹת FP; זִקְנֵי MP NIS	ADJ old
זֶ֫רַע; זְרָעִים P, זַרְעֵי P NIS	NOUN M seed

חוּץ	NOUN M outside
חוֹתָם, חוֹתַם NIS	NOUN M seal, signet ring
חֲזָאֵל	PN Hazael
חָזַק	VB Q be strong; HI strengthen, seize
חָזָק	ADJ strong, powerful
חָטָא	VB Q sin
חַטָּאת, חַטַּאת NIS; חַטָּאוֹת P, חַטֹּאת P NIS	NOUN F sin, sin-offering
חַי M, חֵי NIS, חַיִּים MP; חַיָּה F, חַיּוֹת FP	ADJ alive, living
חָיָה	VB Q live, be alive; HI keep alive, let live, revive
חֵיל, חֵל	NOUN M outer rampart, outwork
חֵיק	NOUN M bosom, lap
חָלָה	VB Q grow weak, fall ill, become injured; HO be wounded
חֳלִי	NOUN M sickness, suffering
חָלִיל; חָלִ֫ילָה W. LOC ADV	INTJ far be it that, be it far from
חָלַק	VB Q, PI divide, distribute; NI divide oneself
חִלֵּק	VB PI divide (חָלַק)
חָמֵשׁ, חֲמִשָּׁה F; חֲמִשִּׁים P	CARD five; P fifty
חָסֵר	VB Q decrease, lack
חָפֵץ; חֲפֵצָה F	ADJ willing, delighting
חָצָה	VB Q divide; NI be divided
חָצִיר	NOUN M grass
חֹר; חֹרִים P	NOUN M free, noble ones
חֶ֫רֶב; חֲרָבוֹת P, חַרְבוֹת P NIS	NOUN F sword
חֹרֵב	PN Horeb
חָרָבָה	NOUN F dry land
חָרַשׁ	VB Q plow, engrave, plan
חָשַׂךְ	VB Q keep back, withhold
חָתַם	VB Q seal, confirm

ADJ good, pleasant	טוֹב, טוֹבִים P, טוֹבֵי MP NIS; טוֹבָה F, טוֹבַת F NIS, טוֹבוֹת FP
NOUN M dew	טַל
ADV not yet, before	טֶ֫רֶם
VB Q tear, rend, pluck	טָרַף

VB Q be(come) dry; HI cause to be dry	יָבֵשׁ
NOUN F hand	יָד; יָדַ֫יִם DU, יְדֵי DU NIS; יָדוֹת P, יְדוֹת P NIS
VB Q know	יָדַע
PN Jehu	יֵהוּא
PN Judah	יְהוּדָה
PN YHWH (personal name of Hebrew God)	יְהוָה
PN Jehoram	יְהוֹרָם
PN Jehoshaphat	יְהוֹשָׁפָט
NOUN M day; W. ART today הַיּוֹם; daily יוֹם יוֹם	יוֹם; יָמִים P, יְמֵי P NIS
PN Jezreel	יִזְרְעֶאל
PN Jezreelite	יִזְרְעֵאלִי
VB Q be good, pleasing; HI do (something) well, deal well with	יָטַב
NOUN M boy; F girl	יֶ֫לֶד; יַלְדָּה F
NOUN M sea	יָם; יַמִּים P
VB Q add; HI multiply, do again, continue	יָסַף
CONJ because	יַ֫עַן
PN Jacob	יַעֲקֹב
VB Q go forth; HI bring forth	יָצָא
PN Isaac	יִצְחָק
VB Q pour, pour out; HI pour (oil); HO be poured, cast, molten, firmly established	יָצַק
VB Q awake	יָקַץ
VB Q be precious	יָקַר
VB Q fear	יָרֵא
ADJ afraid	יָרֵא
PN Jeroboam	יָרָבְעָם
VB Q go down, descend	יָרַד
PN Jordan (River)	יַרְדֵּן
PN Jericho	יְרִיחוֹ
NOUN M greens, vegetable	יָרָק
VB Q take possession, inherit	יָרַשׁ
PN Israel	יִשְׂרָאֵל
COP is; EXST there is	יֵשׁ

VB Q sit, dwell (Q PTCP inhabitant, dweller); HI set, cause to sit, inhabit, settle	יָשַׁב
VB Q sleep	יָשַׁן
ADJ sleeping	יָשֵׁן
NOUN M remainder, what is left behind	יֶ֫תֶר

PREP like, as	כְּ
NOUN F jar, pitcher	כַּד
ADV thus, so	כֹּה
NOUN M strength, power	כֹּחַ
CONJ because, when, if, though, but; COMP that	כִּי
CONJ but	כִּי אִם
ADJ all, every; NOUN M everything	כָּל־, כֹּל, כֻּלֵּךְ W. ENCL PRON
NOUN M dog	כֶּ֫לֶב; כְּלָבִים P, כַּלְבֵי P NIS
VB Q be complete; PI complete, finish; PU be completed, finished	כָּלָה
NOUN M vessel, utensil	כְּלִי; כֵּלִים P
VB PILPEL contain, sustain, keep (כול)	כִּלְכֵּל
ADV so, thus, yes	כֵּן
NOUN M silver, money	כֶּ֫סֶף; כְּסָפִים P, כַּסְפֵּי P NIS
VB Q be vexed; HI provoke to anger	כָּעַס
NOUN M vexation, anger	כַּ֫עַס; כְּעָסִים P
NOUN F hand, palm	כַּף; כַּפַּ֫יִם DU, כַּפֵּי DU NIS
PN Cherith	כְּרִית
NOUN M/F vineyard	כֶּ֫רֶם; כְּרָמִים P, כַּרְמֵי P NIS
PN Carmel	כַּרְמֶל
VB Q bend one's knee, bow down, kneel	כָּרַע
VB Q cut, cut off, cut down	כָּרַת
VB Q write	כָּתַב

PREP to, for	לְ
ADV no, not	לֹא
not translated (= Q INF אמר); COMP *used to introduce direct speech*	לֵאמֹר
NOUN M heart, mind	לֵב, לֵבָב; לִבְּךָ, לֵבַבְךָ W. ENCL PRON
VB Q wear; HI clothe	לָבֵשׁ, לָבַשׁ
VB PI lick up (לחך)	לִחַךְ
NOUN M bread, food	לֶ֫חֶם
NOUN M night	לַ֫יְלָה
VB Q spend the night, stay overnight	לִין

PREP according to (לְ + פֶּה)	לְפִי
PREP, CONJ before	לִפְנֵי
VB Q take, receive	לָקַח
VB Q lick, lap up	לָקַק

NOUN M strength; ADV exceedingly	מְאֹד
NOUN F hundred	מֵאָה, מְאַת NIS
PRON anything	מְאֹומָה
VB PI refuse (מאן)	מֵאֵן
NOUN M wilderness	מִדְבָּר
VB Q measure; HITPOEL stretch oneself out	מָדַד
INTER what? how?	מָה
NOUN F haste; ADV hurriedly	מְהֵרָה
PN Moab; Moabite	מוֹאָב; מוֹאָבִי, מוֹאֲבִיָּה F
VB Q die; HI kill	מוּת
NOUN M death	מָוֶת
NOUN M altar	מִזְבֵּחַ; מִזְבָּחוֹת P
PN Meholah	מְחוֹלָה
NOUN M purchase price, equivalent worth	מְחִיר
NOUN M encampment, camp	מַחֲנֶה; מַחֲנִים/מַחֲנוֹת P
NOUN M tomorrow	מָחָר
NOUN F bed, couch	מִטָּה, מִטַּת NIS; מִטּוֹת P
NOUN F rain	מָטָר
NOUN M water	מַיִם; מֵי/מֵימֵי NIS
NOUN F blow, wound	מַכָּה; מַכּוֹת P
VB Q be full, fill; PI fill	מָלֵא
NOUN M fullness, full measure	מְלֹא
VB PI fill (מָלֵא)	מִלֵּא
NOUN M messenger, angel	מַלְאָךְ; מַלְאָכִים P, מַלְאֲכֵי P NIS
NOUN F kingdom	מְלוּכָה
NOUN F war, battle	מִלְחָמָה; מִלְחָמוֹת P, מִלְחֲמוֹת P NIS
VB Q reign, be(come) king	מָלַךְ
NOUN M king	מֶלֶךְ; מְלָכִים P, מַלְכֵי P NIS; מַלְכִּי W. ENCL PRON
NOUN F kingdom, rule	מַמְלָכָה, מַמְלֶכֶת NIS; מַמְלָכוֹת P
PREP from; more than	מִן־ and מִ·
NOUN F gift, grain offering	מִנְחָה, מִנְחַת NIS
NOUN M number, quantity	מִסְפָּר, מִסְפַּר NIS
NOUN M cake, (fine) food	מָעוֹג
ADJ little, few	מְעַט

מַעְיָן, מַעְיַן NIS; מַעְיָנִים P, מַעְיְנֵי P NIS	NOUN M spring, source, headwaters
מְעָרָה, מְעָרַת NIS; מְעָרוֹת P, מַעֲרוֹת P NIS	NOUN F cave
מִפְּנֵי	PREP, CONJ from before (מִן + פְּנֵי)
מָצָא	VB Q find
מִצְוָה; מִצְוֹת P	NOUN F commandment
מִקְוֶה, מִקְוֵה NIS	NOUN M collection, collected mass
מָקוֹם, מְקוֹם NIS; מְקֹמוֹת P	NOUN M place
מְרַאֲשׁוֹת	NOUN FP place of the head
מֶרְכָּבָה	NOUN F chariot
מָשַׁח	VB Q anoint
מָשַׁךְ	VB Q seize, carry off; pull, drag
מִשְׁפָּט, מִשְׁפַּט NIS; מִשְׁפָּטִים P, מִשְׁפְּטֵי P NIS	NOUN M judgment, justice; custom
מָתַי	INTER when?
מָתְנַיִם, מָתְנֵי NIS	NOUN DU hips, loins

נָא	*illocutionary signal equivalent to "I tell you," or a marker of politeness, "please"*
נִבָּא	VB NI prophesy (נבא)
נָבוֹת	PN Naboth
נִבֵּט	VB PI look, gaze (נבט)
נְבָט	PN Nebat
נָבִיא, נְבִיא NIS; נְבִיאִים P, נְבִיאֵי P NIS	NOUN M prophet
נֶגֶד	ADV, PREP in front of, in sight of, opposite to
נָגַע	VB Q touch, reach, strike
נָגַשׁ	VB Q draw near, approach
נוּחַ	VB Q rest; HI cause to rest, make quiet; set down; let remain, leave
נוֹתַר	VB NI be left over, remain over (יתר)
נַחַל	NOUN M torrent (valley)/run-off ravine, wadi
נַחֲלָה, נַחֲלַת NIS	NOUN F possession, property, inheritance
נִחַם	VB NI be sorry/regret, comforted (נחם)
נִחֵם	VB PI comfort, console (נחם)
נֶחְצָה	VB NI be divided (חָצָה)
נֹכַח	PREP in front of, before, opposite to
נִכְנַע	VB NI humble oneself, submit (כנע)
נִלְחַם	VB NI fight (לחם)
נִמְלַט	VB NI escape (מלט)
נִמְשִׁי	PN Nimshi
נִסְתַּר	VB NI hide oneself (סתר)
נְעוּרִים	NOUN MP time of youth

NOUN M lad, young boy	נַ֫עַר; נְעָרִים P, נַעֲרֵי P NIS
VB Q fall	נָפַל
NOUN F life, self	נֶ֫פֶשׁ; נְפָשׁוֹת P, נַפְשׁוֹת P NIS
VB NI be slight, trifling, unimportant (קלל)	נָקַל
VB Q lift up, carry; NI be deceived; HI deceive	נָשָׂא
NOUN F breath	נְשָׁמָה
VB Q kiss	נָשַׁק
VB PI cut up (נתח)	נִתַּח
VB Q give, place, set	נָתַן

NOUN F seah (dry measure equivalent to about 7 quarts)	סְאָה; סָאתַ֫יִם DU; סְאִים P
VB Q turn about, go around, surround	סָבַב
ADV/PREP around, about	סָבִיב
NOUN M horse, stallion	סוּס; סוּסִים P, סוּסֵי P NIS
VB Q turn aside, depart; HI cause to depart, remove	סוּר
NOUN M rock	סֶ֫לַע
NOUN FP crutches made of branches; divided opinion	סְעִפִּים
NOUN F stormwind	סְעָרָה
NOUN M scroll, document, book	סֵ֫פֶר; סְפָרִים P; סִפְרִי W. ENCL PRON
VB Q stone; PU be stoned	סָקַל
VB PU be stoned (סָקַל)	סֻקַּל
ADJ ill-humored, sullen	סַר; סָרָה F

NOUN F cloud	עָב, עַב NIS; עָבִים P
VB Q serve, work	עָבַד
NOUN M servant	עֶ֫בֶד; עֲבָדִים P, עַבְדֵי P NIS
PN Obadiah	עֹבַדְיָ֫הוּ
VB Q pass over; HI allow to pass over	עָבַר
NOUN F round flat loaf of bread	עֻגָה, עֻגַת NIS; עֻגוֹת P
PREP unto, as far as; CONJ while, until	עַד
ADV still, yet, again	עוֹד
NOUN M transgression, iniquity	עָוֹן; עֲוֹנוֹת P
NOUN M flying creatures, fowl, insects	עוֹף
NOUN M skin, (animal) hide	עוֹר
VB Q abandon, forsake	עָזַב
NOUN F eye	עַ֫יִן; עֵינַ֫יִם DU, עֵינֵי DU NIS
NOUN F city	עִיר; עָרִים P, עָרֵי P NIS
VB Q put into disorder, bring disaster, throw into confusion, ruin	עָכַר

עַל	PREP upon, over
עָלָה	VB Q go up; HI cause to rise up, lead up
עֹלָה, עֹלַת NIS; עֹלוֹת P	NOUN F burnt offering
עֲלִיָּה, עֲלִיַּת NIS	NOUN F upper room
עִם; עִמִּי/עִמָּדִי W. ENCL PRON	PREP with; with me, at my side
עַם; עַמִּים P, עַמֵּי P NIS; עַמִּי W. ENCL PRON	NOUN M people
עָמַד	VB Q stand; HO be set up, caused to stand
עָמְרִי	PN Omri
עָנָה	VB Q answer, respond
עָפָר, עֲפַר NIS	NOUN M dust, dirt, dry earth
עֵץ; עֵצִים P, עֲצֵי P NIS	NOUN M tree; P wood
עָצַר	VB Q hold back, restrain
עֶקְרוֹן	PN Ekron
עֶ֫רֶב; הָעַרְבַּ֫יִם DU	NOUN M evening, sunset
עֹרֵב; עֹרְבִים P	NOUN M raven
עָרַךְ	VB Q set out, lay in rows
עָשָׂה	VB Q do, make, act
עֵשָׂו	PN Esau
עֶ֫שֶׂר, עֲשָׂרָה FS; עֶשְׂרִים P	CARD S ten; P twenty
עֵת; עִתּוֹת/עִתִּים P	NOUN F time
עַתָּה	ADV now

פֶּה, פִּי NIS	NOUN M mouth (*with* ל, *see* לְפִי)
פֹּה	ADV here
פָּנָה	VB Q turn
פָּנֶה; פָּנִים P	NOUN M (*always* P) face
פָּסַח	VB Q limp, leap; PI limp about
פִּסֵּחַ	VB PI limp about (פָּסַח)
פַּ֫עַם; פְּעָמִים P, פַּעֲמֵי P NIS	NOUN M step, time
פַּר; פָּרִים P	NOUN M young bull, steer
פֶּ֫רֶד; פְּרָדִים P	NOUN M mule
פָּרַק	VB Q, PI tear away
פֵּרֵק	VB PI tear away (פָּרַק)
פָּרָשׁ; פָּרָשִׁים P	NOUN M horseman
פָּשַׁע	VB Q rebel, break away, act disloyally
פַּת; פִּתִּים P	NOUN M scrap, piece
פֶּ֫תַח; פְּתָחִים P, פִּתְחֵי P NIS	NOUN M opening

צָבָא, צְבָא NIS; צְבָאוֹת P, צִבְאוֹת P NIS	NOUN M host, army; hard service
צָהֳרַ֫יִם	NOUN M DU noon; midday

VB PI command (צוה)	צִוָּה
VB Q fast	צוּם
NOUN M fast	צוֹם; צֹמוֹת P
PN Sidon, Sidonian	צִידוֹן, צִידֹנִי
NOUN M pair	צֶ֫מֶד; צְמָדִים P
VB Q, PI cry out	צָעַק
VB PI cry out (צָעַק)	צִעֵק
NOUN F jar, jug, pitcher	צַפַּ֫חַת
PN Zarephath	צָרְפַת, צָרְפַ֫תָה W. LOC ADV

VB Q collect, gather together	קָבַץ
VB Q bury	קָבַר
ADV eastward	קֶ֫דֶם, קֵ֫דְמָה W. LOC ADV
NOUN M voice, sound	קוֹל; קוֹלוֹת P
VB Q rise, stand up; HI raise, erect	קוּם
ADJ small	קָטָן, קְטַנָּה F; קְטַנִּים MP, קְטַנּוֹת FP; קְטַנֵּי MP NIS
ADJ MS small; F, P supplied by קָטָן	קָטֹן
NOUN M wall	קִיר; קִירוֹת P
PN Kishon	קִישׁוֹן
NOUN M flour	קֶ֫מַח
VB PI be jealous, be envious of (קנא)	קִנֵּא
NOUN M end, extremity	קֵץ
VB Q call, proclaim, read aloud	קָרָא (I)
VB Q meet someone, encounter, happen	קָרָא (II)
PREP in the midst, among	קֶ֫רֶב
ADJ near	קָרוֹב, קְרוֹבָה F; קְרוֹבִים MP, קְרוֹבוֹת FP
VB Q tear, rend; NI be rent, split asunder	קָרַע
NOUN MP pieces of cloth, rags	קְרָעִים
NOUN M attention	קֶ֫שֶׁב
VB POEL gather (קשׁשׁ)	קֹשֵׁשׁ
NOUN F bow	קֶ֫שֶׁת; קְשָׁתוֹת P; קַשְׁתִּי W. ENCL PRON

VB Q see, look; NI show oneself, appear; HI show, exhibit	רָאָה
PN Ramoth	רָאמוֹת
NOUN M head	רֹאשׁ; רָאשִׁים P, רָאשֵׁי P NIS
ORD first	רִאשׁוֹן, רִיאשֹׁנָה F; רִיאשֹׁנִים MP, רִאשֹׁנוֹת FP
ADJ many, much	רַב, רַבָּה F, רַבַּת F NIS; רַבִּים MP, רַבּוֹת FP
NOUN F spirit, wind	רוּחַ; רוּחוֹת P

רוּץ	VB Q run
רָחוֹק; רְחוֹקִים MP	ADJ far, distant; NOUN M distance, at a distance (רָחוֹק)
רָחַץ	VB Q wash, bathe
רָכַב	VB Q ride, mount
רֶ֫כֶב	NOUN M (COLL) chariot, war chariot(s)
רַכָּב	NOUN M driver, charioteer
רֹ֫מַח	NOUN M lance, spear
רִנָּה	NOUN F cry, shout
רַע, רָעָה F; רָעִים MP, רָעֵי MP NIS; רָעוֹת FP	ADJ bad, evil
רָעָב	NOUN M famine, hunger
רָעָה	NOUN F evil, misfortune, calamity
רָעַע	VB Q be bad, evil; HI do evil, treat badly
רַ֫עַשׁ	NOUN M earthquake
רִפֵּא	VB PI heal, repair (רָפָא)
רָצַח	VB Q kill, murder
רִצְפָּה; רְצָפִים P	NOUN F glowing coal, glowing stone
רַק	ADV only, still, but, however, nevertheless
רֹ֫תֶם	NOUN M gorse plant, broom bush, juniper

שְׂבָכָה	NOUN F net, grid
שָׂדֶה; שָׂדוֹת P, שְׂדֵי P NIS	NOUN M field
שׂוּם	VB Q put, place, set
שִׂיג	NOUN M journey, a stepping away/aside
שִׂיחַ	NOUN M musing, complaint
שִׂים	VB Q put, place, set
שֵׂעָר, שְׂעַר NIS	NOUN M hair
שָׂפָה, שְׂפַת NIS; שְׂפָתַ֫יִם DU, שִׂפְתֵי DU NIS	NOUN F lip, shore
שַׂק; שָׂקִּים P, שָׂקֵּי P NIS	NOUN M sack(cloth)
שַׂר; שָׂרִים P, שָׂרֵי P NIS	NOUN M official, captain, prince

שָׁאַל	VB Q inquire, ask
שֵׁ֫בֶט; שְׁבָטִים P, שִׁבְטֵי P NIS	NOUN M rod; tribe
שְׁבִיעִי, שְׁבִיעִית F	ORD seventh
שֶׁ֫בַע, שְׁבַע NIS, שִׁבְעָה F, שִׁבְעַת F NIS; שִׁבְעִים P	CARD seven; P seventy
שָׁבַר	VB Q break; PI shatter, break
שִׁבֵּר	VB PI shatter, break (שָׁבַר)
שׁוּב	VB Q turn back, return
שָׁחַט	VB Q slaughter

VB Q overflow, gush, pour down, rinse	שָׁטַף
VB Q urinate	שִׁין
VB Q lie (down)	שָׁכַב
VB Q send	שָׁלַח
NOUN M table	שֻׁלְחָן, שֻׁלְחַן NIS; שֻׁלְחָנוֹת P, שֻׁלְחֲנוֹת P NIS
ORD third; P thirtieth	שְׁלִישִׁי, שְׁלִישִׁית F; שְׁלִשִׁים P
VB PI divide into three; do a third time (שׁלשׁ)	שִׁלֵּשׁ
ADV there	שָׁם
NOUN M name	שֵׁם; שֵׁמוֹת P
NOUN M heavens	שָׁמַ֫יִם, שְׁמֵי NIS
NOUN M oil, fat	שֶׁ֫מֶן
CARD eight; P eighty	שְׁמֹנֶה, שְׁמֹנָה F; שְׁמֹנִים P
VB Q hear, listen; obey W. בְּקוֹל	שָׁמַע
PN Samaria	שֹׁמְרוֹן
NOUN M/F sun	שֶׁ֫מֶשׁ
NOUN F tooth, ivory	שֵׁן, שִׁנַּ֫יִם DU
NOUN F year	שָׁנָה, שְׁנַת NIS; שָׁנִים P, שְׁנֵי P NIS
VB Q repeat, do again	שָׁנָה
ORD second	שֵׁנִי M, שֵׁנִית F
CARD two	שְׁנַ֫יִם M, שְׁתַּ֫יִם F
VB PI gird (שׁנס)	שִׁנֵּס
PN Shaphat	שָׁפָט
VB Q pour out, shed (blood)	שָׁפַךְ
NOUN M scale armor, body armor	שִׁרְיוֹן
VB PI serve, attend to (שׁרת)	שֵׁרֵת
VB Q drink	שָׁתָה
NOUN M resident alien, sojourner, inhabitant	תּוֹשָׁב
PREP under, beneath	תַּ֫חַת, תַּחְתַּי W. ENCL PRON
NOUN M perfection	תֹּם, תָּם NIS; תֻּמִּי W. ENCL PRON
NOUN F watercourse, aqueduct, conduit, channel	תְּעָלָה, תְּעָלַת NIS
VB Q lay hold of, seize	תָּפַשׂ
PN Tishbite	תִּשְׁבִּי